1  12/98

# WILLIAM MAKEPEACE THACKERAY

# Modern Critical Views

*These and other titles in preparation*

*Modern Critical Views*

# WILLIAM MAKEPEACE THACKERAY

*Edited and with an introduction by*
Harold Bloom
Sterling Professor of the Humanities
Yale University

CHELSEA HOUSE PUBLISHERS ◊ 1987
New York ◊ New Haven ◊ Philadelphia

Library of Congress Cataloging-in-Publication Data

William Makepeace Thackeray.

   (Modern critical views)
   Bibliography: p.
   Includes index.
   Summary: A collection of thirteen critical essays,
arranged in chronological order of publication, devoted
to the works of the nineteenth–century English writer.
   1. Thackeray, William Makepeace, 1811–1863—
Criticism and interpretation. [1. Thackeray, William
Makepeace, 1811–1863—Criticism and interpretation.
2. English literature—History and criticism]
I. Bloom, Harold.  II. Series.
PR5638.W5     1987          823'.8          87–8024
ISBN 1–55546–288–X (lib. bdg.)

# Contents

# *Editor's Note*

This book gathers together a representative selection of the best modern criticism devoted to the writings of William Makepeace Thackeray. The critical essays are reprinted here in the chronological order of their original publication. I am grateful to Wendell Piez for his work as a researcher on this volume.

My introduction explores Thackeray's implicit identification with the superb Becky Sharp in *Vanity Fair*, despite the novelist's excessively overt ironies, or defenses against seeing his own ambivalences reflected in his protagonist. Robert Kiely begins the chronological sequence with an analysis of the humor in Thackeray's nonfictional prose, after which R. D. McMaster explores the Pygmalion myth in *The Newcomes*.

Wolfgang Iser, theorist of the reader's share, traces that role in *Vanity Fair*, while Ina Ferris uncovers in *Lovel the Widower* the breakdown of another narrative role, the story's teller, which was exploited so brilliantly in *Vanity Fair*. Another kind of breakdown, that of the characters' selves, is examined by Joan Garrett-Goodyear, after which Peter K. Garrett considers Thackeray's double perspectives, which enter also into Maria DiBattista's account of the charades in *Vanity Fair*.

Juliet McMaster studies "the alignment of love and death" in *Phillip*, Thackeray's last novel, an alignment prefigured in George Levine's exegesis of *Pendennis*, with its complex refraction of the novelist's hopeless love for Jane Brookfield.

Thackeray's familiar essays, *Roundabout Papers*, are analyzed by Richard W. Oram as instances of the skeptical Thackeray's investment of what hopes he had in the possibilities of the recurrence of vision through the mediation of time and memory. Repetition, in another sense, is the subject of J. Hillis Miller's reading of *Henry Esmond*, which is deconstructed here as "a large-scale expression of the negative relation between irony and repetition."

Thackeray's temporal disorderings of the passions are examined by Barbara Hardy, who finely catches the curious balance Thackeray achieves between comedy and a sombre intensity in representing the feelings of his protagonists. In this book's final essay, Craig Howes considers *Pendennis* from the aspect of the controversy it provoked on the issues of the status of writers and on the aesthetic dignity of literature.

# *Introduction*

G. K. Chesterton, saluting Thackeray as the master of "allusive irrelevancy," charmingly admitted that "Thackeray worked entirely by diffuseness." No celebrator of form in the novel has ever cared for Thackeray, who, like his precursor Fielding, always took his own time in his writing. Thackeray particularly follows Fielding, who was the sanest of novelists, in judging his own characters as a magistrate might judge them, a magistrate who was also a parodist and a vigilant exposer of social pretensions. Charlotte Brontë, Thackeray's fierce admirer, in her preface to the second edition of *Jane Eyre*, said that he "resembles Fielding as an eagle does a vulture." This unfortunate remark sounds odd now, when no critic would place Thackeray anywhere near Fielding in aesthetic eminence. Nor would any critic wish to regard Thackeray as Dickens's nearest contemporary rival, a once fashionable comparison. Thackeray, we all agree, is genial but flawed, and until recently he did not have much following among either novelists or critics. Trollope and Ruskin sometimes seem, respectively, the last vital novelist and great critic to regard Thackeray with the utmost seriousness. Splendid as he is, Thackeray is now much dimmed.

Though *Henry Esmond* is a rhetorical triumph in the genre of the historical novel, *Vanity Fair*, itself partly historical, is clearly Thackeray's most memorable achievement. Rereading it, one encounters again two superb characters, Becky Sharp and William Makepeace Thackeray. One regrets that Becky, because of the confusion of realms that would be involved, could not exercise her charms upon the complaisant Thackeray, who amiably described his heroine's later career as resembling the slitherings of a mermaid. Anyway, Thackeray probably shared the regret, and what I like best in *Vanity Fair* is how much Thackeray likes Becky. Any reader who does not like Becky is almost certainly not very likeable herself or himself. Such an observation may not seem like literary criticism to a formalist or some other kind of plumber, but I would insist that Becky's vitalism is the critical center in any strong reading of *Vanity Fair*.

Becky, of course, is famously a bad woman, selfish and endlessly design-ing, and rarely bothered by a concern for truth, morals, or the good of the community. But Thackeray, without extenuating his principal personage, situates her in a fictive cosmos where nearly all the significant characters are egomaniacs, and none of them is as interesting and attractive as the energetic Becky. Her will to live has a desperate gusto, which is answered by the gusto of the doubtlessly fictive Thackeray who is the narrator, and who shares many of the weaknesses that he zestfully portrays in his women and men. Perhaps we do not so much like Becky because Thackeray likes her, as we like Becky because we like that supreme fiction, Thackeray the narrator. Sometimes I wish that he would stop teasing me, and always I wish that his moralizings were in a class with those of the sublime George Eliot (she would not have agreed, as she joined Trollope and Charlotte Brontë in admiring Thackeray exorbitantly). But never, in *Vanity Fair*, do I wish Thackeray the storyteller to clear out of the novel. If you are going to tour Vanity Fair, then your best guide is its showman, who parodies it yet always acknowledges that he himself is one of its prime representatives.

Does Thackeray overstate the conventional case against Becky in the knowing and deliberate way in which Fielding overstated the case against Tom Jones? This was the contention of A. E. Dyson in his study of irony, *The Crazy Fabric* (1965). Dyson followed the late Gordon Ray, most genial and Thackerayan of Thackerayans, in emphasizing how devious a work *Vanity Fair* is, as befits a narrator who chose to go on living in Vanity Fair, however uneasily. Unlike Fielding, Thackeray sometimes yields to mere bit-terness, but he knew, as Fielding did, that the bitter are never great, and Becky refuses to become bitter. An excessively moral reader might observe that Becky's obsessive lying is the cost of her transcending of bitterness, but the cost will not seem too high to the imaginative reader, who deserves Becky, and who is not as happy with her foil, the good but drab Amelia. Becky is hardly as witty as Sir John Falstaff, but then whatever other fictive personage is? As Falstaff seems, in one aspect, to be the child of the Wife of Bath, so Becky comes closer to bring Falstaff's daughter than any other female character in British fiction. Aside from lacking all of the Seven Deadly Virtues, Becky evidently carries living on her wits to extremes in whoredom and murder, but without losing our sympathy and our continued pleasure in her company.

I part from Dyson when he suggests that Becky is Vanity Fair's Volpone, fit scourge for its pretensions and its heartlessness, of which she shares only the latter. Becky, like her not-so-secret sharer, Thackeray the narrator, I judge to be too good for Vanity Fair, though neither of them has the undivided inclination to escape so vile a scene, as we might wish them to do. Becky's most famous reflection is "I think I could be a good woman if I had five thousand a year." This would go admirably as the refrain of one of those ballads that Brecht kept lifting from Kipling, and helps us to see that Becky Sharp fits better into Brecht's world than into Ben Jonson's. What is most winning about her is that she is never morose. Her high-spirited courage does us good, and calls into question the aesthetics of our morality. Thackeray never allows us to believe that we live anywhere except in Vanity Fair, and we can begin to see that the disreputable Brecht and the reputable Thackeray die one another's lives, live one another's deaths, to borrow a formulation that W. B. Yeats was too fond of repeating.

Thackeray, a genial humorist, persuades the reader that Vanity Fair is a comic novel, when truly it is as dark as Brecht's The Threepenny Opera, or his Rise and Fall of the City of Mahagonny. The abyss beckons in nearly every chapter of Vanity Fair, and a fair number of the characters vanish into it before the book is completed. Becky survives, being indomitable, but both she and Thackeray the narrator seem rather battered as the novel wanes into its eloquent and terribly sad farewell:

> Ah! Vanitas Vanitatum! Which of us is happy in this world? Which of us has his desire? or, having it, is satisfied?—Come children, let us shut up the box and the puppets, for our play is played out.

ROBERT KIELY

# Victorian Harlequin: The Function of Humor in Thackeray's Critical and Miscellaneous Prose

In *Roundabout Papers*, Thackeray tells an anecdote which, as usual, is partly at his own expense. He was visiting a church in Antwerp when the beadle told him that his walking about was disturbing the service. Thakeray pointed to others who seemed to be moving around less quietly than he: "'They come to pray,' says the beadle. 'You don't come to pray, you ———, 'When I come to pray,' says I, 'I am welcome,' and with this withering sarcasm, I walk out of church in a huff. I don't envy the feelings of that beadle after receiving point blank such a stroke of wit."

It is the kind of story that Boswell probably would have let pass unrecorded, for, despite his love of the eighteenth century, Thackeray was not a great creator of bons mots. The sharp retort and the well-shaped epigram were not his style. He was not a wit and, as his tone of exaggerated satisfaction makes plain, he knew it.

Thackeray's gift was for something less taut, less pointed and quick than what is usually called wit. His best effects are cumulative, indirect, and elusive. By his own definition, he was a humorist—a term which may seem comfortably imprecise, but one which may also be used to imply brainless geniality or a tendency to conceal one's own vices while ridiculing those of others. Thackeray himself was restless in any single role, but throughout his career he was fond of comparing himself, as well as his subjects, to clowns and jesters. One of his favorite words was "quack," and his most typical metaphorical guises were those of Harlequin and Punchinello. The usual ex-

From *Veins of Humor*, edited by Harry Levin. © 1972 by the President and Fellows of Harvard College. Harvard University Press, 1972.

planation for this—indeed, one that Thackeray sometimes offers—is that all men are, in one way or another, actors and frauds; that each of us shows sides of himself in public which are different from the man within.

A famous passage at the beginning of the lectures on *The English Humourists* tells the story of a man in deep depression who asks his physician for a cure and is advised to visit the theater where Harlequin is playing. The advice turns out to be useless because the patient is himself the actor who plays Harlequin. At first, the anecdote seems to suggest that the humorist is one who puts up a good front, conceals with tricks and laughter the sorrow that he really feels. But it is always dangerous to quote from the beginning of a paragraph by Thackeray without following the rest. For as he expands his definition, humor becomes something much more than surface gaiety: "If Humour only meant laughter, you would scarcely feel more interest about humourous writers than about the private life of poor Harlequin just mentioned, who possesses in common with these the power to make you laugh."

Harlequin, whose public and private selves are as different as night and day, is not the model humorist after all, but only a convenient contrast to the genuine article: "The humourous writer professes to awaken and direct your love, your pity, your kindness—your scorn for untruth, pretension, imposture—your tenderness for the weak, the poor, the oppressed, the unhappy." It is such a familiar Victorian catalogue that one is tempted to pass quickly over it in search of something more "original." But that would be a mistake, for the core of Thackeray's idea of humor is here. Obviously, but also very importantly, humor, for Thackeray, is not a cover-up, a simplification of reality, but an evocation of complex, even contradictory, responses. The seriousness and sadness of the true humorist show through his best jokes, not in spite of them, but in subtle combination with them.

It is also clear from the catalogue that the humorist appeals to the heart more than to the mind—to love, pity, tenderness, even to "scorn" rather than to reasoned disapproval. He is one who "feels the truth" and therefore "takes upon himself to be the week-day preacher." The idea that the capacity to feel things deeply gives a man special moral insight is, in part, a Romantic legacy familiar in much Victorian literature. The wit shows himself to be superior to other men through his ability to make quick and sharp distinctions. The humorist, on the other hand, is just like everybody else, only more so. His art depends less on his power to surprise or impress his reader than on his ability to create an affective bond with him. The humorist, defined as a passionate and, especially, compassionate moralist, becomes the descendant not so much of Swift and Pope as of Wordsworth and Keats. As George

Eliot put it in 1856, "Humour, in its higher forms, and in proportion as it associates itself with the sympathetic emotions, continually passes into poetry; nearly all great modern humourists may be called prose poets."

Thackeray's distaste for Romantic extravagance and his sympathy for the eighteenth century make it difficult to consider his work in terms even remotely connected with the Romantic imagination. Yet there is something to be gained from examining his humor not as a faltering attempt at balance and intellectual clarity but as a continuing process, a feeling into things and situations, making judgments and withdrawing them, forever enlarging possibilities and resisting conclusions. Like many Romantics, he seeks at his best to imitate the movement of life rather than a preconceived idea of it. His moral force comes not so much from taking positions, but from widening and enriching the ground from which moral positions are taken.

But, of course, as all readers of Thackeray know, though he could be subtle and evasive, he could also be heavy-handed and obvious. If he could imitate the general flow and confusion of life, he could also mimic very specific mannerisms and habits of speech and, in so doing, make what appear to be emphatic, rapid, and sometimes ruthless moral judgments. Thackeray was a droll caricaturist, an expert at detecting buffoonery. The question is whether the arch, wicked, and sometimes silly side of him fits in with his concept of the humorist as compassionate moralist. Does he succeed at putting cap and bells at the service of an open mind and benevolent heart? Or is he merely another "quack"—as he sometimes claims—pretending one thing while doing something else?

Of course, the answers to these questions vary with particular works; but one general observation is worth making at the outset. For Thackeray the humorist, in contrast to the tragedian and philosopher, is a bold entertainer—one who snatches the attention of his audience by almost any means rather than earning it through patient reasoning or gradual development of character and situation. The tonal nuances and meditative digressions may come later, but first it is important to capture the spectator's fancy. For Thackeray beginnings are important and, in his own work, they are often filled with memorable displays of posing and face-pulling.

Despite his persistent references to the artificiality, the sham posturing of comedians, nothing was more natural to him than to play the mimic. One sees it everywhere in his writing, in letters, reviews, lectures, and journals as well as in novels, tales, and burlesques. Just as he could sketch while receiving visitors or attending an opera, so too his ear could apparently work away while the rest of his mind was on other things. Some of the early imitations are little more than aural doodles—fragments of tea-talk, diplomatic pronouncements, pedantic rumblings, odds and ends of a brogue. They do not represent carefully worked out or even very conscious attitudes. They are unguarded reactions, almost absentminded ways of seeing and hearing.

Readers are still irritated by his travel books because of his habit of mimicking accents and expressions, exaggerating modes of dress and social intercourse, in short, appearing to ridicule customs of every sort simply because they are not British. There is no denying that he had most of the prejudices of his nation and class. The *Irish Sketch Book* and *From Cornhill to Grand Cairo* tell relatively little about foreign places and a great deal about the middle-class Victorian baggage which the traveler was so often unable to put down and forget. But, like many tourists, Thackeray often felt an urge to become part of the very scenes which he could hardly describe without a cliché or a laugh. However, unlike the student abroad who thinks he can stop shaving and blend in, Thackeray was acutely aware of his unmistakable Englishness. When in his prose he does adopt a foreign guise, he seeks some of the pleasure of masquerade without, for any length of time, mistaking it for assimilation.

Thackeray's foreign sketches are partial admissions of his own limitations as well as comments on strange places and people. The initial pleasure in imitation is no less genuine for being undercut by a sense of that aspect of the self which can never be other than that which is solidly and rather sadly is. The point is that even at his least supple and imaginative, Thackeray displays an irrepressible urge to try on voices, expressions, and styles other than his ponderous own.

One of the first characters introduced in the *Paris Sketch Book* is Sam Pogson, a young Englishman who is hardly in Calais before trying out French ways—or what he thinks are French ways—flirting with every woman in sight, drinking champagne constantly, and dropping fashionable phrases. Thackeray, unable to resist mimicking an Englishman trying to be French, quotes from a letter in which Pogson describes one of his successes to a friend:

> I'll tell you how it occurred. Everybody in France, you know, dines at the ordinary—it's quite distangy to do so. . . . You know my way with women: champagne's the thing; make 'em drink, make 'em talk—make 'em talk, make 'em do anything. So I orders a bottle, as if for myself; and "Ma'am," says I, "will you take a glass of Sham—just one?" Take it she did. . . . Bob Irons told me that he had made some slap-up acquaintances among the genteelest people at Paris, nothing but by offering them Sham.

Pogson's performance is a sham of class as well as of nationality, and Thackeray enjoys ridiculing it. But, in a way, he also understands the impulse behind it. Pogson's folly is not so much in wanting to enter into the spirit of things by imitating foreign ways, but in his adoption of a self-congratulatory tone in the midst of his failure to see the difference between his copy and the real thing. Pogson has no perspective on the world or himself and therefore lacks the power of successful imitation as well as the saving grace of irony.

Nothing so much preoccupied Thackeray—even in his seemingly offhand criticism of society, literature, and art—as the nature and value of imitation. He revered and wanted originality, yet it was his peculiar gift to "take off" from what others had already said and done. His nonfiction is a gallery of borrowed poses, but his imagination never lodges very long or happily in any single one. If we are searching for the author's own voice, we can find it in the characters he chooses to imitate so long as we recognize that there is a continual "trying on" during which some parts seem to fit and others do not. Thackeray is not all Pogson any more than he is all Michael Angelo Titmarsh or Pendennis. We can discover him—or, at least, his imagination—only if we follow his movement to and from, in and out of such creatures. Imitation, role-playing, even mimicry are, for Thackeray, essential to humor; for, unlike the wit, who continually distinguishes between himself and others, the humorist is one who seeks a common ground and risks, like Pogson, looking like a fool if he cannot find it.

The parallel between Pogson's problem—his inability to distinguish between a true copy and a sham—and the humorist's dilemma, though not explicitly drawn, is everywhere in evidence in the *Paris Sketch Book*. The work is a journal and therefore one does not expect much in the way of form, yet Thackeray is continually searching in it for a meeting place between moral rigor, sympathy, and a light heart. One sees it in the typical pattern of his approach to French character. Stage one is the detached view (which usually means rather harsh criticism of French ways on moral grounds); stage two is an amiable warming to the color and vivacity of the subject (often accompanied by wishful ejaculations—"Would that we English had their wit, their museums, their elegance!"); stage three is a self-consciously exaggerated imitation of someone or something French in which the joke is double-edged because based on the incompatibility of the French and English temperaments; stage four is a return to the sensible and comfortable English voice, still moralizing, but less strident than at the outset.

Thackeray, the humorist, like Pogson, the tourist, wants somehow to enter into an unfamiliar life—to become, if only very briefly, that which he contemplates. He is able to see that Pogson's vulgarity and condescension, his lack of feeling and respect for French life, make his role-playing farcical; but that insight does not quite enable Thackeray to eliminate every trace of Pogson in himself. His solution, not a philosophical choice so much as a psychological compromise, is to keep his vulgar feelings of superiority separate from his moments of sympathetic identification. What results is a radical and rapid alternation of mood and perspective—usually regarded as a virtue in Thackeray's fiction, often looked on as a form of weakmindedness or hypocrisy in his travel writing and criticism.

It is certainly true that Thackeray was unable to work out a coherent system by which the two tendencies could be logically reconciled; but this is not an unfamiliar problem to the student of the nineteenth-century mind. If Thackeray's habit of shifting tone and distance is thought of as an aesthetic strategy based on psychological need rather than as a form of moral cowardice, it becomes apparent how much it resembles the strategy of many nineteenth-century writers, particularly the Romantics. To approach one's subject cautiously from a distance, to move closer to it, to unite with it imaginatively, and again to return to the remove created by habit is to express in sequential, dramatic terms an experience of the mind and heart which appears to defy coherent rational justification and intellectual consistency.

A striking example of the pattern can be seen in Thackeray's treatment of young French painters in the *Paris Sketch Book*. At first, he calls their existence "the easiest, dirtiest, merriest . . . possible" and makes it clear that he disapproves of their arrogance, vanity, and immorality. But as he proceeds to scorn their foppish ways, he becomes fascinated and then charmed by the very details he had seemingly been preparing for his own indignation. Their ingenious hairstyles and beards, their fancy jackets and incredible caps—at first taken up as objects of ridicule are suddenly used by Thackeray, despite his earlier reservations, as badges of honor. He seems to turn on his English reader and on the Pogson side of himself and, almost without warning, he is speaking, not as a disapproving tourist, but as a defender of French culture. He borrows French phrases and French sarcasm to pour out invective against an England where "a grocer's daughter would think she made a *mésalliance* by marrying a painter, and where a literary man . . . ranks below . . . the apothecary, the attorney, and the wine-merchant." Warming to his subject and to his sheer pleasure in role-playing, he imitates, not the English traveler trying to sound French, but the way a Frenchman might mimic an English conversation: " 'Who is that monstrous pleasant fellow?' 'Don't you know? . . . It's Asterisk, the author of so-and-so, and a famous contributor to such-and-such.' 'Good Heavens! a literary man! I thought he had been a gentleman!' "

But Thackeray, as usual, cannot keep up the pretense for very long. "To our muttons," he says, and returns to his sensible English voice. Calling himself back once again to the ostensible subject of the chapter—the French school of painting—he takes up neoclassicism and appears, by a shift in tone, to be avoiding the consequences of his own wishful thinking. In a broader sense, however, he does not change his real subject at all. He is still preoccupied with the artist's role and with the nature of imitation in art and life. He criticizes French classicism not because he thinks the ancients are unworthy of imitation but because he thinks the moderns are incapable of matching their achievement: "Because to these lofty heights giants had scaled, behold the race of pigmies must get upon stilts and jump at them likewise! and on the canvas, and in the theatre, the French frogs (excuse the pleasantry) were instructed to swell out and roar as much as possible like bulls. What was the consequence . . .? In trying to make themselves into bulls, the frogs made themselves into jackasses, as might be expected."

Thackeray's language here is harsh and his English prejudice bursts unpleasantly to the surface (though the echo of Aesop and La Fontaine's "La Grenouille qui veut se faire aussi grosse que le Boeuf" suggests that even in this he was the mimic). But there is more at issue than national rivalry. Having abandoned a career as a painter, he knew what it was to try to scale the "lofty heights" and to realize that he, like all the rest, was a member of a new race of pigmies. Considering his own stylistic habits and indeed the paragraphs filled with posturing and role-playing which precede his discussion of neoclassicism, Thackeray's attack on imitative artists takes on a significance and even a poignancy beyond its value as a general critical statement:

> And yet we, O foolish race! must try our very best to ape some one or two of our neighbours, whose ideas fit us no more than their breeches! It is the study of nature, surely, that profits us, and not of these imitations of her. A man, as a man, from a dustman up to Aeschylus, is God's work, and good to read, as all works of nature are; but the silly animal is never content; is ever trying to fit himself into another shape; wants to deny its own identity, and has not the courage to utter its own thoughts.

Clearly, Thackeray is referring as much to his own problems as a writer as he is to the French school of painting. Once again, the rhetoric, at least, appears to be built upon Romantic formulations. One cannot assume that Thackeray meant the same thing that Wordsworth or Coleridge did when they spoke of nature; nonetheless, it would be a mistake to discount such passages altogether. One of Thackeray's basic objections to French classicism was that it perpetuated a myth of heroism which, if it ever had validity, certainly seemed in the nineteenth century to have it no longer. For Thackeray, as for many Victorians, the classical hero was a thing out of nature. The writer who wished to be true to nature (that is, to himself and his times) wrote about common, ordinary people and was, therefore, in one very old-fashioned sense of the word, bound to be a comic artist.

But Thackeray recognized that a successful imitation of nature depends on more than choice of subject matter and a will to tell the truth. Supposing a writer does have the "courage to utter his own thoughts," how does he shape these thoughts in such a way that they will make sense to others? What are the stylistic resources, the formal conventions, the vocabulary, the syntax of the honest man? These are questions which Thackeray often posed, and sought in his roundabout way to get at.

One tends to remember the lectures on *The English Humourists* for their many outbursts of moral indignation, but the fact is that Thackeray was willing to forgive almost anything in a writer whose style struck him as somehow natural and authentic. After condemning Swift's grossness, he praises his "elaborately simple" style; he admires Congreve's "energy" despite his "heathen immorality"; he says of Addison that "he came to that artificial age, and began to speak with his noble, natural voice"; he admits that Steele was coarse, but praises the naturalness of his writing too, which he says comes from the fact that "he wrote so quickly and carelessly that he was forced to make the reader his confidant, and had not the time to deceive him"; he calls Gay "such a natural good creature"; and he excuses Fielding's lapses in taste on the grounds of what he calls his "vast health."

Though Thackeray does not try to suggest that there is a single key to the method by which all this naturalness is conveyed through language, he does make it clear that the public display of private emotion is not what he had in mind. His harshest criticism is reserved for Sterne and not, as is sometimes supposed, primarily because of Sterne's bawdy humor, but because of his habitual parading of sentiment. "A perilous trade, indeed, is that of a man who has to bring his tears and laughter, his recollections, his personal griefs and joys, his private thoughts and feelings to market." Thackeray had a horror of self-exposure which extended into his literary judgment. As he goes on to explain in the lecture on Sterne, the peril for the artist who is too intimate with his reader lies in one of two extremes: either he loses all control, all sense of the difference between art and life (Thackeray asks of Sterne, "Where did the lie begin, and did he know where?"), or else the control is so taut as to make the personal effusiveness part of a calculated hoax. In the former case, emotion is reduced to self-pity and art to self-indulgence. But it is the latter view which Thackeray finally adopts toward Sterne: "The humour of Swift and Rabelais, whom he pretended to succeed, poured from them as naturally as song does from a bird. . . . But this man . . . is a great jester, not a great humourist. He goes to work systematically and of cold blood."

It is important to be sure that a post-Freudian conception of the distinction between wit and humor does not lead to a misinterpretation of Thackeray's point. In his 1928 essay "Humour," Freud argues that wit is the result of a "preconscious thought (being) given over for a moment to unconscious revision. A joke (witticism) is thus the contribution made to the comic by the unconscious. In just the same way, humour would be the contribution made to the comic through the agency of the superego. . . . In bringing about the humourous attitude, the superego is actually repudiating reality and serving an illusion. It means, 'Look! here is the world, which seems so dangerous! It is nothing but a game for children—just worth making a jest about!' "

For Freud, wit is amoral and, to some degree, discomforting *because* it is spontaneous, irrational, and born of a hidden reality. Humor, on the other hand, rationalizes, moralizes, comforts, and therefore falsifies reality. Thackeray's vocabulary is different from Freud's, and one cannot with precision equate "heart" with "unconscious" and "mind" with "superego." Still, it is clear that in an important respect his psychological assumptions are the reverse of Freud's. Sterne is a mere jester, a false and immoral wit *because* his works are cool, cerebral calculations. What is good *and* true, in Thackeray's view, usually comes spontaneously and unsystematically from man's heart, not from his brain which is the real source of egocentricity. There is no necessary split between the "felt response" and a good conscience. Indeed, the humorist may be one who is willing to sacrifice logic, structural coherence, and even moral consistency to that principle.

But, of course, to repudiate the value of a systematic use of intellect— even lightheartedly—is to risk chaos or, at the very least, verbal confusion. For poets the risk has always seemed more adventuresome and heroic than it has for novelists, especially novelists with a sense of humor. Thackeray was never in danger of turning into a Blake or a Pound; he was very much in danger of turning into a Barthelme, celebrating his freedom from the extremes of confessional sentimentality and cool rationality by producing warmed-over trivia. What saved him was his great gift for mimicry. He did not have to have a mind and ideas of his own so long as he inhabited other people's. His range and depth may not have been Shakespearian, but his ability to observe human nature, coupled with his willingness to borrow whatever he found useful from other writers, saved him from maudlin egoism and incoherent abstraction.

Thackeray's imitative habits may at times seem in direct contradiction to his diatribes against neoclassicism. Yet, if one follows his circuitous argument closely, it becomes clear that his objections are to pretentiousness and static formalism rather than to imitation in general. He admitted, for example, that there were cases in which an author might truly find a mind congenial to his own among classical writers and therefore best be able to express himself in reference to the works of that writer. He praises Matthew Prior without claiming originality for him: "Horace is always in his mind; and his song, and his philosophy, his good sense, his happy easy turns and melody, his loves and his Epicureanism bear a great resemblance to that most delightful and accomplished master."

But, from Thackeray's point of view, few writers have Prior's luck in discovering a perfect soul mate in the past; for others to persist in headlong and solemn imitation was a masquerade of the most foolish and inadvertently farcical sort. Yet Thackeray's alternative was not quite mock-heroic either. He was not sufficiently sure of himself nor fixed in his opinion of ancient and modern writers to carry off a sustained and consistent piece of ironic imitation. His approach to other writers—like his approach to the characters in his novels—is a mixture of whimsy, compassion, respect, ridicule, and affection. According to his own definition, he was a humorist even in his criticism.

Thackeray prefers talking about men to talking about books, and he insists that the crucial question for the critical biographer to ask about his subject is not "what are his works like?" but "would we have liked to live with him?" In the early pages of *The English Humourists* he is up to his familiar trick of trying on various roles, imagining what it would be like to have been the friend of Swift, of Fielding, of Dr. Johnson. Warming to the idea, he writes: "I should like to have been Shakespeare's shoeblack—just to have lived in his house, just to have worshipped him—to have run on his errands." It is the sort of remark which seems to a modern reader to be neither biographical nor critical. One might almost conclude that, despite some misleading labels, all of Thackeray's works are fictions. But it would be more accurate to say that there is no clear boundary between fiction and criticism in Thackeray's prose, that the critic, like the novelist, is continually meandering between evaluation and collaboration, between detachment and sympathy.

The general impression of Thackeray's literary criticism is one of inconsistency and excess. He either praises or blames too much. One reason for this is that, though most of his critical pieces were written for public occasions, many of them are in fact conversations between the artist and himself, a kind of shoptalk in monologue. He may, as he says, go to the lives and works of other writers for moral uplift and so on, but he also goes, like any artist, to learn his craft. The results of such inquiries are more like an artist's sketchbook than like a sustained piece of academic criticism. It would be a mistake to interpret his denunciation of certain writers as a sign that he wished to disregard their work. There is a wonderful story in *Roundabout Papers* about his being asked to admire the work of an American sculptor who had never seen a statue. Thackeray got himself in trouble with the American press for saying that looking at other statues would have done the man no harm.

For all his impatience with certain kinds of imitativeness, Thackeray most definitely believed in looking at other men's "statues." But if we wish to know what he thought of another writer's style, we should look not at what he says about it or its author, but at how he treats (and mistreats) it in his own prose. The quality and resonance of an echo must be considered, not the solidity of a critical formulation. *Novels by Eminent Hands* are humorous imitations rather than strict parodies, because in them Thackeray was studying his art as well as lampooning the habits of other writers. There is a warming to the very mannerisms which are selected for ridicule, even a kind of collaboration, because the humorist could not quite keep his curiosity and sympathy out of the picture.

It is therefore a mistake to dismiss the fictional burlesques as mere barbs aimed at authors whom Thackeray disliked. Though each author parodied by Thackeray obviously possessed traits which he found amusing, each also provided him with techniques he adapted to his own purposes in his fiction. The burlesques are entertainments, but they are also critical statements and laboratories in which Thackeray tested his powers. Among those parodied are Disraeli, Fenimore Cooper, Mrs. Gore, G. P. R. James, and Charles Lever. Two of the most distinctive pieces are one based on Bulwer-Lytton's *Eugene Aram* and one on *Ivanhoe* which, though much longer than any one of the group collected under the heading *Novels by Eminent Hands*, was begun in the same spirit.

Though always fascinated by the works of Bulwer-Lytton, Thackeray found much in them objectionable and silly. He disliked the snobbish Francophilia and forced elegance of *Pelham*; he disliked presumptuous inventions of dialogue between great historical and literary figures, as in *Devereaux* where Bolingbroke, Swift, Pope, Addison, Voltaire, and Condorcet are paraded before the reader in a series of "accidental" encounters with the hero; and he disliked the glorification of vice in the person of a glamorous criminal. All of these Bulwerisms are exaggerated and ridiculed in *George de Barnwell*, but the most amusing and telling aspect of the parody is Thackeray's imitation of Bulwer's style which seeks at the same time to be dramatic and philosophical, sublime and picturesque, classical and modern—all things to all readers.

Thackeray opens his burlesque with a prefatory statement by the author explaining—as Bulwer often liked to—that the seemingly vulgar nature of his subject did not make it unworthy of epic treatment: "Is Odysseus less august in his rags than in his purple? Fate, Passion, Mystery, the Victim, the Avenger, the Hate that harms, the Furies that tear, the Love that bleeds, are not these with us still?"

Then, after a long catalogue of the passing parade on the streets of London, the narrator becomes reflective: "And the Philosopher, as he regarded the hot strife and struggle of these Candidates in the race for God, thought with a sigh of the Truthful and the Beautiful, and walked on, melancholy and serene."

Thackeray seizes upon Bulwer's inflated language, his meaningless strings of abstractions, his apostrophes and forced alliterations, and shows them as part of one long cliché. The implication is that Bulwer is writing in the mock-heroic vein without knowing it. He is another laughable, humorless Pogson, a maker of shams, except that his condescension is not restricted to the French. From Thackeray's point of view, Bulwer was a literary as well as a social snob. Despite his protestations about writing romances of "real life," he was not primarily interested in common experience or the broad types of human nature in which all men could recognize something of themselves. He explained in the preface to the 1840 edition of *Eugene Aram* that he chose to write about this supposedly benevolent and sensitive criminal because he "presents such an anomaly in human conduct so rare and surprising."

In an article in *Fraser's*, Thackeray elaborated upon his objection to Bulwer's persistent quest for the rare and exotic. A young English journalist had recently died, and Bulwer had published a long eulogy in which he attributed death to a fever brought on by the young man's refusal to take shelter in a rainstorm and getting "heroically wet through." According to Thackeray, Bulwer went about telling the tale in precisely the wrong way, enveloping "the chief personage in fine words, as statuaries do their sitters in Roman togas," rather than giving the episode fully and "in detail." What Thackeray means by "detail" is partly visual imagery—more of the storm and the color of the man's jacket—but also circumstantial material drawn from the character's life to that point. The situation is thus made interesting not because of any inherent or isolated quality, but because of the way it intersects with the rest of the character's life and the way the pattern of that life may resemble the lives of other men.

There is no doubt that Thackeray had a keen eye for Bulwer's faults, but he saw it as no contradiction for the critic to emulate what he found worthwhile in an imperfect model. The humorist-as-critic retains his notion that life and art are mixed affairs and that the careful observer may often find reason to praise and blame in very nearly the same breath. The true humorist is as wary of the perfect scapegoat as he is of the perfect hero. Thackeray admitted later in his life that he had learned much from Bulwer. But even if he hadn't said so, we might have guessed that his use of historical figures in *Henry Esmond* owes part of its success to a close and critical observation of Bulwer's attempt at the same thing.

Thackeray also enjoys ridiculing Bulwer's philosophical narrator meditating on the follies of humanity; yet, of course, the opening of *Vanity Fair* shows him resorting to the same convention. After describing the noise and confusion of the Fair, the narrator says:

> A man with a reflective turn of mind, walking through an exhibition of this sort, will not be oppressed, I take it, by his own or other people's hilarity . . . but the general impression is one more melancholy than mirthful. When you come home, you sit down in a sober, contemplative, not uncharitable frame of mind, and apply yourself to your books and your business. I have no other moral than this to tag to the present story of "Vanity Fair."

The relative simplicity of diction and the disclaimer of a clear moral issue immediately distinguish this passage from a comparable one by Bulwer. But a subtler and more crucial difference is reflected by the way in which Thackeray switches smoothly from third person to first to second and back to first again in such a short space. The narrator here, as throughout the novel, changes his perspective and tone by slipping like a salamander from role to role. He may be the stage manager who manipulates the whole show, or a character as vain and helpless as the others, or an observer just watching the spectacle with the reader. Bulwer lets himself become frozen in the convention of the melancholy philosopher while Thackeray darts in and out of it like a quick-change artist.

Thackeray's way of avoiding a pose was to keep moving. He admired but also mistrusted Scott's "big bow-wow strain," yet could not sustain the controlled understatement of an Austen either. His realm—and what he considered to be the realm of the humorist—lay between heroic drama and comedy. The humorist forever wavers between laughter and tears. Thackeray never strikes an emotionally sublime note because his feelings are continually qualifying and diluting one another. *Rebecca and Rowena* is one of his most curious and, in some ways, most instructive critical imitations because it contains such an uncoordinated mixture of modes and tones. It is part sequel, part parody, and part meditation. The terms takeoff and put-on—which sound like opposites, but aren't—suggest the nature of Thackeray's peculiar approach to Scott. There is an air of whimsy and fraud throughout the piece, which sometimes parallels and sometimes entangles itself with a serious putting on of the very costumes and conventions which are being mocked. It is a less successful variant on the puppet theater theme in *Vanity Fair* which can, by contrast, make other episodes in the book appear more like life.

Many of the reservations he had about Bulwer as a novelist, Thackeray had about Scott as well. The static descriptions, the hero worship, the false archaisms struck him as being silly. Thackeray liked to think in terms of probabilities and demanded that even characters in novels should occasionally reveal a bit of common sense. If Ivanhoe had had any sense, for example, he obviously would not have settled for the bloodless and vapid Rowena but would have married the intelligent, virtuous, and beautiful Rebecca. The piece contains a good deal of fun at the expense of Scott and the fashion of Romantic medievalism, but it also contains many passages of straightforward adventure narrative, and it concludes on a pathetic note about the early deaths of the heroine and hero which is quite extraordinary for a so-called parody.

The work is so rich in itself that one might take it up at almost any point and learn much about Thackeray as a humorist. Of particular interest is the way it reveals Thackeray's use of humor in order to explore the possibilities of historical fiction. One of the major problems facing the writer of historical novels—and one which Thackeray did not think Scott had adequately solved—was to evoke the atmosphere of another era while, at the same time, making the characters and events credible to contemporary readers. Scott's habit of mixing archaic and pseudo-archaic language with colloquial expressions of his own time was to Thackeray a constant source of amusement. Rather than endowing the past with an authentic vitality, it created a stage setting peopled by characters who seemed to forget their lines from time to time and say things in their own words and accents. Even the prompter or narrator was often guilty, as can be seen in Thackeray's imitation of Scott describing Ivanhoe leaving his castle for battle:

> Then Ivanhoe's trumpet blew: then Rowena waved her pocket handkerchief; then the household gave a shout; then the pursuivant of the good knight, Sir Wilfrid the Crusader, flung out his banner (which was argent, a gules cramoisy with three Moors impaled sable): then Wamba gave a lash on his mule's haunch, and Ivanhoe, heaving a great sign, turned the tail of his warhorse upon the castle of his fathers.

> As they rode along the forest, they met Athelstane the Thane
> powdering along the road in the direction of Rotherwood on his
> great dray-horse of a charger. "Goodbye, good luck to you, old
> brick," cried the Prince, using the vernacular Saxon. "Pitch into
> those Frenchmen; give it 'em over the face and eyes; and I'll stop
> at home and take care of Mrs. I."

The humor here is a bit too obvious—but, among other things,
Thackeray is playing with words and moods, making discord almost too easily
but listening through it for the possibilities of harmony. One of the lessons
Thackeray learned from Scott's successes as well as his failures was not to
strive too feverishly for the antique effect. His reasoning is the same as that
which we come upon again and again in his dissertations on the imitative
possibilities of art. The imitation, however conscientiously attempted, will
simply not match the original. The more earnest and exact the writer tries
to be, the more awkward and apparent will be his failure. The artist must
remain sufficiently conscious of the representational nature of his art so that
he will not deceive himself into trying to make it do what it never can.

In accepting the limitations of language and of all literary conventions,
the humorist is able to free himself from wasting his energy on the wrong
problems—that is, the ones he cannot solve. Similarly, the historical novelist
who realizes that he cannot "recreate" another age may free his imagination
to play with its shadows, to hint and evoke rather than to repeat. The success of *Henry Esmond* is the result of many things, but surely one of them
is the tactful and unobtrusive way in which Thackeray suggests the style of
Augustan English without attempting an exact copy of it. One recognizes
a tone, a cadence, here and there a word or phrase, but the attention is never
stopped by it. One way to describe the achievement is to say that it would
be impossible to parody.

One could go on citing the ways in which Thackeray put humor to work
for him outside of the novels, but the pattern already emerges clearly enough.
The humorous imitation—whether of a foreigner or a fellow novelist—is the
epitome of the qualified response, the art of making up your mind and then
changing it. Thackeray's criticism is nearly always tempered by sympathy,
his sentimentality undercut by irony. But everywhere in his work the voice
of the mimic can be heard. In the early sketches the fun seems to be for its
own sake, but soon the adoption and exaggeration of accents and gestures
becomes a way for the artist to draw near his subject without identifying
himself with it altogether. Thackeray came to see that a momentary flash
of truth may be captured indirectly by edging up to things and treating them
obliquely. And the only way he knew of keeping the approximation from
absorbing and reducing the reality was continually to change it. In his criticism

and short sketches as well as in his novels, he threw exactness and consistency to the winds and aimed, like most great humorists, at the variety and energy of life—"the great aggregate experience"—rather than at its meaning abstractly conceived.

Thackeray's imitative mode is rarely simple or purely negative. Some of the traits he most enjoyed lampooning in Bulwer-Lytton and Scott show up in altered form in his own novels. But then, he would have been willing to admit that the humorist must be a persistent and shameless scavenger if he is to keep his devices varied and changing. Almost any old trick will do if it is not allowed to stand so long as to become stale. Harlequin can console himself that his art is in a serious relation to life only if he resists the rigidity which comes of growing too fond of one mask. Then he can achieve what George Eliot called "that wonderful and delicious mixture of fun, fancy, philosophy, and feeling, which constitutes modern humour."

R. D. McMASTER

# The Pygmalion Motif
## *in* The Newcomes

With an indirect kind of narcissism, the mind falling in love with its own creation, Pygmalion produces a statue, the figment of his imagination, worships it, and seeks to bring it to life. This kind of activity, including the worship of statues, is a recurrent pattern in Thackeray's *The Newcomes*. Thackeray is peculiarly interested in the role fictions play in the lives of his characters. Some, like Pygmalion, fall in love with visions they have summoned forth from their own imaginations and try to bring these ideal patterns to life by imposing them on the raw material of other people's lives. Others fashion their own lives according to stylized patterns. Ethel Newcome, for example, at one stage describes herself and other young ladies fashioned for the marriage market as works of art like paintings in a gallery, and the personality she presents to others is made up of various highly artificial projections. Clive Newcome, as a painter, perceives Ethel primarily in terms of statuary and paintings, falling in love with his own imagination of her. The world Thackeray describes is one of perpetual tension between the ordering imagination and the resisting raw material of life. To the individual at the vivid center of his moment of time, his schemes seem unique and substantial. In a long view, however, he encounters the frustrations that all men encounter in a world of limitations, and there is nothing new under the sun. That is the point of "the farrago of old fables" with which *The Newcomes* begins. And the contrast between the patterns the mind wishes to see fulfilled and the realities of life in the fallen world occasions Thackeray's

From *Nineteenth-Century Fiction* 29, no. 1 (June 1974). © 1974 by the Regents of the University of California.

postscript after he has, like George Bernard Shaw in his play *Pygmalion*, chopped his story short, leaving the reader's romantic longings frustrated.

In familiar moral terms, this idealizing drive of the imagination can be seen as the attempt of fallen humanity to rebuild paradise. And if we examine the first number of *The Newcomes* with the kind of care that is now given to the serial parts of Dickens's novels, we find Thackeray carefully setting up these themes and modes of vision both in setting and character. The first number keeps moving back and forth between a paradisal pastoral vision of the world and a more vulgar, commercial, urban view of it. In the first chapter, where the curtain rises, the animals in the introductory fable come to grief with the sudden incursion of reality in the form of butcher, ploughboy, and farmer. Another golden and pastoral world, but containing the threat of its own destruction, immediately follows, the narrator looking far back to a time "when the sun used to shine brighter than it appears to do in this latter half of the nineteenth century." This world, colored by the narrator's nostalgia and by the green youth of the company he is remembering, centers on a coffee-house called the "Cave of Harmony," a citified Arcadia where "the roses bloom again, and the nightingales sing by the calm Bendemeer," and where the songs are "chiefly of the sentimental class." The innocent swain, who enters with his son, "a fine tall young stripling" with "bright blue eyes," is Colonel Newcome, the instant sport of the barely more than adolescent rakes assembled, including Pendennis, who dubs him "Don Ferolo Whiskerandos." For a moment the Arcadian note is in danger from the impulse of the wags to "low mimetic," but "'*Maxima debetur pueris*,' says Jones (a fellow of very kind feeling, who has gone into the Church since), and writing on his card to Hoskins hinted to him that a boy was in the room, and a gentleman, who was quite a greenhorn: hence that the songs had better be carefully selected." The Colonel's contribution of "Wapping Old Stairs," sung before an initially embarrassed Clive, is another triumph of finer feeling over fallen nature: "It was like Dr. Primrose preaching his sermon in the prison. There was something touching in the *naïveté* and kindness of the placid and simple gentleman." The moment is achieved, the mood harmonious, "we could see he was thinking about his youth—the golden time—the happy, the bright, the unforgotten."

The moment fails, however, the romance turns ironic, with Captain Costigan's entrance "in his usual condition at this hour of the night." A kind of Irish Silenus, with "a horrid grin, and leering," he launches into a song so outrageous that the scandalized Colonel interrupts him with a moral tirade, amusing, offending, and upsetting the onlookers. Then:

> shouldering his stick, and scowling round at the company of

scared bacchanalians, the indignant gentleman stalked away, his boy after him.

Clive seemed rather shamefaced; but I fear the rest of the company looked still more foolish.

"Aussique diable venait-il faire dans cette galère?" says King of Corpus to Jones of Trinity; and Jones gave a shrug of his shoulders, which were smarting, perhaps; for that uplifted cane of the Colonel's had somehow fallen on the back of every man in the room.

There is nothing casual about this pastoral embroidery; the next chapter, "Colonel Newcome's Wild Oats," heads unerringly to yet another paradise as we look back upon the elder Thomas Newcome's marriage to a girl with a quarter of a million, a Quaker connection, and a mansion at Clapham "surrounded by lawns and gardens, pineries, graperies, aviaries, luxuries of all kinds." It was, however,

> a serious paradise. As you entered at the gate, gravity fell on you; and decorum wrapped you in a garment of starch. The butcherboy who galloped his horse and cart madly about the adjoining lanes . . . fell into an undertaker's pace. . . . The rooks in the elms cawed sermons at morning and evening; the peacocks walked demurely on the terraces; the guineafowls looked more quakerlike than those savoury birds usually do. . . . The head-gardener was a Scotch Calvinist, after the strictest order, only occupying himself with the melons and pines provisionally, and until the end of the world.

The chapter ends with young Tom, the Colonel-to-be, having rebelled against "that stifling garden of Eden" and scandalized his step-mother by wishing to marry a Papist, embarking for India and the army, his father afraid to leave him his fortune "on account of his terror of Sophia Alethea, his wife."

The third chapter, and end of the first number, consists of a series of letters establishing family relationships and bringing the Colonel's son, Clive, on the scene as a child sent home from India. The cycle of generations is ready to begin again, and Thackeray's complex lacing back and forth in time between the Colonel's youth and Clive's is an important element in the "argument" Thackeray will unfold.

With its blending and offsetting of stylized outlooks and environments, its ironic playing with pastoral and cynical conventions, the first number of *The Newcomes* is a skilled and efficient exordium. Its oscillating visions of the world function in two ways: as they are accepted or expressed by the

characters themselves, they are examples of life attempting to conform to
imaginative pattern and threatened by the unforeseen, the chaos of reality,
or else by the impingement of one man's paradise on another's; as they jostle
one another for the reader's attention, they implicitly and ironically call into
question the very idea of nature as opposed to art. And here one may recall
a renowned feature of Thackeray's style that makes him a delight to literate
readers. Few novelists, other than Joyce, imbue character and plot with such
a range of supplementary fabulation. Not only are we to see the story as
a fable with characters as typical as the fable animals, but as fairy tale, with
Clive, Ethel, and Lady Kew as Prince, Princess, and Witch, or again as myth,
with Clive as Hercules enslaved by Ethel as Omphale, and again as elegant
pastoral theatre, in which Ethel plays shepherdess to Clive's swain. In another
complex stream of allusion, Ethel repeatedly calls to mind the sculpture of
Diana in the Louvre. Head letters often provide pictorial glosses to the narrative, as in chapter 52, in which Lady Kew, pictured as a witch, casts a
spell over a teapot as Macbeth wielding a stick (Barnes) approaches to con-
sult her. In another perspective, *The Newcomes* is a moral progress. The
head letter of chapter 2, in which the elder Thomas Newcome, like Dick
Whittington, comes to London to make his fortune, "marrying his master's
daughter, and becoming sheriff and alderman of the City," shows Hogarth's
industrious apprentice. For the marriage market at Baden, Thackeray invokes
*Marriage à la Mode*, and later, Lord Highgate hangs about Barnes's wife,
Clara, "just in such an attitude as the bride is in Hogarth's 'Marriage à la
mode' as the counsellor talks to her." In John Harvey's view, Thackeray expected his readers to see he was taking his theme from *Marriage à la Mode*,
and indeed two reviewers, one of them Edward Burne-Jones, did (*Victorian
Novelists and Their Illustrators*). Behind all these figurative allusions and
rephrasings hover the tone and perspective of Ecclesiastes with its themes
of recurrence and frustration. My intention, however, is not to labor the obvious point of Thackeray's manifold allusiveness, but to argue that in *The
Newcomes* these compounded stories and allusions are essential not only to
the decoration but to the principal theme of the work, a theme that has its
center in Colonel Newcome's attempt to mold life according to his imaginary
pattern.

The colonel's appearance as a derided but morally triumphant innocent,
Don Ferolo Whiskerandos, in the ironic pastoral context of the first number
invites us to reconsider a letter Thackeray wrote as the book was just under
way: "I read Don Quixote nearly through when I was away. What a vitality
in those two characters! What gentlemen they both are! I wish Don Quixote
was not thrashed so very often. There are sweet pastoralities through the
book, and that piping of shepherds and pretty sylvan ballet which dances

always round the principal figures is delightfully pleasant to me." Thackeray read *Don Quixote* in the summer of 1853 while writing the first four numbers of *The Newcomes*. The connection is evident not only in the ironic pastoralities of the first number, a type of satire Thackeray enjoys in *Vanity Fair* and *Pendennis* as well, but directly in his emphatic conclusion to the second number. Encountering the Colonel's supercilious nephew Barnes, whom he despises as a "dashed little prig," General Sir Thomas de Boots says of the Colonel:

> "I tell you what, young man, if you were more like him it wouldn't hurt you. He's an odd man; they call him Don Quixote in India; I suppose you have read *Don Quixote*."
>
> "Never heard of it, upon my word; and why do you wish I should be more like him? I don't wish to be like him at all, thank you."
>
> "Why, because he is one of the bravest officers that ever lived," roared out the old soldier. "Because he's one of the kindest fellows; because he gives himself no dashed airs, although he has reason to be proud if he chose. That's why, Mr. Newcome."
>
> . . . the indignant general walks away gobbling and red.

This vignette is significant in showing the enmity between Barnes and the Colonel, but the identification of the Colonel with Don Quixote, recurrent throughout the novel, adds another somber tinge. In Don Quixote we have, par excellence, the man who has inherited a conventional vision that fires his imagination and who, trading the world's brass for its gold, insists that it be *the* world, thus creating for himself the tragedy that Sir Philip Sidney attributed to "that first accursed fall of Adam: since our erected wit maketh us know what perfection is, and yet our infected will keepeth us from reaching unto it" (*An Apology for Poetry*). As both Cervantes and Thackeray knew, our infected wills can also contribute to the doggedness of our convictions about what virtue and perfection are. As Thackeray wrote, "The wicked are wicked no doubt, and they go astray and they fall, and they come by their deserts: but who can tell the mischief which the very virtuous do?" Any number of characters in *The Newcomes* live encapsulated in thoroughly conventional visions which they nevertheless regard as highly singular and singularly realistic: " 'Know the world, young man!' cries Newcome; 'I should think if I don't know the world at my age, I never shall.' And if he had lived to be as old as Jahaleel a boy could still have cheated him."

Wonderful in its orchestration of time and memory, the Colonel's career is a cycle, starting and ending in childhood, a cycle that under his influence will partly repeat itself in the life of his son. Having lost his first love Léonore in a conflict of class and family interests, the Colonel settles for a pitiful little marriage of second choice from which Clive is born. When the Colonel returns from India as a distinguished officer and meets Clive's cousin Ethel, the past and present merge:

> they fell in love with each other instantaneously. . . . There was no point of resemblance, and yet a something in the girl's look, voice, and movements, which caused his heart to thrill, and an image out of the past to rise up and salute him. . . . It is an old saying, that we forget nothing. . . . No doubt, as the old soldier held the girl's hand in his, the little talisman led him back to Hades, and he saw Leonora.

As the chapter ends, the Colonel's work of art takes shape in his imagination and his great enterprise begins. The passage is worth quoting at length:

> The Colonel from his balcony saw the slim figure of the retreating girl, and looked fondly after her; and as the smoke of his cigar floated in the air, he formed a fine castle in it, whereof Clive was lord, and that pretty Ethel, lady. . . . "What a fine match might be made between that child and Clive! She reminds me of a pair of eyes I haven't seen these forty years. I would like to have Clive married to her; to see him out of the scrapes and dangers that young fellows encounter, and safe with such a sweet girl as that. If God had so willed it, I might have been happy myself, and could have made a woman happy. But the Fates were against me. I should like to see Clive happy, and then say *Nunc dimittis*."

Seeing a present colored by his own youthful romance, the Colonel fashions from these materials a dream that will serve both to complete vicariously the pattern of his own frustrated love story and to bring happiness to his son. God did not will his own ideal marriage; now he can be God and arrange things more perfectly. His aspiration is not at first sight arrogant, for the vision arises from the unselfish love of parent for child (and here one might note in passing that readers irritated by the wandering and slow-paced way Thackeray develops the "sentimental question" of Clive's love for Ethel are on the wrong scent—the great and moving love in *The Newcomes* is between Colonel Newcome and his son). The paragraph is nevertheless ominous. Not only do we anticipate what comes of playing God, but that reiterated word, happy, happy, happy—"I might have been happy myself. . . . I should like to see Clive happy"—rings with a frail sound against the burden of Thackeray's moral vision: "Ah! *Vanitas Vanitatum*! Which of us is happy in this world? Which of us has his desire? or, having it, is satisfied?" (*Vanity Fair*, chap. 67).

Boethius explains man's misery as arising from his pursuit of false felicity; we can see the process at work in the Colonel, who, "having fixed his whole heart upon this darling youth, his son, was punished." While the Colonel devotes himself to Clive, Clive devotes himself to art. "Thomas Newcome had now been for three years in the possession of that felicity which his soul longed after. . . . And yet, in spite of his happiness, his honest face grew more melancholy." The impassioned controversies about art between Clive and his youthful friends go over the Colonel's head, and though he longs to share in the camaraderie, "the party would be hushed if he went in to join it—and he would come away sad at heart to think that his presence should be a signal for silence among them; and that his son could not be merry in his company." As he confronts this dilemma, toiling away hour after hour in the National Gallery "before the ancient statues, desperately praying to comprehend them," and asking himself, "why can't I love the things which he loves? . . . why am I blind to the beauties which he admires so much?" we come to the central tragedy in Thackeray's world of ardently cherished schemes and patterns. It is the obverse of the book's more cheerful introductory version of Ecclesiastes, that is, "there may be nothing new under and including the sun; but it looks fresh every morning." Now

a sickening and humiliating sense of the reality came over him: and he sadly contrasted it with the former fond anticipations. Together they were, yet he was alone still. His thoughts were not the boy's: and his affections rewarded but with a part of the young man's heart. Very likely other lovers have suffered equally. Many a man and woman has been incensed and worshipped, and has shown no more feelings than is to be expected from idols. There is yonder statue in St. Peter's, of which the toe is worn away with kisses, and which sits, and will sit eternally, prim and cold. As the young man grew, it seemed to the father, as if each day separated them more and more. He himself became more melancholy and silent. His friend the civilian marked the ennui, and commented on it in his laughing way. Sometimes he announced to the club, that Tom Newcome was in love: then he thought it was not Tom's heart but his liver that was affected, and recommended blue-pill. O thou fond fool! who art thou, to know any man's heart save thine alone? . . . As if Thomas Newcome, by poring over poems or pictures ever so much, could read them with

Clive's eyes!—as if, by sitting mum over his wine, but watching till the lad came home with his latchkey (when the Colonel crept back to his own room in his stockings), by prodigal bounties, by stealthy affection, by any schemes or prayers, he could hope to remain first in his son's heart!

Thackeray is both specific and general here. The Colonel's frustration in his lovingly elaborated scheme for happiness is not singular: his lot is everyone's. However perfect the Colonel's vision of bliss, it is his alone. Instead of Pygmalion's happy result in loving his work of imagination so much that it comes alive, we have here the reverse. The statue sits "eternally prim and cold." The trouble is twofold: not only does the vision disintegrate to a "sickening and humiliating sense of reality," but, even if it did not, it is in its very essence incommunicable. Don Quixote is judged to be mad.

The Colonel's further fantasy of marrying Clive to Ethel founders against Ethel's determination to marry an aristocrat with a fortune, and against the lies, hatred and machinations of her brother Barnes. Frustrated and embittered, the Colonel, as he has done before, falls back on secondary targets, alternative ways of making Clive be happy. The Colonel has become a great bank director, but "this Bundelcund Banking Company, in the Colonel's eyes, was in reality his son Clive." Angered by Barnes's duplicity, the Colonel contests the Newcome election with him: "I have long had the House of Commons in my eye," he says, "but not for me. I wanted my boy to go there." And having failed to win Ethel for Clive, as he had failed to win Léonore for himself, he promotes Clive's marriage to Rosey, the milksop daughter of terrible Mrs. Mackenzie, just as he had settled for his own vain and silly Emma. In addition, since Clive is so unenthusiastic, the Colonel "performs all the courtship part of the marriage." In a combination of love for his father, despair of Ethel, and the sheer inertia that also plagues his career as an artist, Clive falls in with the Colonel's plan, bringing misery to them both. He suffers in silence while the Colonel rages at what seems to him his son's perverse unhappiness. "With every outward appliance of happiness, Clive was not happy." "His very silence angered the old man." "His life had been a sacrifice for that boy! What darling schemes had he not formed in his behalf, and how superciliously did Clive meet his projects! The Colonel could not see the harm of which he had himself been the author." The grand vision ends in wreck and, for the Colonel, poverty-stricken, and enfeebled by the bitter shrewishness of Mrs. Mackenzie, death. The cycle ends with the pieces from which it started, on the one hand a delirious vision of Léonore, on the other, suggesting a separation he has ever since been trying to overcome, a recollection of his own father beating him for a childish escapade: " 'It wasn't the pain you know: it wasn't the pain, but. . . .' Here tears came into his eyes and he dropped his head on his hand, and the cigar from it fell on to the floor, burnt almost out, and scattering white ashes."

Mrs. Mackenzie, surely one of the most dreadful women in all literature, is a savage counterpart to the Colonel in the novel's design, molding Rosey according to her scenario, as the Colonel with more benign intent arranges life for Clive. As Thackeray wrote, "the kind scheme of the two elders was, that their young ones should marry and be happy ever after, like the prince and princess of the fairy-tale." With that aim in view, Mrs. Mackenzie, the Campaigner, scolds Rosey, angrily beats her, laces her "so tight, as nearly to choke the poor little lass," then simpers downstairs with her, arms entwined, to weep touchingly at sentimental songs before the gentlemen. Like Clive with the Colonel, Rosey "acquiesced gladly enough in her mamma's opinion, that she was in love with the rich and handsome young Clive, and accepted him for better or worse." Unsuspected depths in Rosey appear only at the end, when Ethel comes to visit the harassed and poverty-stricken Clive. Miserable and jealous, Rosey tears her hand away from her posturing mother's proprietary clutch, leaving behind her wedding ring. Symbolically freed from the sour fairy tale her mother has contrived, standing alone, she finds herself confronting utter emptiness. Without the sustaining framework of an imposed pattern, she has no existence. Her illness deepens, and to the accompaniment of Mrs. Mackenzie's stamping, raging hysterics, she weakens and dies.

If the Colonel and Mrs. Mackenzie show the effects of shaping others' lives according to one's own idea of happiness, Ethel shows the structuring imagination at work within herself. In her career Thackeray compounds two visions of the world, and as she affects one convention or the other she becomes worldly cynic or innocent shepherdess. Like Rosey and Clive, she too is the victim of an imposed vision. Old Lady Kew, "sister of the late lamented Marquis of Steyne," works at shaping Ethel's destiny, but Ethel proves to be a more aggressive and interesting character than Clive. It is customary to see her as clear-sighted in her sense of the family sordidness, especially in view of the famous scene in which she provokes Lady Kew by suggesting that young ladies should wear green tickets with "Sold" on them, like the paintings in a gallery, and then turns up for dinner with a ticket on her frock as "a *tableau vivant*." Certainly her credo seems straightforward in its priorities: "I believe in elder sons, and a house in town, and a house in the country." Ethel, nevertheless, is a complex and sardonic creature, not so easy to classify. Even her insistence on the Newcome sordidness has about it a degree of defiant affectation. She too suits her life to an involved fiction. At one level she is aware, aloof, and direct, repeatedly telling Clive that she

is of the world worldly because she chooses to be so. "She chose to be
Countess of Kew because she chose to be Countess of Kew. . . . Clive was
but a fancy." But in her relationship with Lady Kew, she is governed by a
ferocity that intimidates even that tough manager. Her bullying brother Barnes
fears her. And her rage appears again in her scornful treatment of the lovers
who try to claim her, whether Clive or Kew or Farintosh. Though committed to a mercenary, status-seeking society, she is harshly satirical of it. As
a result, there is at times a good deal of ambivalence, self-excuse, and easy
fatalism in her, as in her observations to Lady Kew or Clara Pulleyn's marriage
to Barnes:

> That poor wretch, that poor girl whom my brother is to marry,
> why did she not revolt and fly? I would, if I loved a man suffi-
> ciently, loved him better than the world, than wealth, than rank,
> than fine houses and titles—and I feel I love these best—I would
> give up all to follow him. But what can I be with my name and
> my parents? I belong to the world like all the rest of my family.
> It is you who have bred us up; you who are answerable for us.
> Why are there no convents to which we can fly? . . . you make
> me what you call happy, and I would rather be at the plough like
> the women here.

Accusation, hasty qualification, fatalism, blame shifting, absurd primitivism
—as Lady Kew replies, quite rightly: "No, you wouldn't Ethel. . . . These
are the fine speeches of schoolgirls." And there is the crux of Ethel's complicated character: she moves between two fictions of the world, one all hard-
ness for which she is not responsible and one all artless primitivism which
she implies is the real Ethel.

   This tension makes for some fine comedy that carries on the pastoral
imagery of the novel's first number and reaches its height in chapter 47, entitled "Contains Two or Three Acts of a Little Comedy" and introduced by
a head-letter sketch of an elegant swain and shepherdess à la Watteau. Further to stress the fact that life is now going to follow the formulas of fiction,
Thackeray writes the chapter as play dialogue in three conversations à la
Marivaux, setting the scene in the "quaint old garden of the Hôtel de Florac,"
with a dry fountain, a moss-eaten Triton, and, in a parody of Keats, "a
broken-dosed damp Faun, with a marble panpipe, who pipes to the spirit
ditties which I believe never had any tune," and a "Cupid, who has been at
the point of kissing Psyche this half-century at least, though the delicious
event has never come off, through all those blazing summers and dreary
winters." "After some talk about nuns, Ethel says, 'There were convents once
in England. She often thinks she would like to retire to one'; and she sighs

as if her heart were in that scheme." She now turns to reproaching Clive for worldliness—stage direction: "(*She heaves a sigh and looks down towards a beautiful new dress of many flounces which Madame de Flouncival, the great milliner, has sent her home that very day.*)" Clive enters only a touch ironically into Ethel's fantasy by describing himself as "like the Peri who looks into Paradise and sees angels within it," signifying thereby that he dotes on her London house. And he adds sadly that when he first saw her she was "like that fairy-princess who came out of the crystal box. . . . *Ethel (innocently).* Have I ever made any difference between us?"

Conversation 2 proceeds from a low comedy scene between servants to another contrived meeting between Clive and Ethel, Ethel continuing her vein of world weariness: "Oh, dear me, who is happy in the world? What a pity Lord Highgate's father had not died sooner!" and "O what a life of vanity ours is!" In Conversation 3, Madame de Florac, the Colonel's Léonore, lost long ago to a marriage of interest, puts an end to these "singular coincidences" of Clive's and Ethel's meetings and reproaches Ethel's schemes of union without love. Moved by the discourse, Ethel admits her ambivalence, her simultaneous love and contempt for jewels, great names, and admiration. Back again in her worldly vision, she once more reproaches Clive for his low social position and his artist's profession, dismissing him with a number of excuses and the dreadful word, brother: "Now do you see, *brother*, why you must speak to me so no more?"

The whole comedy, of course, is a refinement (in its much more elaborate interweaving of strands) on the superb "Phillis and Corydon" chapter of *Pendennis*, in which Blanche Amory tunes her pastoral emotions stage by stage to the titles of her books of poetry, from *Mes Soupirs* to *Mes Larmes*. Ethel is more intriguing, perhaps, because neither of her visions is altogether false. The pastoral, though it is largely humbug, does show a streak of conscience in Ethel's avowed sordidness, as when she is talking to the Colonel: "Thus the young lady went on talking, defending herself whom nobody attacked, protesting her dislike to gaiety and dissipation—you would have fancied her an artless young country lass, only longing to trip back to her village, milk her cows at sunrise, and sit spinning of winter evenings by the fire." She thoroughly takes in Laura Pendennis, whose Christian discourses sound so ponderously edifying that she has on occasion been regarded as the voice of Thackeray himself setting a moral standard. Rehearsing Ethel's familiar account of being bred to vanity, Laura credits her with fresh insight: "Ethel's simple talk," she says, "made me smile sometimes, do you know, and her *strenuous* way of imparting her discoveries. I thought of the shepherd boy who made a watch, and found on taking it into the town how very many watches there were, and how much better than his. . . . She told me very

artlessly her little history, Arthur; it affected me to hear her simple talk, and—
and I blessed God for our mother, my dear, and that my early days had had
a better guide." Here is yet another case of self-centered vision—Laura inspired by her own vein of moral enthusiasm and selecting from Ethel's variety
of artifices the one she wants to believe is artless.

Just as the Colonel in adoring his son figuratively confronts the prim
cold statue that resists his love, so Clive confronts the statue of the virgin
huntress, Diana. As a painter, Clive naturally idealizes Ethel in works of imagination: "A frequenter of his studio might see a whole gallery of Ethels
. . . one face and figure repeated on a hundred canvases and papers." Before
the works of the great masters, "Clive's heart sang hymns, as it were . . .
and, somewhat as he worshipped these masterpieces of his art he admired
the beauty of Ethel." More especially, however, he identifies her with the
statue of Diana in the Louvre: the "famous Parisian marble" could not be
"more perfect in form than this young lady." Thackeray, nevertheless, suggests the flaw in Clive's imaginary portrait and the latent menace in Ethel
even in the midst of Clive's encomiums: " 'By Jove, how handsome she is
. . . how grand she would look as Herodias's daughter . . . with the muscles
accented like that glorious Diana at Paris—a savage smile on her face and
a ghastly, solemn, gory head on the dish—I see the picture, sir, I see the picture!' and he fell to curling his moustache—just like his brave old father."
In the same passage, Clive moves from "a fond eulogium of his sire" to the
excited statement "that if his father wanted him to marry, he would marry
that instant. And why not Rosey?" The answer to this rhetorical question
is evident in his unconsciously ominous comment on how to paint poor Rosey:
"You ought to paint her in milk, sir!" Pendennis, as narrator, makes clear
the social significance of the Diana image, saying of the most sordid part
of Ethel's career, "I was not present when Diana and Diana's grandmother
hunted the noble Scottish stag . . . Lord Farintosh." But Thackeray also emphasizes "the haughty virginal expression" of the Diana, thereby underscor-
ing both the complexities of Ethel's psychology and the poor chances of her
worshipers, for her prey once caught is spurned—Lord Kew, Farintosh, and
always Clive. Worship as he may, Clive cannot bring this statue alive to suit
his artistic vision.

The fault is not simply in Ethel. Clive is a submissive son, an irresolute
lover, and a half-hearted artist. Clive's loving compliance combined with the
Colonel's loving readiness to pattern lives creates tragedy. If there is a standard in the book against which these pursuers of imaginary designs can be
measured, it is probably to be found in Clive's fellow painter, J. J. Ridley,
the butler's son whom Clive befriends, patronizes, and gradually learns to
respect. While Clive plays at art, Ridley works at it. But Ridley is unobtrusive

by nature and a background figure in the novel. To the extent that his presence is felt, however, he does distinguish the genuine from the false, the inspired from the shabby, both in his friend Clive and in art. The two concerns come together for a moment at the height of the Colonel's prestige, when, at the annual dinner of the Bundelcund Banking Company, Rosey is presented with

> a superb silver coco-nut-tree, whereof the leaves were dexterously arranged for holding candles and pickles; under the coco-nut was an Indian prince on a camel giving his hand to a cavalry officer on horseback—a howitzer, a plough, a loom, a bale of cotton, on which were the East India Company's arms, a brahmin, Britannia, and Commerce, with a cornucopia were grouped round the principal figures . . . [a] chaste and elegant speciment of British art.

Amidst the splendid speeches, Pendennis notices "J. J. eyeing the trophy, and the queer expression of his shrewd face. The health of British Artists was drunk à propos of this splendid specimen of their skill, and poor J. J. Ridley, Esq., A.R.A., had scarce a word to say in return." J. J. and Clive sit gloomily together, neither satisfied with Clive's condition. The coco-nut tree in its monstrosity is a miniature version of Clive's home as Rosey and the Colonel have embellished it and where "Clive, in the midst of all these splendours, was gaunt, and sad, and silent."

As a mercenary creature of facts, figures, and malice, Barnes would seem to be far removed from these indulgers in quixotic, artistic, and social fantasies. He hates the Colonel and Clive for the daily beauty of their lives as compared with his own cowardly, simpering snobbery. Warrington sees Barnes as one of "Nature's rogues," far superior to the imaginary villains of novelists—though it may be noted that Warrington has to call on Swift, Pope, and Zoroaster to describe him adequately. But Barnes, too, acts out imaginary designs: the impersonal man of business as he maliciously plots against the Colonel, the doughty warrior as he threatens duels with Belsize or the Colonel (but quaking in terror all the time lest they get around his excuses and actually fight him), the banker with a heart of gold as he lectures on the Poetry of Childhood and the Poetry of Womanhood and the Affections (this after rejecting the girl he seduced and beating his wife until she deserts him). If Barnes is the harsh reality of the world against which fairy-tale schemes and visions are to be measured, what a maze of fantasy that reality encompasses.

Surrounding these major figures, the minor characters of the novel further illustrate the patterns I have suggested, either living within an enclosing conventional fable, or imposing a predetermined pattern on others. While Clara Pulleyn and Jack Belsize on one level show us the frustrations and con-

sequences of the marriage market and are therefore part of Thackeray's
renowned and shrewd assessment of society, they are nevertheless presented
in terms of thoroughly conventional fantasy and artifice. Lady Clara belongs
to the animal fable of the novel's beginning, as her name, Pulleyn, suggests.
Her father's estate is Chanticlere, her brother is Viscount Rooster, and
Rooster's grandfather once "played two nights and two days at a sitting with
Charles Fox." Belsize, threatening general destruction when Clara is sold to
Barnes, puts the Vicomte de Florac in mind of Corneille's *Le Cid*: "Suppose
you kill ze Fazér, you kill Kiou, you kill Roostere, your Chimène will have
a pretty moon of honey." Lord Kew protests the folly of seeing Belsize and
Clara as "Jenny and Jessamy falling in love at first sight, billing and cooing
in an arbour, and retiring to a cottage. . . . Pshaw! what folly is this!" In
addition to these containing fictions of Clara and Belsize are the further versions drawn from *Marriage à la Mode* and the contrary fictions of the lawyers
in Barnes's divorce trial.

The Duchesse d'Ivry, whose jealous plotting sabotages the marriage of
Ethel and Lord Kew, is otherwise known as Mary Queen of Scots. She
resembles "the master of the theatrical booth" in that "this lady with her
platonic lovers went through the complete dramatic course,—tragedies of
jealousy, pantomimes of rapture, and farces of parting." "She was Phèdre.
. . . She was Medea." When in a pique of jealousy she plots to have Lord
Kew killed, she hires a poet who is a compound of literary and nationalistic
clichés to do the job. The author of *Les Râles d'un Asphyxié*, "he drank great
quantities of absinthe of a morning; smoked incessantly: played roulette when
he could get a few pieces: contributed to a small journal, and was especially
great in his hatred of *l'infâme Angleterre. Delenda est Carthago* was tatooed
beneath his shirtsleeve," and he shook his fist at the lion in the Garden of
Plants. Fantastic but convincing, indeed all too familiar in his bizarre enthusiasm, this poetic patriot may well remind us of Oscar Wilde's comment
on the boy burglar inspired by tales of Jack Sheppard: "He is Fact, occupied
as Fact usually is, with trying to reproduce Fiction, and what we see in him
is repeated on an extended scale throughout the whole of life" ("The Decay
of Lying").

To conclude, then, at close range in *The Newcomes* we see two related
patterns of action: on the one hand, attempts to impose the imagination's
daydreams and formulas on the lives of others, as with the Colonel; on the
other, stylization of behavior according to conventional fancies as with Ethel.
Standing farther back from Thackeray's canvas, we see life as a series of recurrent formulas, so that, as he says, all stories are old. Everywhere the narrative is saturated with traditional and familiar fictions from art, literature,
mythology and social convention that not only adorn reality and displace

reality but become reality. A depiction of the world so highly fictive may lead us to reconsider Thackeray's long-standing reputation as a realist, but not because he eschews the accidents of experience for the patterns of imagination—rather, the two are in perennial tension. What seems unique, chaotic, and real is merely segmented from the eternal pattern, and he keeps both before us. Put another way, he is portraying an affliction of the imagination. Man imagines style, order or perfection, but he lives in a world of limitation. As Camus says: "There is not one human being who, above a certain elementary level of consciousness, does not exhaust himself in trying to find formulas or attitudes that will give his existence the unity it lacks. . . . The same impulse . . . also leads to creative literature which derives its serious content from this source" (*The Rebel: An Essay on Man in Revolt*). In short, the impulse that shapes both life and art is a reflex from the consciousness that, though imagination and reason would order it otherwise, "the race is not to the swift, nor the battle to the strong, neither yet bread to the wise, nor yet riches to men of understanding, nor yet favour to men of skill; but time and chance happeneth to them all" (Eccles. 9:11).

Traditionally and rightly, readers have considered *The Newcomes* a masterly depiction of a certain social milieu: that of "the most polite, and most intelligent, and best informed, and best dressed, and most selfish people in the world." It is a much richer book than that might suggest, however, and I have been at pains to illustrate one of the several dimensions of that richness. Thackeray himself remarked: "I can't jump further than I did in *The Newcomes*." Since everyone knows Henry James irritably labeled *The Newcomes* a "baggy monster" (Preface to *The Tragic Muse*), it may be well to conclude with his wonderful recollection in *Notes of a Son and Brother* of the great Victorian serial novels in general and *The Newcomes* in particular: "These various, let alone numerous, deeper-toned strokes of the great Victorian clock were so many steps in the march of our age. . . . I witnessed, for that matter, with all my senses, young as I was, the never-to-be-equalled degree of difference made, for what may really be called the world-consciousness happily exposed to it, by the prolonged 'coming-out' of The Newcomes, yellow number by number, and could take the general civilised participation in the process for a sort of basking in the light of distinction."

WOLFGANG ISER

# The Reader as a Component Part
# of the Realistic Novel: Esthetic Effects
# in Thackeray's Vanity Fair

"You must have your eyes forever on your Reader. That alone constitutes
. . . Technique!" Ford Madox Ford's exhortation to the novelist draws attention to one of the few basic rules that have governed the novel throughout
its relatively short history. This awareness as a prerequisite for steering the
reader has always exerted a fundamental influence on the form of the narrative. From the start the novel as a "genre" was virtually free from traditional constraints and so the novelists of the eighteenth century considered
themselves not merely as the creators of their works but also as the law-
makers. The events they devise also set out the standards regarded as necessary
for judging the events; this is shown clearly by Defoe and Richardson in their
prefaces and commentaries, and especially by Fielding in the innumerable
essays with which he permeates his narrative. Such interventions are meant
to indicate how the author wants his text to be understood, and also to make
the reader more deeply aware of those events for the judgment of which his
own imagination has to be mobilized. With the author manipulating the
reader's attitude, the narrator becomes his own commentator and is not afraid
to break into the world he is describing in order to provide his own explana-
tions. That this is a deliberate process is demonstrated by a sentence from
Fielding's *Tom Jones*: "And this, as I could not prevail on any of my actors
to speak, I myself was obliged to declare."

And so the novel as a form in the eighteenth century is shaped by the
dialogue that the author wishes to conduct with his reader. This simulated

From *The Implied Reader: Patterns of Communication in Prose Fiction from Bunyan
to Beckett.* © 1974 by the Johns Hopkins University Press, Baltimore/London.

relationship gives the reader the impression that he and the author are part-
ners in discovering the reality of human experience. In this reader-oriented
presentation of the world, one can see an historical reflection of the period
when the possibility of a priori knowledge was refuted, leaving fiction as
the only means of supplying the insight into human nature denied by em-
pirical philosophy.

The author-reader relationship, which was thus developed by the
eighteenth-century novel, has remained a constant feature of narrative prose
and is still in evidence even when the author seems to have disappeared and
the reader is deliberately excluded from comprehension. While Fielding offers
this reassurance to his readers: "I am, indeed, set over them for their own
good only, and was created for their use, and not they for mine," Joyce, at
the other end of the scale drops only the ironic information that the author
has withdrawn behind his work, "paring his fingernails." The reader of
modern novels is deprived of the assistance which the eighteenth-century
writer had given him in a variety of devices ranging from earnest exhortation to satire and irony. Instead, he is expected to strive for himself to unravel
the mysteries of a sometimes strikingly obscure composition. This development reflects the transformation of the very idea of literature, which seems
to have ceased to be a means of relaxation and even luxury, making demands
now on the capacity of understanding because the world presented seems
to have no bearing on what the reader is familiar with. This change did not
happen suddenly. The stages of transition are clearly discernible in the nineteenth century, and one of them is virtually a half-way point in the development: the so-called "realistic" novel. An outstanding example of this is
Thackeray's *Vanity Fair*. Here, the author-reader relationship is as different
from the eighteenth-century "dialogue" as it is from the twentieth-century
demand that the reader find for himself the key to a many-sided puzzle. In
Thackeray, the reader does have to make his own discoveries, but the author
provides him with unmistakable clues to guide him in his search.

The first stage in our discussion must be to modify the term "author."
We should distinguish, as Wayne Booth does in his *Rhetoric of Fiction*, between the man who writes the book (author), the man whose attitudes shape
the book (implied author), and the man who communicates directly with
the reader (narrator): "The 'implied author' chooses, consciously or unconsciously, what we read; . . . he is the sum of his own choices. . . . This
implied author is always distinct from the 'real man'—whatever we may take
him to be—who creates a superior version of himself, a 'second self,' as he
creates his work." The narrator, of course, is not always to be identified with
the implied author. In the novels of the nineteenth century it happens again
and again that the narrator moves even further and further away from the

implied author by virtue of being an actual character in the story itself. Traces of this kind of narrator are already apparent in Dickens's novels, and in Thackeray's *Vanity Fair* he is a complete character in his own right. It is almost as if the implied author, who devised the story, has to bow to the narrator, who had a deeper insight into all the situations. What the implied author describes is interpreted by the narrator to a degree far beyond what one might normally deduce from the events. One is bound to ask the purpose of this clear though sometimes complex separation between narration and commentary, especially in a "realistic" novel which is supposed to represent reality as it is. The justification lies in the fact that even a realistic novel cannot encompass total reality. As Arnold Bennett once remarked: "You can't put the whole of a character into a book." If the limitations of the novel are such that one cannot reveal a complete character, it is even more impossible to try to transcribe complete reality. And so even a novel that is called realistic can present no more than particular aspects of a given reality, although the selection must remain implicit in order to cloak the author's ideology.

## II

Thackeray's *Vanity Fair* is also governed by this principle, which is clearly reflected by the differing titles of the original version and the final one. The first, consisting of eight chapters, was called "Pen and Pencil Sketches of English Society," indicating that the reality described was meant primarily as a reproduction of social situations; the final version, "Vanity Fair," is concerned less with depicting social situations than with offering a judgment of them. This quality is commented on by Thackeray himself in a letter written a few years after the publication of *Vanity Fair*: "the Art of Novels *is* . . . to convey as strongly as possible the sentiment of reality—in a tragedy or a poem or a lofty drama you aim at producing different emotions; the figures moving, and their words sounding, heroically." "Sentiment of reality" implies that the novel does not represent reality itself, but aims rather at producing an idea of how reality can be experienced. This *Vanity Fair* not only offers a panorama of contemporary reality but also reveals the way in which the abundance of details has been organized, so that the reader can participate in the organization of events and thus gain the "sentiment of reality." This is the reason why the novel continues to be effective even today, though the social conditions it describes are only of historical interest. If the past has been kept alive, this is primarily due to the structural pattern through which the events are conveyed to the reader: the effect is gained by the interplay between the implied author who arranges the events, and the narrator who comments on them. The reader can only gain real access to the social reality presented by the implied author, when he follows the adjustments of perspective made by the narrator in viewing the events described. In order to ensure that the reader participates in the way desired, the narrator is set up as a kind of authority between him and the events, conveying the impression that understanding can only be achieved through this medium. In the course of the action, the narrator takes on various guises in order to appear as a fully developed character and in order to control the distance from which the reader has to view the scenes unfolded before him.

At the start of the novel, the narrator introduces himself as "Manager of the Performance," and gives an outline of what the audience is to expect. The ideal visitor to "Vanity Fair" is described as a "man with a reflective turn of mind"; this is an advance indication of what the reader has to accomplish, if he is to realize the meaning of the proceedings. But at the same time, the Manager promises that he has something for everyone: "Some people consider Fairs immoral altogether, and eschew such, with their servants and families: very likely they are right. But persons who think otherwise, and are of a lazy, or a benevolent, or a sarcastic mood, may perhaps like to step in for half an hour, and look at the performances. There are scenes of all sorts: some dreadful combats, some grand and lofty horse-riding, some scenes of high life, and some of very middling indeed; some love-making for the sentimental, and some light comic business." In this way the Manager tries to entice all different types of visitors to enter his Fair—bearing in mind the fact that such a visit will also have its aftereffects. When the reader has been following the narrator for quite some time, he is informed: "This, dear friends and companions, is my amiable object—to walk with you through the Fair, to examine the shops and the shows there; and that we should all come home after the flare, and the noise, and the gaiety, and be perfectly miserable in private." But the reader will only feel miserable after walking through the Fair if, unexpectedly, he has come upon himself in some of the situations, thereby having his attention drawn to his own behavior, which has shone out at him from the mirror of possibilities. The narrator is only pretending to help the reader—in reality he is goading him. His reliability is already reduced by the fact that he is continually donning new masks: at one moment he is an observer of the Fair, like the reader; then he is suddenly blessed with extraordinary knowledge, though he can explain ironically that "novelists have the privilege of knowing everything"; and then, toward the end, he announces that the whole story was not his own at all, but that he overheard it in a conversation. At the beginning of the novel the narrator is presented as Manager of the Performance, and at the end he presents himself as the reporter of a story which fell into his hands purely by chance. The further away he stands from the social reality depicted, the clearer is the outline of the part he is meant to play. But the reader can only view the social panorama in the constantly shifting perspectives which are opened up for him by this Protean narrator. Although he cannot help following the views and interpretations of the narrator, it is essential for him to understand the motivations behind this constant changing of viewpoints, because only the discovery of the motivations can lead to the comprehension of what is intended. Thus the narrator regulates the distance between reader and events, and in doing so brings about the esthetic effect of the story. The reader is given only as much information as will keep him oriented and interested, but the narrator deliberately leaves open the inferences that are to be drawn from this information. Consequently, empty spaces are bound to occur, spurring the reader's imagination to detect the assumption which might have motivated the narrator's attitude. In this way, we get involved because we react to the viewpoints advanced by the narrator. If the narrator is an independent character, clearly separated from the inventor of the story, the tale of the social aspirations of the two girls Becky and Amelia takes on a greater degree of objectivity, and indeed one gains the impression that this social reality is not a mere narration but actually exists. The narrator can then be regarded as a sort of mediator between the reader and the events, with the implication that it is only through him that the social reality can be rendered communicable in the first place.

### III

The narrator's strategy can be seen even more clearly in his relations with the characters in the novel and with the reader's expectations. *Vanity Fair* has as the subtitle, *A Novel without a Hero*, which indicates that the characters are not regarded as representing an ideal, exemplary form of human conduct, as established by the conventions of the eighteenth-century novel. Instead, the reader's interest is divided between two figures who, despite the contrast in their behavior, can under no circumstances be regarded as complementary or even corrective. For Becky, no price is too high for the fulfillment of her social ambitions; her friend Amelia is simple and sentimental. And so right at the beginning we are told:

> As she is not a heroine, there is no need to describe her person;
> indeed I am afraid that her nose was rather short than otherwise,
> and her cheeks a great deal too round and red for a heroine; but
> her face blushed with rosy health, and her lips with the freshest
> of smiles, and she had a pair of eyes which sparkled with the
> brightest and honestest good-humour, except indeed when they

> filled with tears, and that was a great deal too often; for the silly
> thing would cry over a dead canary-bird; or over a mouse, that
> the cat haply had seized upon; or over the end of a novel, were
> it ever so stupid.

The details of such a description serve only to trivialize those features that
were so important in the hero or heroine of the traditional novel. These details
give the impression that something significant is being said about the person
described, but the succession of clichés, from the round red cheeks and
sparkling eyes to the soft-hearted sentimentality, achieve their purpose precisely by depriving the character of its representative nature. But if Amelia is
deprived of traditional representative qualities and is not to be regarded as
the positive counterpart to the unscrupulous, sophisticated Becky, then the
novel denies the reader a basic focal point of orientation. He is prevented
from sympathizing with the hero—a process which till now had always provided the nineteenth-century reader with his most important means of access
to the events described—as typified by the reaction of a reviewer to Charlotte
Brontë's *Jane Eyre*: "We took up *Jane Eyre* one winter's evening, somewhat
piqued at the extravagant commendations we had heard, and sternly resolved
to be as critical as Croker. But as we read on we forgot both commendations and criticism, identified ourselves with Jane in all her troubles, and finally married Mr. Rochester about four in the morning" (quoted by Kathleen
Tillotson in *Novels of the Eighteen-Forties*). In contrast, *Vanity Fair* seems
bent on breaking any such direct contact with the characters, and indeed
the narrator frequently goes out of his way to prevent the reader from putting himself in their place.

   This occurs predominantly through the narrator's comments on the particular patterns of behavior developed by Amelia and Becky in critical situations. He reveals the motives behind their utterances, interpolating consequences of which they themselves are not aware, so that these occasions serve
to uncover the imbalance of the characters. Often the behavior of the
characters is interpreted far beyond the scope of the reactions shown and
in the light of knowledge which at best could only have been revealed by
the future. In this way the reader is continually placed at a distance from the
characters. As Michel Butor once pointed out, in a different context: "If
the reader is put in the place of the hero, he must also be put in the hero's
immediate present; he cannot know what the hero does not know, and things
must appear to him just as they appear to the hero." In *Vanity Fair*, however,
the characters are illuminated by a knowledge to which they themselves have
no access. They are constantly kept down below the intellectual level of the
narrator, whose views offer the reader a far greater stimulus to identifica-

tion than do the characters themselves. This detachment from the characters is part of the narrator's avowed intention: "as we bring our characters forward, I will ask leave, as a man and a brother, not only to introduce them, but occasionally to step down from the platform, and talk about them: if they are good and kindly, to love them and shake them by the hand; if they are silly, to laugh at them confidentially in the reader's sleeve: if they are wicked and heartless, to abuse them in the strongest terms which politeness admits of." The characters in this novel are completely hedged in by such judgments, and the reader sees all their actions only when they have been refracted by the narrator's own critical evaluation. The immensity of his presence makes it impossible for the reader to live their lives with them, as did the reviewer we have quoted, during his reading of *Jane Eyre*. The actual gap between the characters' actions and the narrator's comments stimulates the reader into forming judgments of his own—thereby bridging the gaps—and gradually adopting the position of critic himself.

It is mainly this intention that shapes the composition of the characters, and there are two dominant techniques to be observed. The first part of the novel reproduces letters which Becky and Amelia write to each other. The letter makes it possible to reveal the most intimate thoughts and feelings to such a degree that the reader can learn from the correspondents themselves just who they are and what makes them "tick." A typical example is Becky's long letter telling Amelia all about her new surroundings at the Crawley family's country seat. Becky's impressions end with the spontaneous self-revelation: "I am determined to make myself agreeable." Fitting in with present circumstances remains her guiding principle throughout her quest for social advancement. Such a wish is so totally in keeping with her own character that the maneuvers necessary for its fulfillment constitute for Becky the natural way to behave. Thus we see that in society, self-seeking hypocrisy has become second nature to man. In the letters, however, Becky's self-esteem remains so constant that she is clearly quite unaware of her two-facedness. The obvious naiveté of such self-portraits is bound to provoke the reader into critical reaction, and the heading of the chapter that reproduces Becky's letter is already pointing in this direction, for the unmistakably ironic title is: "Arcadian Simplicity." Thus the self-revelation of the letter actually justifies the narrator for not taking the character as it is, but setting it at a critical distance so that it can be seen through. Elsewhere we read: "Perhaps in Vanity Fair there are no better satires than letters." But the invention of the satire is for the reader himself to uncover, for the narrator never offers him more than ironic clues. The narrator's keen concern to give the impression that he never commits himself to ultimate clarity reveals itself at those times when he accidentally reaches an "understanding" with his reader, but then remembers that such an exchange of experiences goes beyond the limits of his narrative: "but we are wandering out of the domain of the story."

The second technique designed to rouse the critical faculties of the reader is revealed in Amelia's almost obsessive habit of "building numberless castles in the air . . . which Amelia adorned with all sorts of flower-gardens, rustic walks, country churches, Sunday schools, and the like." This daydreaming is typical of Amelia, who devises these beautiful visions as an escape from the narrow confines of her social existence. Her whole outlook is governed by expectations that generally arise out of chance events in her life and are therefore as subject to fortuitous change as the social situations she gets into. The dependence of these often very sentimental daydreams on the circumstances of the moment shows not only the fickleness of her behavior but also the disorientated nature of her desires, the fulfillment of which is inevitably frustrated by the apparently superior forces of her environment. The projection of hopes which cannot be realized leads to an attitude which is as characteristic of Amelia as it is of Becky, who for different motives also covers up what she really is, in order to gain the social position she hankers after. Despite the difference in their motives, both Amelia's and Becky's lives are largely governed by illusions, which are shown up for what they are by the fact that whenever they are partially realized, we see how very trivial the aspirations really were. The characters themselves, however, lack this awareness, and this is hardly surprising, as their ambitions or longings are often roused by chance occurrences which are not of sufficient lasting importance to give the characters a true sense of direction. Becky certainly has greater drive in her quest for social advancement, and one would therefore expect a greater degree of continuity in her conduct; but this very ambition requires that she should adapt her conduct to the various demands made by the different strata of society; and this fact in turn shows how malleable and therefore illusory are the conventions of social life. What is presented in Becky's life as continuity should not be confused with the aspirations of the eighteenth-century hero, who went forth in order to find out the truth about himself; here it is the expression of the many-sided sham which is the very attribute of social reality.

When the narrator introduces his characters at the beginning of the novel, he says of Becky: "The famous little Becky Puppet has been pronounced to be uncommonly flexible in the joints, and lively on the wire." As the characters cannot free themselves from their illusions, it is only to be expected that they should take them for unquestionable reality. The reader is made aware of this fact by the attitude of the narrator, who has not only seen through his "puppets," but also lets them act on a level of consciousness far below his own. This almost overwhelming superiority of the narrator over his characters also puts the reader in a privileged position, though with the unspoken but ever-present condition that he should draw his own conclusions from the extra knowledge imparted to him by the narrator. There is even an allegory of the reader's task at one point in the novel, when Becky is basking in the splendor of a grand social evening:

> The man who brought her refreshment and stood behind her chair, had talked her character over with the large gentleman in motley-coloured clothes at his side. Bon Dieu! it is awful, that servants' inquisition! You see a woman in a great party in a splendid saloon, surrounded by faithful admirers, distributing sparkling glances, dressed to perfection, curled, rouged, smiling and happy:—Discovery walks respectfully up to her, in the shape of a huge powdered man with large calves and a tray of ices—with Calumny (which is as fatal as truth) behind him, in the shape of the hulking fellow carrying the wafer-biscuits, Madam, your secret will be talked over by those men at their club at the public-house to-night. . . . Some people ought to have mutes for servants in Vanity Fair—mutes who could not write. If you are guilty, tremble. That fellow behind your chair may be a Janissary with a bowstring in his plush breeches pocket. If you are not guilty, have a care of appearances: which are as ruinous as guilt.

This little scene contains a change of standpoints typical of the way in which the reader's observations are conditioned throughout this novel. The servants are suddenly transformed into allegorical figures with the function of uncovering what lies hidden beneath the façades of their masters. But the discovery will only turn into calumny from the standpoint of the person affected. The narrator compares the destructive effect of calumny with that of truth and advises his readers to employ mutes, or better still illiterate mutes, as servants, in order to protect themselves against discovery. Then he brings the reader's view even more sharply into focus, finally leaving him to himself with an indissoluble ambiguity: if he feels guilty, because he is pretending to be something he is not, then he must fear those around him as if they were an army of Janissaries. If he has nothing to hide, then the social circle merely demands of him to keep up appearances; but since this is just as ruinous as deliberate hypocrisy, it follows that life in society imposes roles on all concerned, reducing human behavior to the level of playacting. All the characters in the novel are caught up in this play, as is expressly shown by the narrator's own stage metaphor at the beginning and at the end. The key word for the reader is "discover," and the narrator continually prods him along the road to discovery, laying a trail of clues for him to follow.

The process reveals not only the extent to which Becky and Amelia take their illusions for reality but also—even more strikingly—the extent to which reality itself is illusory, since it is built on the simulated relationships between people. The reader will not fail to notice the gulf between "illusion" and "reality," and in realizing it, he is experiencing the esthetic effect of the novel: Thackeray did not set out to create the conventional illusion that involved the reader in the world of the novel as if it were reality; instead, his narrator constantly interrupts the story precisely in order to prevent such an illusion from coming into being. The reader is deliberately stopped from identifying himself with the characters. And as the aim is to prevent him from taking part in the events, he is allowed to be absorbed only to a certain degree and is then jerked back again, so that he is impelled to criticize from the outside. Thus the story of the two girls serves to get the reader involved, while the meaning of the story can only be arrived at by way of the additional manipulations of perspective carried out by the narrator.

This "split-level" technique conveys a far stronger impression of reality than does the illusion which claims that the world of the novel corresponds to the whole world. For now the reader himself has to discover the true situation, which becomes clearer and clearer to him as he gets to know the characters in their fetters of illusion. In this way, he himself takes an active part in the animation of all the characters' actions, for they seem real to him because he is constantly under obligation to work out all that is wrong with their behavior. In order that his participation should not be allowed to slacken, the individual characters are fitted out with different types and degrees of delusion, and there are even some, like Dobbin, whose actions and feelings might mislead one into taking them for positive counterparts to all the other characters. Such a false assumption is certainly perceived, even if not intended, by the narrator, who toward the end of the novel addresses the reader as follows: "This woman [i.e., Amelia] had a way of tyrannising over Major Dobbin (for the weakest of all people will domineer over somebody), and she ordered him about, and patted him, and made him fetch and carry just as if he was a great Newfoundland dog. . . . This history has been written to very little purpose if the reader has not perceived that the Major was a spooney." What might have seemed like noble-mindedness was in fact the behavior of a nincompoop, and if the reader has only just realized it, then he has not been particularly successful in the process of "discovering."

The esthetic effect of *Vanity Fair* depends on activating the reader's critical faculties so that he may recognize the social reality of the novel as a confusing array of sham attitudes, and experience the exposure of this sham as the true reality. Instead of being expressly stated, the criteria for such

judgments have to be inferred. They are the blanks which the reader is supposed to fill in, thus bringing his own criticism to bear. In other words, it
is his own criticism that constitutes the reality of the book. The novel, then,
is not to be viewed as the mere reflection of a social reality, for its true form
will only be revealed when the world it presents has, like all images, been
refracted and converted by the mind of the reader. *Vanity Fair* aims not at
presenting social reality, but at presenting the way in which such reality can
be experienced. "To convey as strongly as possible the sentiment of reality"
is Thackeray's description of this process, which he regarded as the function
of the novel. If the sense of the narrative can only be completed through the
cooperation of the reader (which is allowed for in the text), then the borderline
between fiction and reality becomes increasingly hazy, for the reader can
scarcely regard his own participation as fictional. He is bound to look on
his reactions as something real, and at no time is this conviction disputed.
But since his reactions are real, he will lose the feeling that he is judging a
world that is only fictional. Indeed, his own judgments will enhance the impression he has that this world is a reality.

How very concerned Thackeray was to confront the reader with a reality
he himself considered to be real is clear from the passage already quoted,
in which the narrator tells the reader that his object is to walk with him
through the Fair and leave him "perfectly miserable" afterward. Thackeray
reiterates this intention in a letter written in 1848: "my object . . . is to indicate, in cheerful terms, that we are for the most part an abominably foolish
and selfish people . . . all eager after vanities . . . I want to leave everybody
dissatisfied and unhappy at the end of the story—we ought all to be with
our own and all other stories. For this insight to take root in the reader, the
fictional world must be made to seem real to him. Since, in addition, the
reader is intended to be a critic of this world, the esthetic appeal of the novel
lies in the fact that it gives him the opportunity to step back and take a
detached look at that which he had regarded as normal human conduct. This
detachment, however, is not to be equated with the edification which the
moral novel offered to its readers. Leaving the reader perfectly miserable after
his reading indicates that such a novel is not going to offer him pictures of
another world that will make him forget the sordid nature of this one; the
reader is forced, rather, to exercise his own critical faculties in order to relieve
his distress by uncovering potential alternatives arising out of the world he
has read about. "A man with a reflective turn of mind" is therefore the ideal
reader for this novel. W. J. Harvey has remarked, in a different context:

> A novel . . . can allow for a much fuller expression of this sensed
> penumbra of unrealized possibilities, of all the what-might-have-

beens of our lives. It is because of this that the novel permits a
much greater liberty of such speculation on the part of the reader
than does the play. Such speculation frequently becomes, as it does
in real life, part of the substantial reality of the identity of any
character. The character moves in the full depth of his conditional
freedom; he is what he is but he might have been otherwise. Indeed the novel does not merely *allow* for this liberty of speculation; sometimes it *encourages* it to the extent that our sense of
conditional freedom in this aspect becomes one of the ordering
structural principles of the entire work.

(Character and the Novel)

## IV

The aspect of the novel which we have discussed so far is the narrator's
continual endeavor to stimulate the reader's mind through extensive commentaries on the actions of the characters. This indirect form of guidance is supplemented by a number of remarks relating directly to the expectations and
supposed habits of the novel-reader. If the fulfillment of the novel demands
a heightened faculty of judgment, it is only natural that the narrator should
also compel the reader—at times quite openly—to reflect on his own situation, for without doing so he will be incapable of judging the actions of the
characters in the novel. For this process to be effective, the possible reader
must be visualized as playing a particular role with particular characteristics,
which may vary according to circumstances. And so just as the author divides
himself up into the narrator of the story and the commentator on the events
in the story, the reader is also stylized to a certain degree, being given attributes which he may either accept or reject. Whatever happens he will be
forced to react to those ready-made qualities ascribed to him. In this manner
the double role of the author has a parallel in that of the reader, as W. Booth
has pointed out in a discussion on the narrator:

> the same distinction must be made between myself as reader and
> the very often different self who goes about paying bills, repair-
> ing leaky faucets, and failing in generosity and wisdom. It is only
> as I read that I become the self whose beliefs must coincide with
> the author's. Regardless of my real beliefs and practices, I must
> subordinate my mind and heart to the book if I am to enjoy it
> to the full. The author creates, in short, an image of himself
> and another image of his reader; he makes his reader, as he
> makes his second self, and the most successful reading is one in

which the created selves, author and reader, can find complete agreement.

Such an agreement can, however, be reached along widely differing lines, for instance through disagreement—i.e., a subtly instituted opposition between reader and narrator—and this is what happens in *Vanity Fair.*

When the narrator pretends to be at one with the reader in evaluating a certain situation, the reverse is usually the case. For instance, he describes an old but rich spinster who is a member of the great Crawley family, into which Becky is going to marry, in fulfillment of her social aspirations:

> Miss Crawley was . . . an object of great respect when she came to Queen's Crawley, for she had a balance at her banker's which would have made her beloved anywhere. What a dignity it gives an old lady, that balance at the banker's! How tenderly we look at her faults if she is a relative (and may every reader have a score of such), what a kind good-natured old creature we find her! . . . How, when she comes to pay us a visit, we generally find an opportunity to let our friends know her station in the world! We say (and with perfect truth) I wish I had Miss Mac-Whirter's signature to a cheque for five thousand pounds. She wouldn't miss it, says your wife. She is my aunt, say you, in an easy careless way, when your friend asks if Miss MacWhirter is any relative. Your wife is perpetually sending her little testimonies of affection, your little girls work endless worsted baskets, cushions, and footstools for her. What a good fire there is in her room when she comes to pay you a visit, although your wife laces her stays without one! . . . Is it so, or is it not so?

By using the first-person plural, the narrator gives the impression that he is viewing through the reader's eyes the many attentions paid to the old lady with the large bank balance; for the reader such conduct is scarcely remarkable—indeed it is more the expression of a certain *savoir vivre.* By identifying himself with this view, the narrator seems to reinforce rather than to oppose this attitude, which is symptomatic of human nature. But in pretending merely to be describing "natural" reactions, he is in fact seeking to trap the reader into agreeing with him—and as soon as this is accomplished, the reader realizes for himself the extent to which consideration of personal gain shapes the natural impulses of human conduct.

In this way, the difference between the reader and the characters in the novel is eliminated. Instead of just seeing through them, he sees himself reflected in them, so that the superior position which the narrator has given him over the pretences and illusions of the characters now begins to fade. The reader realizes that he is similar to those who are supposed to be the objects of his criticism, and so the self-confrontations that permeate the novel compel him to become aware of his own position in evaluating that of the characters. In order to develop this awareness, the narrator creates situations in which the characters' actions correspond to what the reader is tricked into regarding as natural, subsequently feeling the irresistible urge to detach himself from the proceedings. And if the reader ignores the discreet summons to observe himself, then his critical attitude toward the characters becomes unintentionally hypocritical, for he forgets to include himself in the judgment. Thackeray did not want to edify his readers, but to leave them miserable, though with the tacit invitation to find ways of changing this condition for themselves.

This predominantly intellectual appeal to the mind of the reader was not always the norm in the realistic novel. In Dickens, for example, emotions are aroused in order to create a premeditated relationship between the reader and the characters. A typical illustration of this is the famous scene at the beginning of Oliver Twist, when the hungry child in the workhouse has the effrontery (as the narrator sees it) to ask for another plate of soup. In the presentation of this daring exploit, Oliver's inner feelings are deliberately excluded, in order to give greater emphasis to the indignation of the authorities at such an unreasonable request. The narrator comes down heavily on the side of authority, and can thus be quite sure that his hard-hearted attitude will arouse a flood of sympathy in his readers for the poor starving child. The reader is thus drawn so far into the action that he feels he must interfere. This effect, not unlike the tension at a Punch and Judy show, enables Dickens to convey contemporary reality to his readers. He follows traditional practice insofar as he brings about a total involvement of the reader in the action. In Thackeray things are different. He is concerned with preventing any close liaison between reader and characters. The reader of Vanity Fair is in fact forced into a position outside the reality of the novel, though the judgment demanded of him is not without a tension of its own, as he is always in danger of sliding into the action of the novel, thereby suddenly being subjected to the standards of his own criticism.

The narrator does not aim exclusively at precipitating his reader into such situations of involuntary identification with the characters. In order to sharpen the critical gaze, he also offers other modes of approach, though these demand a certain effort at discrimination on the part of the reader— for instance, when he wishes to describe, at least indirectly, the various aspects of the important love affair between Amelia and Osborne:

The observant reader, who has marked our young Lieutenant's previous behaviour, and has preserved our report of the brief conversation which he has just had with Captain Dobbin, has possibly come to certain conclusions regarding the character of Mr. Osborne. Some cynical Frenchman has said that there are two parties to a love-transaction: the one who loves and the other who condescends to be so treated. Perhaps the love is occasionally on the man's side; perhaps on the lady's. Perhaps some infatuated swain has ere this mistaken insensibility for modesty, dullness for maiden reserve, mere vacuity for sweet bashfulness, and a goose, in a word, for a swan. Perhaps some beloved female subscriber has arrayed an ass in the splendour and glory of her imagination; admired his dullness as manly simplicity; worshipped his selfishness as manly superiority; treated his stupidity as majestic gravity, and used him as the brilliant fairy Titania did a certain weaver at Athens. I think I have seen such comedies of errors going on in the world. But this is certain, that Amelia believed her lover to be one of the most gallant and brilliant men in the empire: and it is possible Lieutenant Osborne thought so too.

Apparently simple situations are taken apart for the reader and split up into different facets. He is free to work his way through each one and to choose whichever he thinks most appropriate, but whether this decision favor the image of the cynical Frenchman or that of the infatuated swain, there will always remain an element of doubt over the relationship under discussion. Indeed the definite view that Amelia has of her relationship with Osborne acts as a warning to the reader, as such a final, unambiguous decision runs the risk of being wrong.

The reader is constantly forced to think in terms of alternatives, as the only way in which he can avoid the unambiguous and suspect position of the characters is to visualize the possibilities which they have not thought of. While he is working out these alternatives the scope of his own judgment expands, and he is constantly invited to test and weigh the insights he has arrived at as a result of the profusion of situations offered him. The esthetic appeal of such a technique consists in the fact that it allows a certain latitude for the individual character of the reader, but also compels specific reactions—often unobtrusively—without expressly formulating them. By refusing to draw the reader into the illusory reality of the novel, and keeping him at a variable distance from the events, the text gives him the illusion that he can judge the proceedings in accordance with his own point of view.

To do this, he has only to be placed in a position that will provoke him to pass judgments, and the less loaded in advance these judgments are by the text, the greater will be the esthetic effect.

The "Manager of the Performance" opens up a whole panorama of views on the reality described, which can be seen from practically every social and human standpoint. The reader is offered a host of different perspectives, and so is almost continually confronted with the problem of how to make them consistent. This is all the more complicated as it is not just a matter of forming a view of the social world described, but of doing so in face of a rich variety of viewpoints offered by the commentator. There can be no doubt that the author wants to induce his reader to assume a critical attitude toward the reality portrayed, but at the same time he gives him the alternative of adopting one of the views offered him, or of developing one of his own. This choice is not without a certain amount of risk. If the reader adopts one of the attitudes suggested by the author, he must automatically exclude the others. If this happens, the impression arises, in this particular novel, that one is looking more at oneself than at the event described. There is an unmistakable narrowness in every standpoint, and in this respect the reflection the reader will see of himself will be anything but complimentary. But if the reader then changes his viewpoint, in order to avoid this narrowness, he will undergo the additional experience of finding that his behavior is very like that of the two girls who are constantly adapting themselves in order to ascend the social scale. All the same, his criticism of the girls appears to be valid. Is it not a reasonable assumption then that the novel was constructed as a means of turning the reader's criticism of social opportunism back upon himself? This is not mentioned specifically in the text, but it happens all the time. Thus, instead of society, the reader finds himself to be the object of criticism.

## V

Thackeray once mentioned casually: "I have said somewhere it is the unwritten part of books that would be the most interesting." It is in the unwritten part of the book that the reader has his place—hovering between the world of the characters and the guiding sovereignty of the "Manager of the Performance." If he comes too close to the characters, he learns the truth of what the narrator told him at the beginning: "The world is a looking-glass, and gives back to every man the reflection of his own face." If he stands back with the narrator to look at things from a distance, he sees through all the activities of the characters. Through the variableness of his own position, the reader experiences the meaning of *Vanity Fair*. Through the characters he undergoes a temporary entanglement in the web of his own illusions, and through the demand for judgment he is enabled to free himself from it and to get a better view of himself and of the world.

And so the story of the two girls and their social aspirations forms only one aspect of the novel, which is continually supplemented by views through different lenses, all of which are trained on the story with the intention of discovering its meaning. The necessity for these different perspectives indicates that the story itself does not reveal direct evidence as to its meaning, so that the factual reality depicted does not represent a total reality. It can only become total through the *manner* in which it is observed. Thus the narrator's commentary, with its often ingenious provocations of the reader, has the effect of an almost independent action running parallel to the story itself. Herein lies the difference between Thackeray and the naturalists of the nineteenth century, who set out to convince their readers that a relevant "slice of life" was total reality, whereas in fact it only represented an ideological assumption which, for all the accuracy of its details, was a manipulated reality.

In *Vanity Fair* it is not the slice of life, but the means of observing it that constitute the reality, and as these means of observation remain as valid today as they were in the nineteenth century, the novel remains as "real" now as it was then, even though the social world depicted is only of historical interest. It is in the preoccupation with different perspectives and with the activation of the reader himself that *Vanity Fair* marks a stage of transition between the traditional and what we now call the "modern" novel. The predominant aim is no longer to create the illusion of an objective outside reality, and the novelist is no longer concerned with projecting his own unambiguous view of the world onto his reader. Instead, his technique is to diversify his vision, in order to compel the reader to view things for himself and discover his own reality. The author has not yet withdrawn "to pare his fingernails," but he has already entered into the shadows and holds his scissors at the ready.

INA FERRIS

# The Breakdown of Thackeray's Narrator: Lovel the Widower

So few readers have even dipped into the pages of Thackeray's late fiction that an immediate and lengthy plunge is necessary to convey its peculiar features. The following segment constitutes the opening pages of chapter 5 of *Lovel the Widower*, a short fiction first serialized in the *Cornhill Magazine* in 1860. The narrator, Charles Batchelor, has proposed to the governess heroine, Bessy Prior, and waits in the garden for her reply. From there he sees her enter the morning-room and witnesses the egregious young alcoholic, Captain Baker, suddenly reveal his awareness of her former disreputable profession of dancer. Chapter 4 closes with Bessy's startled cry and Batchelor's promise that "what happened I shall tell in the ensuing chapter." Chapter 5 opens:

> If, when I heard Baker call out Bessy Bellenden [her stage name], and adjure Jove, he had run forward and seized Elizabeth by the waist, or offered her other personal indignity, I too should have run forward on my side and engaged him. Though I am a stout elderly man, short in stature and in wind, I know I am a match for *that* rickety little captain on his high-heeled boots. A match for him? I believe Miss Bessy would have been a match for both of us. Her white arm was as hard and polished as ivory. Had she held it straight pointed against the rush of the dragon, he would have fallen backwards before his intended prey: I have no doubt he would. It was the hen, in this case, was stronger than the liber-

From *Nineteenth-Century Fiction* 32, no. 1 (June 1977). © 1977 by the Regents of the University of California.

tine fox, and *au besoin* would have pecked the little marauding vermin's eyes out. Had, I say, Partlet been weak, and Reynard strong, I *would* have come forward: I certainly would. Had he been a wolf now, instead of a fox, I am certain I should have run in upon him, grappled with him, torn his heart and tongue out of his black throat, and trampled the lawless brute to death.

Well, I didn't do any such thing. I was just *going* to run in,— and I didn't. I was just going to rush to Bessy's side to clasp her (I have no doubt) to my heart: to beard the whiskered champion who was before her, and perhaps say, "Cheer thee—cheer thee, my persecuted maiden, my beauteous love—my Rebecca! Come on, Sir Brian de Bois Guilbert, thou dastard Templar! It is I, Sir Wilfred of Ivanhoe." (By the way, though the fellow was not a *Templar*, he was a *Lincoln's Inn* man, having passed twice through the Insolvent Court there with infinite discredit.) But I made no heroic speeches. There was no need for Rebecca to jump out of window and risk her lovely neck. How could she, in fact, the French window being flush with the ground floor? And I give you my honour just as I was crying my war-cry, couching my lance, and rushing *à la recousse* upon Sir Baker, a sudden thought made me drop my (figurative) point: a sudden idea made me rein in my galloping (metaphorical) steed, and spare Baker for that time.

Suppose I had gone in? But for that sudden precaution, there might have been a Mrs. Batchelor. I might have been a bullied father of ten children. (Elizabeth has a fine high temper of her own.) What is four hundred and twenty a year, with a wife and perhaps half-a-dozen children? Should I have been a whit the happier? Would Elizabeth? Ah! no. And yet I feel a certain sort of shame, even now, when I think that I didn't go in. Not that I was in a fright, as some people choose to hint. I swear I was not. But the reason why I did not charge was this:—

Nay, I *did* charge part of the way, and then, I own, stopped. It was an error in judgment. It wasn't a want of courage. Lord George Sackville was a brave man, and as cool as a cucumber under fire. Well, *he* didn't charge at the battle of Minden, and Prince Ferdinand made the deuce and all of a disturbance, as we know. Byng was a brave man,—and I ask, wasn't it a confounded shame executing him? So with respect to myself. Here is my statement. I make it openly. I don't care. I am accused of seeing a woman insulted, and not going to her rescue. I am not guilty, I say. That is, there were reasons which caused me not to attack.

Even putting aside the superior strength of Elizabeth herself to the enemy—I vow there were cogent and honourable reasons why I did not charge home.

You see I happened to be behind a blue lilac bush (and was turning a rhyme—Heaven help us!—in which *death* was only to part me and Elizabeth) when I saw Baker's face surge over the chair-back. I rush forward as he cries "by Jove." Had Miss Prior cried out on her part, the strength of twenty Heenans, I know, would have nerved this arm; but all she did was to turn pale, and say, "Oh, mercy! Captain Baker! Do pity me!"

Returning to the suspended external event, Batchelor records the confrontation between Bessy and Baker up to the moment when Baker seizes her hands. Narration then again ceases as Batchelor stops to ask, "Now do you understand why I paused?" and goes on to depict himself first as smitten with jealousy, then as anxious lest he might be contaminated by union with a woman whose disreputable past is known to others. (Batchelor himself has always known.) While Batchelor continues to hesitate ("just as I was going to step forward—to step?—to *rush* forward"), Bessy sends Baker sprawling to the floor. The door opens; Bedford the butler (also in love with Bessy) rushes in and "pitches into" Baker furiously until Bessy, laughing, calls him off. Batchelor, in a "rage of mortification" at Bedford's successful action, sneaks into the house by another path, "arriving like Fortinbras in *Hamlet*, when everyone is dead and sprawling, you know, and the whole business is done" (chap. 5).

What are we to make of this? Narrative has fallen apart. The sequence is permeated with false starts, failed modes, confused ironies. After asserting that he will record "what happened," Batchelor abruptly drops his narrative, withdraws from the reality he has established, and proceeds to experiment with a series of speculative fictions prompted by a hypothesis about what might have happened ("If . . . he had . . . I too should have"). The primary impulse here is defensive: Batchelor attempts to justify what did not happen—he did not act. So he suspends the narrative to generate fantasies that play with ways of reinventing the actual event in an attempt to mitigate the guilt aroused by contemplation of that event. Behind this lies not only Batchelor's particular psychological need but a more general uncertainty about the nature of his narrative effort. He cannot deal with the events at hand; cannot find a way to tell his story. Traditional modes enter as Batchelor transforms Bessy and Baker into figures from moral fable (hen and fox) but inverts their traditional roles, an inversion in which awareness of the inadequacy of conventional categories mingles with the impulse to justify his own failure of intention. This particular fable is quickly abandoned. Batchelor moves on to try out another fable ("Had he been a wolf now") but then discards this mode to set up an excursion into romance, imagining himself as Ivanhoe. Romance releases heroic fantasies, but Batchelor is unable to sustain the idiom ("the fellow was not a *Templar*, he was a *Lincoln's Inn* man"), as uneasy parody mingles with comic images of his own impotence.

With the failure of romance, Batchelor switches abruptly from re-creating his past to conjecture about the present that might have resulted had he performed the conventional action: "Suppose I had gone in?" Emphasis shifts from fantasy about what Batchelor would have done to defense of what he did not do. Turning to yet another narrative mode, he draws on history, creating a fiction that justifies the actual past and provides a context for his present narrative role. Invoking the controversial trials of Sackville and Byng, both convicted of failure to take required action in battle but not of cowardice, Batchelor imagines himself as a frank and spirited defendant addressing the court: "I am not guilty, I say." This assertive stance is immediately and expectedly qualified: "That is, there were reasons which caused me not to attack." These reasons are never made clear—Batchelor himself does not seem to know for certain—and he continues to advance hypotheses even after returning to his narrative. The reluctance to narrate and the experimentation with traditional modes to try out yet another self-image, yet another way of telling the story, persist to the end of the sequence. The ignominious entrance that concludes the episode brings in another literary tradition as Batchelor playfully presents the possibility of casting himself in the tragic mode ("arriving like Fortinbras in *Hamlet*"). Like J. Alfred Prufrock he knows he is not Prince Hamlet; but unlike Prufrock he does not cast himself as an anonymous "attendant lord," preferring the more exalted fiction of Fortinbras, the potential leader.

The fragmentation of narrative here demonstrates Batchelor's inability to write his own story. But Batchelor's story is not supposed to be the subject of the narrative. The striking thing about the above passage is that Batchelor not only fails to tell his own tale but abandons the story he set out to relate. Batchelor—it must be stressed—is the narrator of a work entitled *Lovel the Widower* that purports to be an account of how Frederick Lovel married Bessy Prior and so ceased to be a widower. Batchelor announces in the prologue that "I am but the Chorus of the Play." This chorus, however, gradually takes over the play. The main external plot recedes, and Batchelor's internal plot—the story of his unfulfilled intentions and emotional failure—assumes the dominance exemplified in the above segment. He becomes the center of the fiction, his mind its focal subject. This personal prominence of the narrator is the most significant innovation in Thackeray's late work, distinguishing it sharply from his earlier novels in which the narrator grants his story an independent existence, uses his techniques to establish and interpret his imagined external reality. In late novels like *Lovel* and *The Adventures of Philip*, with their more highly personalized, increasingly problematic and central narrators, the ostensible world of the narrative dissolves and technique turns inward, transforming the entire narrative into an expression of the narrator's consciousness.

Batchelor develops out of Michael Angelo Titmarsh, who narrates *The Kickleburys on the Rhine* (1850) in which the character of Lovel (there called Horace Milliken) first appears. The two narrators are similar in their bachelorhood, their halfhearted and always frustrated love affairs (though in the Titmarsh tales these always remain minor motifs), and their comic self-presentation. But their narratives differ dramatically in the experience they create and the questions they raise. Here is Titmarsh in the *Kickleburys* describing an occasion on which he—like Batchelor—"would have" acted but did not. Titmarsh finds himself alone on deck with Fanny Kicklebury (with whom he is smitten), the other passengers having succumbed to seasickness:

> I would have talked with her; I would have suggested images of poesy, and thoughts of beauty; I would have whispered the word of sentiment—the delicate allusion—the breathing of the soul that longs to find a congenial heart—the sorrows and aspirations of the wounded spirit, stricken and sad, yet not quite despairing; still knowing that the hope-plant lurked in its crushed ruins— still able to gaze on the stars and the ocean, and love their blazing sheen, their boundless azure. I would, I say, have taken the opportunity of that stilly night to lay bare to her the treasures of a heart that, I am happy to say, is young still: but circumstances forbade the frank outpouring of my poet soul; in a word, I was obliged to go and lie down on the flat of my back, and endeavour to control *other* emotions which struggled in my breast.

The passage is obviously a set piece, a comic rhetorical extravaganza that Titmarsh delights in creating. He relishes his artifice and concentrates on it, clearly in control of both language and material. Did he experience this situation—the desire, hesitation, and humiliating bout of seasickness? It does not matter, for the passage is not the expression of character but the dramatization and debunking of a literary attitude. Sentimental love poetry is the subject here and not Titmarsh; his love plot merely provides an occasion for undercutting conventional attitudes. Language and technique move outward, beyond the specific fiction, and absorb the reader's attention. As

Titmarsh carefully builds up his parodic images ("wounded spirit," "hope-plant," "stilly night"), we wait for the expected comic deflation. When it comes ("I was obliged to go and lie down"), our sense of appropriate form is satisfied; the anticipated experience has been properly completed. But it is a literary experience; language itself is the event here.

Titmarsh's control and outward focus contrast decisively with Batchelor's internal focus and inability to handle his technique. The skillfully managed rhythm and flowing style of Titmarsh are replaced by the broken, indecisive movements of Batchelor's prose as language now functions mimetically, not rhetorically, evoking the ambivalent movements of his consciousness. The advance and retreat of his technique mirror a mind in which the dominant impulse to evade exists in tension with intermittent impulses toward self-recognition. "I feel a certain sort of shame, even now, when I think that I didn't go in," Batchelor admits finally, but retreats immediately by delaying explanation and then absorbing himself in creating yet another defensive fiction (the Sackville-Byng analogy). While Titmarsh confidently manipulates his parodic images, certain of intention and effect, Batchelor is unable to use his allusions. The Ivanhoe image crumbles—its purpose uncertain. The point of the parody—if it is parody—remains unclear. Romance functions uneasily as a satiric target ("no need for Rebecca to jump"), a wish-fulfilling projection ("I, Sir Wilfred of Ivanhoe"), and an ideal standard that points up Batchelor's failure ("But I made no heroic speeches"). Clarity and purpose are further diffused as Batchelor mingles self-mockery with self-indulgence, crosses self-justification with self-castigation. Irony operates here but its target remains obscure. Batchelor himself is too uncertain, too involved in internal conflicts to direct irony successfully, to manipulate purposefully perspectivist techniques like allusion.

His confusion of the time of the action with the time of narration ("I am a stout elderly man") points to the breakdown of conventional narrative distance that Titmarsh is able to maintain. The retrospective stance that characterizes Thackeray's narrators here collapses. Assuming the expected pose, Batchelor is unable to make it work. Retrospection has not led to the understanding that it is supposed to generate. Whereas memory discovered for Henry Esmond an order informing the discreet moments of his existence, so enabling him to affirm a continuous realization of the self, Batchelor's memory reflects his own fragmentation. Throughout Thackeray memory plays a crucial role in the self-definition of both narrators and protagonists. In an early work like *Pendennis* memory can create for the hero the sustaining fiction of Helen Pendennis that provides him with a sense of self and purpose. But by *Lovel* this is no longer possible. Batchelor's frantic experimentation with successive borrowed fictions only underlines his failure to discover within his experience any shaping fiction. He has lost control of his world and his narrative, has become entangled in his own fiction, and can no longer distinguish himself from it.

The contrast between Titmarsh and Batchelor brings into sharp focus the disintegration that marks Thackeray's late works. But it also points to the increasingly exploratory fiction that emerges out of this disintegration. Batchelor's failed narrative, with its psychological dimensions and its more daring and complex use of fiction, expands the potential of narrative as Titmarsh's more successful exercise does not. The interiorization of fiction in the late Thackeray represents a significant shift that remains largely unnoticed. Focusing on the presence of familiar Thackerayan themes and characters now deployed with obvious weariness and uncertain conviction, readers approach the late narratives as conventional nineteenth-century didactic social fictions and dismiss them as mere tired replayings of earlier novels. But Thackeray, while retaining the conventions of the social novel that he helped to set up in *Vanity Fair*, is now writing a different kind of fiction. The established conventions operate in a relativistic, psychological context that absorbs them and exposes their hollowness. His late works—*Lovel, The Virginians, Philip*, and, in oblique fasion, *Denis Duval*—embody Thackeray's radical distrust of the ability of the dominant mode of Victorian fiction to explore and define the reality of contemporary experience.

At the time of *Vanity Fair*, Thackeray remarked that "our profession seems to me as serious as the Parson's own." By the end of his career, novels have become irrelevant "sweets." The early confidence in the moral function of fiction and the acceptance of the novel's capacity to define "the sentiment of reality" (*Letters*) have eroded drastically by the time of *Lovel*. Both the didactic and realistic concepts of the novel, whatever their ultimate incompatibility, rest on the assumption that quotidian reality has an inherent significance that fiction can discover and define. This assumption dissolves under the pressure of the skeptical, probing technique that Thackeray earlier developed to test the adequacy of novelistic conventions and of the moral and cultural assumptions supporting them. The speculative irony of narrative comment, the experimental use of allusive sequences, and the constant exploration and modification of convention forced an increasing recognition of the inadequacy of conventional narrative strategies (including the classic anticonventional strategy of realism) to account for a reality that investigation revealed as ever more uncertain, subjective, and empty. One has only to recall the increasingly bitter exposure of romantic love and domesticity as the Pendennis sequence of novels develops to measure the impact of the working of this technique. The problematic provisional affirmation of *Pendennis* has become contemptuous dismissal by the time of *Philip*. Moving beyond particular conventions, Thackeray comes to question the basic convention that fiction provides a way of making sense of reality. In the curious epilogue to *The Newcomes*, Thackeray defines all fictional structures—not just happy endings—as irrelevant if pleasant fantasies belonging to "fable-land" and emphasizes the futility of novelistic effort by stressing its divergence from the real world and underlining the purely mimic nature of its activity. Here, at the end of his greatest novel, he confesses to the same debilitating conviction of the impotence of his own narrative idiom that pervades the later novels.

This loss of confidence emerges in *Lovel* primarily as an inability to define, an inability apparent from the very beginning, with the highly insecure prologue to the narrative. Batchelor sets out to define his story in terms of narrative conventions—hero, heroine, setting—but ends up blurring the meaning of the categories and their relevance to his narrative. Witness the first two sentences of *Lovel*: "Who shall be the hero of this tale? Not I who write it." This opening, raising a question and invoking a convention only to ignore both by moving immediately in another direction ("Not I who write it. I am but the Chorus of the Play"), typifies the indirect movement of language throughout. This initial question remains an unanswered mark of interrogation; Batchelor moves on to try out other categories, to blur distinctions further by rapidly shifting subjects and qualifying distinctions. Even for a Thackerayan narrator, his prose is heavily qualified, dominated by constructions like "the scene is . . . No; it may be." Batchelor withdraws continually from assertion and definition, even when the matter at hand is not directly problematic or potentially disturbing. In establishing the social setting of his story, for example, he states: "There is no high life, unless, to be sure, you call a baronet's widow a lady in high life; and some ladies may be, while some certainly are not" (chap. 1). The complicated retreat here from making any positive statement is extraordinary. Batchelor empties of substance the whole process of classification and clarification, reduces the entire sentence to the equivocation of: "There may or may not be high life." The introduction of the hero, Lovel, hedged in by qualifications and by negative definitions that abandon the categories they set up and so fail to function as genuine definitions, offers further evidence of Batchelor's striking inability to commit himself to a definite distinction. This resort to qualifications and evasions is an instinctive, habitual gesture, a characteristic of style that reflects a deeply ingrained uncertainty about reality, about the language used to decipher it, and, ultimately, about himself. Batchelor has no sense of narrative purpose, no internal or external standards to form a basis for definition.

The Victorian heroine typically functions as the source of the moral norms of the fiction. But Bessy Prior remains an enigma, serves neither positively nor negatively to define values. Batchelor concludes his prologue with an image of her "unfathomable eyes," and on this note of an unknowable reality at the center of the events about to be portrayed, he begins his narration of Bessy's Cinderella plot. As the narrative continues, Batchelor keeps returning to the pivotal question: has she a heart? No answer is forthcoming. Bessy's motives and thoughts—her very nature—remain elusive. In the penultimate chapter, Batchelor deliberately draws attention to this failure of narrative investigation: "*Do* I know all about her, or anything; or only just as much as she chooses?" (chap. 5). Batchelor's strategy not only subverts this particular plot but raises questions about the power of narrative in general. In an earlier novel like *Pendennis*, fiction still functioned as a technique of discovery and revelation; Thackeray defined clearly his false and true heroines (Blanche Amory and Laura Bell), never in doubt as to the nature of each. Even in *Vanity Fair*, where he may not always have known what to do with Becky Sharp, he knew what she was. But by *The Newcomes*, where Thackeray creates an ambiguous heroine in Ethel Newcome, doubt about such assumptions—recessive in the earlier novels—comes clearly to the surface. By using the heroine as the focus for his skepticism, Thackeray places in question both the didactic and realistic concepts of the novel. Yet Ethel Newcome, despite her complexity, does not remain finally impenetrable as does Bessy Prior, who is presented in shifting contexts that do not coalesce into a coherent image but function to raise the possibility that character may be indefinable, unavailable to traditional novelistic modes of definition.

The presentation of Bessy, with its impressionistic rather than analytical mode of characterization, turns *Lovel* into a fiction of inference. Fiction no longer orders and evaluates the reality which forms its subject but collects impressions that are left unordered and unresolved; does not so much demonstrate a "truth" about experience as speculate about possible truths. The contrast becomes clearer when one thinks of *Lovel* in relation to a novel like *Middlemarch* in which certainty about the demonstrative and analytical power of narrative informs the presentation of its imagined reality. Dorothea, Casaubon, Lydgate—all are clearly defined and understood; the narrator who stresses the uncertain movements and limitations of her characters is herself certain and omniscient. Batchelor, by contrast, works tentatively, gives us only fragments and possibilities.

His insecurity and instability undercut generalizations about Thackerayan narrators as "reassuring" or as calmly surveying the world from an armchair. But such generalizations usefully highlight the dramatic dislocation of the narrator in the later work. Batchelor is Thackeray's earlier narrators turned literally inside out as the internal personal self behind the external public voice moves into central focus. Technique converges on the

narrator, who is at once the source of the fiction and its most significant self.
Thackeray's growing awareness of the inescapable subjectivity and relativi-
ty of modern reality that make the isolated self the crucial problem to be
solved now forces him to turn on his own alter ego and so put himself to
the test. The resulting interiorization of technique transforms the didactic
mode into a psychological one. Internal focus turns the role-playing of
Thackeray's narrators, typically undertaken for didactic purposes, into a personal, compulsive gesture, expressive of a profound insecurity of the self.
Roles no longer define the imagined world (as does the worldly pose in *The
Newcomes*) or involve the reader, as does the celebrated preacher role, in
self-criticism. The stance of implicated narrator—articulated in *Vanity Fair*'s
"brother wearers of motley"—is now less a stance consciously assumed for
rhetorical purposes than the only stance possible. Formerly a technique encouraging the reader's self-recognition, it now boomerangs back onto the
narrator, placing him rather than the reader in question. When Batchelor
attempts to generate the kind of self-scrutiny we associate with Thackeray's
fiction by pointing out that we reject "muffs" like Lovel in novels while honor-
ing them in actual life, technique falters and finally collapses: "Well? *Quid
rides*? Do you mean that I am painting a portrait which hangs before me
every morning. . . . *Après*? Do you suppose that I suppose that I have not
infirmities like my neighbours?" (chap. 1). Involvement of the reader
stimulates not self-scrutiny but scrutiny of the narrator and his fiction.
Rhetorical purpose dissolves into involuntary self-revelation.

Moral theme is translated into psychological exploration when Batchelor
appears in the familiar Victorian role of the heroine's benevolent godfather.
His "dingy loneliness" redefines the role of generous patron as one of frustration and emotional emptiness rather than morally bracing sacrifice. Batchelor's
relationship with Bessy makes clear the sexual fantasies operating in relationships like that between Jarndyce and Esther Summerson; suggests the
masochism and impotence that underlie those sentimental scenes in which
the Batchelor character yields graciously to the lover the heroine desires.
Batchelor is a sardonic, psychological version of a moral type. This shift in
approach absorbs external plot as well. Bedford and Lovel, both in love with
Bessy, serve as doubles for Batchelor, so turning plot into an extension of
his own mind. Through them Batchelor engages in a complex process of wish
fulfillment (both characters gain love and escape from immediate anxieties)
and self-laceration (Bedford acts while Batchelor cowers) that enables him
to avoid confronting the conflicting impulses that constitute his dilemma.

With the attenuation of the external function of narrative, technique
pushes inward, moving deeper into Batchelor's consciousness and exposing
the problem of the self as a psychological rather than a social or moral prob-

lem. Anticipating the methods of later novelists, Thackeray experiments impressively with rendering consciousness in a long internal monologue in the final chapter expressing Batchelor's response to the shattering of his self-image. Reading a letter from Bessy to her suitor, Drencher, Batchelor discovers not only that she is encouraging Drencher but that she ridicules his own failure of action in the garden and regards him as an "old muff." The monologue that follows this crushing revelation penetrates the fragile substructure of Batchelor's outward self and probes directly the irrationality and despair that underlie his ostensibly rational and complacent surface.

We witness a mind unnaturally conscious of an internal/external split, concentrating on maintaining a precarious exterior poise and normality. The peculiarly brittle quality of the prose captures brilliantly the brittle nature of Batchelor's assumed calmness:

> I did not cut any part of myself with my razor. I shaved quite calmly. I went to the family at breakfast. My impression is I was sarcastic and witty. I smiled most kindly at Miss Prior when she came in. Nobody could have seen from my outward behaviour that anything was wrong within. I was an apple. Could you inspect the worm at my core? No. No. Somebody, I think old Baker, complimented me on my good looks. I was a smiling lake. Could you see on my placid surface, amongst my sheeny water-lilies, that a corpse was lying under my cool depths? "A bit of devilled chicken?" "No, thank you. By the way, Lovel, I think I must go to town to-day." "You'll come back to dinner, of course?" "Well—no." "Oh, stuff! You promised me to-day and to-morrow. Robinson, Brown, and Jones are coming to-morrow, and you must be here to meet them." Thus we prattle on. I answer, I smile, I say, "Yes, if you please, another cup," or "Be so good as to hand the muffin," or what not. But I am dead.
>
> (Chap. 6)

This mind is schizoid; madness threatens directly here. "I was an apple," Batchelor calmly announces, and only then reveals that the statement is not so mad as it seems. The image of himself as a smiling lake hiding a corpse captures the complete split between inner and outer selves and signals Batchelor's awareness of an internally dead self which mitigates his pervasive self-pity and renders even more desperate the struggle to keep the deceptive outer self functioning. As the inconsequential breakfast chatter continues, verb tense shifts from past to present as the Batchelor who recalls the experience loses his distance and collapses the distinction between then and now. The last two lines effectively emphasize the split in consciousness as the humdrum passing of tea and muffins ("I answer, I smile, I say ") is over-turned abruptly by the startling "But I am dead."

This monologue continues for several pages, bringing into direct focus the problem of Batchelor's sense of self that underlies the whole narrative. External reality recedes as Batchelor drifts deeper into a fantasy of death and retreat, imagining himself buried with his ghost smiling wryly at the tomb-stone: "Here lies Charles Batchelor, the Unloved One." The self-conscious capitalization suggests less that Batchelor is deliberately posing than that he wants the reader to believe he is. He plunges immediately into a frantic se-quence of swiftly changing literary fictions (ranging from *Robinson Crusoe* to *The Ancient Mariner* to *Hamlet*), marked by an uneasy comedy ("Tell me where the Wandering Jew is, that I may go and sit with him. Is there any place at a lighthouse vacant?") and punctuated by the refrain, "So I am a Muff, am I?" His emotional desolation finds neither relief nor adequate defini-tion in traditional patterns. But the fictions are all he has—and is. Batchelor's interior world is made up of outworn fictions that underline his own hollowness. Darting among various moments of his past and present, Batchelor constantly and consciously turns himself into artifice. The painful memory of an earlier defeat in love (by Glorvina Mulligan) is defused by being stylized as ironic romance. Out of the images, types, and genres of literary tradition, he constructs his self-image. Through fictions, he attempts to fill the internal vacuum and create the illusion of an authentic self. His internal monologue dramatizes the nature and failure of this effort, provides the most extended rendition in the novel of his alienation and fragmenta-tion. Batchelor emerges from *Lovel* as a set of unresolved tensions, fears, poses, and fantasies. Crystallizing the implications of the preceding narrative, the monologue establishes that Batchelor cannot tell a coherent story because he has no coherent self. The breakdown of his narrative is in effect a breakdown of the self.

Were Thackeray in complete control of Batchelor, *Lovel* would stand as a superb study of the self-deception of an individual and of the culture that produced him, anticipating in its technique later experiments in narrative like *The Good Soldier*. What goes wrong? Why is *Lovel*, despite intermit-tent brilliance, not only a dissatisfying but a disturbing work? The answer lies in the fact that Thackeray is deeply implicated in his narrator; Batchelor's failure is largely Thackeray's own. While exposing Batchelor as suspect, Thackeray is unable to create an implied author in the text to guide response to this problematic narrator. He no longer has any value concepts to provide an evaluative context. By contrast, his early experiment with the unreliable narrator, *The Luck of Barry Lyndon*, depends for its success on the play of conventional Victorian notions of vanity, honor, and love to define and discredit Redmond Barry. And despite occasional characteristic wobbling, the main direction of the irony is clear. But in *Lovel* there are no such concepts, no conventions to illuminate Batchelor. The external plot, which could provide a context, is hollow, useful only as a device to enable Thackeray to escape tortuous subjectivity and create a semblance of narrative progression. Irony shoots off in several directions, dissipates itself in various implications. What are we to make of odd outbursts like "*Quid rides?*" or the savage snarling at Lady Baker or, for that matter, of internal sequences like Batchelor's monologue? The irony enveloping such passages has no direction, can commit itself to nothing. Presumably it could perpetuate itself forever since no discernible purpose regulates its working. Even as it reflects Thackeray's own uncertainty, irony becomes finally a technique of evasion, a way of avoiding evaluation and definition. It paralyzes the fiction, creates the illusion of movement while in fact ensuring stasis.

But it also protects Batchelor. We cannot penetrate Batchelor's irony because Thackeray's irony reinforces its self-protective impulse. Batchelor's conscious self-mockery ("If I choose to put my grief in a ridiculous light, why not?") deflects anticipated attack. Thackeray himself had learned early the use of this technique: Charles Lever's satire "can't injure me," he wrote in 1848, "I have pushed the caricaturing of myself almost to affectation" (*Letters*). Behind this self-caricature both Batchelor and his creator stand protected. Batchelor cowering in the garden is a ridiculous figure, but the diffuseness of the irony surrounding him shields him from a final evaluation. The authorial irony operating in the presentation of Batchelor is one of implication, not dissociation.

Thackeray cannot achieve the distance necessary to control Batchelor because Batchelor is part of himself. Writing novels, Thackeray told his daughters, is "thinking about one's self" (*Letters*). And narrative voice was the principal medium for such introspection. Gordon N. Ray tells us that Thackeray's particularized narrators are "so much like himself" as not to be separate characters, and suggests further that these narrative masks encouraged self-expression. Certainly Thackeray experienced a sense of release when he adopted Pendennis as narrator of *The Newcomes* (*Letters*). But, as Thackeray recognized, the creation of fiction was not entirely—perhaps not even primarily—conscious. In "De Finibus" he records whimsically, yet with an undertone of seriousness, his experience that novelists "*must* go a certain way, in spite of themselves." Whitwell Elwin suggested in 1855 that Thackeray's novels contained more than their author was aware of because he "wrote by a sort of instinct," an observation affirmed by Thackeray (*Letters*). The pressured process of writing the novels and the novels themselves support Thackeray's contention that a good part of his fiction is outside conscious control. Batchelor is such, a partially involuntary creation. Through him Thackeray expresses his modern skeptical consciousness, but this skepticism is deeper than he recognizes and, once embodied in the fiction, generates its own motion. Suggestively, Thackeray never indicated any awareness that in writing *Lovel* he had in fact written Batchelor's story. Batchelor takes over involuntarily; Thackeray remains entangled in his narrator. He cannot create an implied author or articulate an authentic irony because Batchelor draws on obscure sources in his own consciousness that work simultaneously to expose and protect the insecure figure they engender. Batchelor represents a significant advance in the development of narrative voice; but he is also the self-projection of a mind that cannot believe even in itself.

In *Lovel* Thackeray's technique has opened up the self for investigation and found nothing there. The skeptical inward turn has destroyed the narrator, revealed him as a hollow shell. There remains nothing to support the narrative, to give it coherence and purpose. The fear of existential emptiness, always threatening Thackeray's fiction, comes to dominate the later novels and subvert narrative effort. Thackeray's skeptical technique has undercut the values set against this demoralizing vision and destroyed finally the remaining prop—his conviction of the ability of his critical fictional mode to define and render intelligible the conditions of existence. With the collapse of this conviction, Thackeray's narrative becomes a painful, partly involuntary exercise in self-destruction, as he places in question himself and his earlier novels and finds there only emptiness. The figure of Batchelor implies the bankruptcy of the culture in which Thackeray participated, points to the failure of its values to cope with the solipsistic, relativistic world that haunted its imagination. The reaction of contemporary readers suggests that they sensed the threat contained in *Lovel*. The violence with which the *Athenaeum* denounces Thackeray's "deleterious beverage" is striking; *Harper's* admits that the work induces the reaction that "if Life were only that, life would be hardly worth living" but hastens to assure its readers that Thackeray is really writing satire. Permeating *Lovel* is the sense of weariness and personal despair that prompted Thackeray in a letter to include as his own the bleak comment by Pendennis in chapter 6 of *Philip* that "Yesterday is gone" and "To-morrow is not going to bring us much" (*Letters*).

Despair vitiates the explorative potential of the late narratives. The interiorization of fiction, the psychological definition of reality are part of a movement of disintegration, not of redefinition. Thackeray's skepticism pushes him into narrative experiment, but the same skepticism ensures that these experiments will be conducted in a vacuum. An image from another skeptic focuses Thackeray's problem. Montaigne, whose essays Thackeray kept by his bedside, wrote that the mind "does nothing but ferret and hunt around, incessantly wheeling about, contriving, involving itself in its own work, like a silkworm, and there suffocating." This restless silkworm, with its creative and destructive movements, stands as a concrete emblem of the process at work in the later Thackeray.

JOAN GARRETT-GOODYEAR

# Stylized Emotions, Unrealized Selves: Expressive Characterization in Thackeray

The skill of Thackeray's characterization is a puzzling matter and has been open to debate. Acclaimed by some readers for his subtlety and profundity, Thackeray is dismissed by others for his easygoing superficiality. While some follow the careers of his characters with gusto, others feel that his fiction "is merely a matter of going on and on" (F. R. Leavis, *The Great Tradition*). It has been common in the past for critics to nod approvingly at Thackeray's panoramic view of society and his sense of history but to feel that his characters lack depth, that they are not presented with much introspective insight. More recently, a number of sensitive and illuminating critical studies have argued persuasively that his characterization is both skillfully expressive and psychologically penetrating. Yet responses to Thackeray have been divided along these lines from the beginning. William Roscoe, who considered Thackeray "probably the greatest painter of manners that ever lived," noted that "man is his study; but man the social animal . . . never man the individual soul. He never penetrates into the interior, secret, *real* life that every man leads in isolation from his fellows." George Henry Lewes, on the other hand, proclaimed that Thackeray "seizes *characters* where other writers seize only characteristics; he does not give you a peculiarity for the man, he places the man himself, that 'bundle of motives,' before you."

Thackeray elicits such divided responses because he often composes his characters from stereotypes, and he prefers to emphasize in each individual a few prominent, essentially unchanging traits; yet he presents these characters with surprising expressive intensity and in ways which suggest the force of

From *Victorian Studies* 22, no. 2 (Winter 1979). © 1979 by the Trustees of Indiana University.

profound emotional compulsions in determining their actions. Thackeray sees very clearly how conceptions of character which are social and literary clichés serve as expressions of irrational psychological energy (Loofbourow). His characters are trapped in rigid responses, given to extravagant extremes. They ask for too much or not enough, are generous or selfish to a fault, abandon desires too readily or pursue them too desperately. Although Thackeray has been particularly celebrated for his sensitivity to the infinite variety of self-delusion, to the vanity which can make even painful situations a matter of self-congratulation, he sees much more than vanity in his characters. The patterns of exploitation so prevalent in his fiction are shaped to inner requirements for conquest and defeat, for self-aggrandizement and for self-denial.

My concern in this essay is not, however, to demonstrate the profundity of Thackeray's psychological conceptions, for that has been done elsewhere. Rather, I am interested in considering some of the techniques which establish the expressive power of Thackeray's characterizations and what those techniques imply about Thackeray's view of the self. They convey the sense of an intense emotional life which eludes expression. Thackeray's characters are very often in situations of deciding that they should conceal or deny their feelings or, worse, of being unable to confront their feelings at all. The frequency of such situations in his fiction suggests a pessimistic doubt that whatever vital energies are within could ever enrich or liberate the articulated shape the self presents to the world. Instead, he sees the deepest reaches of the self as a reservoir of disappointment and despair, of an emotionality which is incompatible with the demands of life as it may be lived in a social context. His characters seem to speak to each other across barriers, and the manner of their speaking dramatizes a sense that their fullest feelings are being held back or are entangled in unresolvable contradictions. Thackeray's ability to convey the pressure such uncharted emotional regions bring to bear on sensitive individuals in an indifferent or even hostile world is one of the major accomplishments of his fiction.

The way a character in a novel by Thackeray can avoid coming to terms with feelings shows very clearly in Amelia Sedley's reflections on her marriage to George Osborne when she visits her parents' home just a short time afterwards. What comes into her head are not fully formed thoughts but a succession of images which stand in their place. First, she recalls "that image of George to which she had knelt before marriage." Then "Rebecca's twinkling green eyes and baleful smile lighted upon her." Next, she looks at "the little white bed" of her girlhood and thinks that "she would like to sleep in it that night"; finally, she thinks "with terror" of her marriage bed, "the great funereal damask pavilion in the vast and dingy state bed-room" (*Vanity Fair*). Her bewilderment when the reality of marriage replaces the fantasy of romance, her longing to return to childish simplicities, her helplessness to combat Rebecca, her sexual immaturity are embodied concretely, without abstract intellectual formulation, just as Amelia would experience them. The effect is that while her understanding is clearly judged inadequate, she is also shown to be pathetically at the mercy of feelings which elude her simplifications.

The point is worth emphasizing because it represents a deliberate restriction on Thackeray's part. Instead of concentrating on a level of subjectivity where thoughts are rationally ordered and move towards clarified perception, Thackeray depicts a less rational, less deliberately conscious level on which anxieties and despairs come as images, one after the other, without the intervening control of directed intention. In this way, he suggests that Amelia is not only unwilling but also unable to come to terms with her own perceptions. The sequence of her thoughts enables the reader to supply the causal links Amelia omits: instead of understanding how far sexual disappointment and even dread have replaced her girlish daydreams, Amelia retreats into prayer; but Thackeray's analysis of the situation is clear enough. At the same time, Thackeray's use of symbolically resonant imagery enables him to convey the emotional intensity of the subjective experience he criticizes: the image of Amelia's funereal bed is movingly suggestive in a way that the enumeration of her timorous misgivings would not be.

Limited characters who are presented with psychological acumen and expressive intensity abound in Thackeray's fiction, but the novels most dominated by the pathos of characters whose passionate feelings must be forever frustrated are *Henry Esmond* and *The Newcomes*. In the fiction before these two novels, many characters are caught in the grip of such wild and extravagant compulsions that the absurdity deflects—without wholly destroying—the pathos, as with the characters in *The Yellowplush Papers*, for example, or the minor characters in *Pendennis*; in the fiction which follows, there is a slackening of Thackeray's artistic grasp, so that the characters are neither as interesting nor as emotionally compelling. That Thackeray should have written his most consistently moving fiction in *Henry Esmond* and *The Newcomes* is not surprising, as these are the two works written most directly after his cherished intimacy with Jane Brookfield was broken off. The stunning impact of this rupture forced Thackeray into a more searching analysis of his own feelings, and of Mrs. Brookfield's, than he had been willing to make in the past. His heightened awareness figures particularly in his brilliant characterizations of the Esmond family, and a sense of terrible deprivation permeates both novels. However much the central characters merit criticism, their feelings are taken with great seriousness, and their suffering is clearly to be mourned.

I

Because *Henry Esmond* and *The Newcomes* are so prominently concerned with characters who cannot or will not acknowledge their feelings,
the use of concrete objects which call attention to those feelings, the sort
of objective correlative already discussed in relation to Amelia, plays an important role. John Loofbourow has described the way recurrent metaphorical
motifs and epical allusions articulate and intensify the emotional experience
of the characters in *Henry Esmond*; but indeed, in this novel even the simplest
repetitions of a phrase or an image can become laden with expressive implications. For example, Esmond's impressions of Lady Castlewood are
studded throughout with apparently casual references to her hands. While
hands traditionally figure in gestures of trust and generosity, they also have
erotic connotations and symbolic connections with marriage—and all of these
associations are important to what Esmond is feeling. In the long course of
his devotion to Lady Castlewood, Esmond frequently misunderstands the
nature of his love for her, but his recurring attention to her hands defines
the increasingly erotic aspect of his feelings even when he imagines himself
wholly infatuated with Beatrix.

Throughout his childhood memories, Esmond's impressions of Lady
Castlewood's graciousness and beauty focus on the loveliness of her hands.
At their first meeting, "she stretched out her hand—indeed when was it that
that hand would not stretch out to do an act of kindness, or to protect grief
and ill-fortune?" (*Henry Esmond*, vol. 1, chap. 1). When she upbraids him
for "polluting" the Castlewood household with smallpox and moral dissolution, he is "bewildered with grief and rage at the injustice of such a stab from
such a hand" (vol. 1, chap. 8). When she blames him for her husband's death,
Esmond is too stunned to protest, "stricken only with the more pain at thinking it was that soft and beloved hand which should stab him so cruelly" (vol.
2, chap. 1). By the time of their reconciliation, Lady Castlewood's hand is
laden with emotional significance for Esmond, so that when "she gave him
her hand, her little fair hand; there was only her marriage ring on it," his
sudden awareness of the wedding band he has never previously mentioned
indicates a specifically erotic direction in his feelings. This erotic emphasis
continues as he muses, "Where lies it? the secret which makes one little hand
the dearest of all? Whoever can unriddle that mystery?" (vol. 2, chap. 6).
Even after Esmond has seen Beatrix in her newly dazzling maturity, his
attention fastens obsessively on Rachel's wedding band: "He . . . took one
of her fair little hands—it was that which had her marriage ring on—and
kissed it" (vol. 2, chap. 8). The note of sensual attraction sounds still more
clearly somewhat later in Esmond's comment that Rachel's hand is "the

prettiest dimpled little hand in the world" (vol. 2, chap. 15). This recurrent pattern of attention suggests that Esmond is passionately, if ambiguously, drawn to Lady Castlewood throughout his courtship of Beatrix; but Rachel, because she lacks the reader's privilege of following Henry's thoughts and can see only his courtly performances, concludes wrongly that his devotion to her is purely filial. That Thackeray dramatizes Edmond's continuing love by emphasizing its subtle influence on the way he perceives reflects his sensitivity to the importance of unconscious desire in shaping subjective experience, and his wish to convey this influence is central to his best fiction.

In *Henry Esmond* both Beatrix and Rachel are torn by powerful feelings which pull in opposite directions and are unresolvable. Thackeray is at his expressive best when he is depicting such situations; he creates for his characters a stylized manner of speaking which impels the reader to look between the lines and recognize the pressure of unacknowledged emotion. The techniques Thackeray adopts may be found throughout his fiction, but they are especially prominent in *Esmond*, which is so decisively flavored with divided longings and frustrated impulse.

When Lady Castlewood attempts to explain to Henry why they were not reconciled earlier, the manner of her speech suggests turbulent passion reined in by decorous convention:

> "I know how wicked my heart has been; and I have suffered too, my dear. I confessed to Mr. Atterbury—I must not tell any more. He—I said I would not write to you or go to you—and it was better even that, having parted, we should part. But I knew you would come back—I own that. That is no one's fault. And to-day, Henry, in the anthem, when they sang it, 'When the Lord turned the captivity of Zion, we were like them that dream,' I thought, yes, like them that dream—them that dream. . . . Do you know what day it is? . . . It is the 29th of December—it is your birthday! But last year we did not drink it—no, no. My lord was cold, and my Harry was likely to die; and my brain was in a fever; and we had no wine. But now—now you are come again, bringing your sheaves with you, my dear."
>
> (*Henry Esmond*, vol. 2, chap. 6)

Rachel constructs her speech around a series of oppositions. She has been wicked, but she has suffered for it; she has confessed, but must say no more. It was better that she and Esmond part, but she knew he would come back. As she half confesses and half struggles not to confess the love she feels for him, her emotional turmoil is expressed both in what she does allow herself to say and in her disjointed manner of saying it. Her style is richly allusive, its implications stopping just short of a direct avowal: the wine and sheaves define her sexual longing (Loofbourow) and her trancelike repetitions suggest her distracted passion. She suppresses any expresssion of causal relationships, although they are obvious to a reader aware of her love for Esmond. She uses the correlative "and" when the subordinate "because" would be more exact; she speaks in brief, simply constructed sentences and offers only sketchy connections between them; she focuses intensely on a series of factual details, which stand in place of the feelings she refuses to express more directly. The effect is one of extreme fragmentation, but the verbal style suggests the very quality of her subjective experience, indicating that she has not yet come to terms with the emotional dislocations of a disintegrating marriage, an adulterous passion, and a sudden widowhood. "My lord was cold, and my Harry was likely to die; and my brain was in a fever; and we had no wine"— she is unable to order these details, unwilling to define precisely the connections between them.

Beatrix's speeches to Esmond, which also center around strongly conflicting feelings, are similarly marked by patterns of emphatic opposition. When she tells him that "a woman of my spirit . . . is to be won by gallantry, and not by sighs and rueful faces," yet also insists that "had you been a great man, you might have been good-humoured; but being nobody, sir, you are too great a man for me; and I'm afraid of you" (*Henry Esmond*, vol. 3, chap. 4), her recurrent paradoxes, accusing Esmond first of being ineffectual and then of being overbearing, suggest that she experiences her own longings and responses in contradictory terms. Typically, she frames her interpretations as extravagant absolutes. Esmond will "never fall into a passion; but . . . never forgive"; she has "no heart," but "would do anything" for "the man that could touch it" (*Henry Esmond*, vol. 3, chaps. 4, 7). Like most of Thackeray's characters, she is too ready to translate situations into incompatible alternatives or intolerable extremes. But Thackeray uses such intractable oppositions expressively as well as critically. His characters' highly mannered speeches testify that ambivalent passions and contradictory emotional drives are integral to his vision of the human experience.

In the more poignant atmosphere of *The Newcomes*, where the central characters find themselves emotionally marooned in a sea of social rapacity, similar stylizations of language may be found, but what is especially striking is a childlike simplicity of speech, most notable in Clive, the Colonel, and Rosey, which evokes a bewildered but radical innocence. Though it may be found elsewhere in Thackeray's fiction, the special prominence of the childlike language here exerts a decisive influence on the tone of the novel as a whole, suggesting how ill-fitted the protagonists are to deal with the stern realities of socio-economic calculation. Clive Newcome is a child who cannot come to terms with the "adult" cynicism of the world around him, and there is an aching tension between his simple, inadequate diction and the emotional desolation it articulates:

> "Still! once means always in these things, father, doesn't it? Once means to-day and yesterday, and for ever and ever. . . . Do you know you never spoke twice in your life about my mother? You didn't care for her . . . your heart was with the other. So is mine. It's fatal; it runs in the family, father. . . . Did Madame de Florac play *you* false when she married her husband? It was her fate, and she underwent it. We all bow to it, we are in the track and the car passes over us."
>
> (*Newcomes*, vol. 2, chap. 30)

Although this passage illustrates Clive's fatalistic passivity and his victimization by self-pity, its gloomy resignation is an appropriate response to the society of *The Newcomes*, which refuses to acknowledge sincerity and demands suppression of tenderness. Clive's readiness to feel doomed in no way diminishes the reality of his ruin. Despite the sentimental pathos of his speech, the very ordinariness of the language plays against the uncompromising extremity of his grief ("once means always," "for ever and ever," "it's fatal") to suggest the impossibility of finding in words an adequate expression for emotional experience. Such thwarted emotionality is a continuing concern of this novel, but Thackeray's manipulations of language suggest that the frustration of feeling comes not simply from a hostile environment but also from the inability of his characters to bring their feelings to creative resolution, whether through failures of will and understanding, or because, as it sometimes seems in Thackeray, emotion ultimately eludes both our knowledge and our control.

In a novel so concerned with society's oppressiveness, Thackeray's device of having characters submerge their feelings in a mass of factual detail works especially well, for the emphasis on externality heightens the sense of limitation imposed by social roles and social situations. The courtship scenes between Clive and Ethel at the Hôtel de Florac derive much of their expressive power from the setting. Only the description of the statues in the garden, so much more eloquent than the conversation of the lovers, expresses the sense of ruin and decay Clive will not permit himself to speak:

> In the centre of that avenue is a fountain, surmounted by a Triton so gray and moss-eaten, that though he holds his conch to his swelling lips, curling his tail in the arid basis, his instrument has had a sinecure for at least fifty years. . . . At the end of the lime-

tree avenue is a broken-nosed damp Faun, with a marble panpipe, who pipes to the spirit ditties which I believe never had any
tune. . . . There is Cupid, who has been at the point of kissing
Psyche this half-century at least, though the delicious event has
never come off through all those blazing summers and dreary
winters; there is Venus and her Boy under the damp little dome
of a cracked old temple.

(Newcomes, vol. 2, chap. 9)

In their talk Clive and Ethel confine themselves to trivialities which express their real feelings only tangentially. Ethel's refusal to acknowledge that
she is attracted to Clive depends on her conviction that she can do without
love in arranging her marriage, but even Clive, who is more open in his love,
underplays it, giving it up too readily, as if not fully aware of what it will
cost him. Again, the childlike tone of his speech betrays his insufficient
awareness of consequences and complexities:

> "I love you so, that if I thought another had your heart, an
> honest man, a loyal gentleman . . . I think I could go back with
> a God bless you, and take to my pictures again, and work on in
> my own humble way. You seem like a queen to me, somehow;
> and I am but a poor, humble fellow, who might be happy, I think,
> if you were. In those balls, where I have seen you surrounded by
> those brilliant young men, noble and wealthy, admirers like me,
> I have often thought, 'How could I aspire to such a creature, and
> ask her to forego a palace to share the crust of a poor painter?' "

(Newcomes, vol. 2. chap. 9)

He deflects the full force of passion into a storybook interpretation of their
love, in which he appears the humble youngest son of an obscure family and
Ethel the exalted princess of a fairytale; and his expression of adoring venera-
tion too readily substitutes a consideration of their respective social positions
for a direct expression of feeling.

Ethel Newcome is even more preoccupied with rank and role than Clive
is; she seems to feel that if one adopts the proper social form, it will guarantee
the proper management of feeling. Her conversations with Clive are constructed out of exemplary but impersonal theories of good behavior: "I won't
say a word about the—the regard which you express for me. I think you
have it. Indeed, I do. But it were best not said, Clive; best for me, perhaps,
not to own that I know it. In your speeches; my poor boy—and you will
please not to make any more, or I never can see you or speak to you again,
never—you forgot one part of a girl's duty: obedience to her parents"

(*Newcomes*, vol. 2, chap. 9). The copybook correctness of these sentiments shows Ethel's immersion in social formulae; her thoughts are so entirely shaped by worldly precepts that she cannot begin to sound her own emotional depths. When she grows impatient with the role she has chosen in life, she talks of retiring to a convent, still clinging to external molds for shaping her thoughts and feelings. Even when she imagines accepting Clive as a lover, it is by casting him in other roles—as an army officer or an artist already successful and wealthy—so that she will not have to relinquish her fantasies of affluence and power. She cannot acknowledge the impulses which draw her to Clive except in a way that distorts and diminishes what he really is.

Even though Clive is exasperated when Ethel defines their relationship in formal terms which deny her feelings, he too gives way to the apparent importance of external definition, as his feeling that she "ought" to have a high place in society shows. That their intimate conversation should be so pervaded with considerations of rank and form testifies to the terrible weight social demands place on private emotion in the world of *The Newcomes*. Although Clive and Ethel neither articulate nor understand the emotional ruin they are creating for themselves, the decaying, moss-grown statues provide an expressive context for their unacknowledged feelings, giving depth and poignancy to designedly inadequate communications. They speak in language so conventional, their few expressions of love are so indirect and subdued, that their emotions seem somehow beyond them, neither comprehended nor effectively realized.

What is striking in *The Newcomes*, indeed, is the way social expectations and social proprieties virtually replace the direct expression of feeling. Rosey can articulate her dissatisfaction with Clive as a husband only by objecting to his discourteous eagerness to go off and paint before breakfast. How or whether this affects her internally the reader is left to guess. In a letter to Laura, Ethel conveys the distress of a chance meeting with Clive simply by summarizing the details of the encounter. Madame de Florac warns Ethel against marriages of convenience by relating her own grief in a narrative dominated by social definitions of obligation:

> "My poor father took the pride of his family into exile with him. Our poverty only made his pride the greater. Even before the emigration a contract had been passed between our family and the Count de Florac. I could not be wanting to the word given by my father. For how many long years have I kept it! But when I see a young girl who may be the victim—the subject of a marriage of convenience, as I was—my heart pities her. . . . There are some laws so cruel that nature revolts against them, and breaks

them—or we die in keeping them. You smile—I have been nearly
fifty years dying—*n'est-ce pas?*—and am here an old woman, complaining to a young girl."

(Newcomes, vol. 2, chap. 9)

As social demands stifle the most vital emotions, a curious sense of
detachment results, a detachment especially clear in the speeches of Madame
de Florac. She calls attention to her immediate situation ("you smile," "an
old woman, complaining to a young girl") as if she were merely watching
herself on stage, setting the prosaic reality of ordinary moments and ordinary
gestures against the years of anguish as one such moment succeeds another.
Her calmly factual tone as she asserts she has been dying for fifty years creates
the impression that her social self has become dissociated from the passionate
one. And in the last chapters of *The Newcomes*, Thackeray's use of Pendennis as narrator comes to reinforce this sense of separation between private
emotion and social reality, for though Pendennis maintains a sympathetically helpful presence throughout the adversities of Clive and the Colonel, he
is powerless to relieve or even share in their anguish. As he himself puts it:
"If Clive came to visit us, as he very rarely did, after an official question or
two regarding the health of his wife and child, no farther mention was made
of his family affairs. . . . I did not press the confidence which he was unwilling to offer, and thought best to respect his silence. I had a thousand affairs
of my own; who has not in London? If you die to-morrow, your dearest friend
will feel for you a hearty pang of sorrow, and go to his business as usual"
(*Newcomes*, vol. 2, chap. 37). Although Ethel relieves their financial plight,
although Florac and his mother resolve that the Colonel "shall not want,"
no one can restore his broken spirit or revive Clive's youthful gaiety and confidence. Friends and narrator alike remain outsiders.


II

The distinctive quality of subjective experience as defined by Thackeray
emerges clearly when he is compared with a writer who makes very different
decisions about how to depict inner realities. George Eliot's novels contrast
strongly with Thackeray's in their style of presenting subjective experience.
When Thackeray's characters think, their thoughts almost never embody a
sustained ratiocinative process. Whereas George Eliot's characters often
follow prolonged and well-ordered lines of thought (even if we do not admire the conclusions they reach), Thackeray's characters shift quickly from
one idea to another, the connective links being associative or emotional, rather
than rational. Their moments of reflection are brief and fragmentary, and

narrative passages designed to follow a character's thoughts usually do so through a proliferation of physical details and external actions which indicate the internal experience. A passage describing Arthur Pendennis's melancholy when he completes his undistinguished college career and comes home to a life without any apparent future catches Thackeray's characteristic flavor:

> Pen came back to Fairoaks, and to his books and to his idleness, and loneliness and despair. He commenced several tragedies, and wrote many copies of verses of a gloomy cast. He formed plans of reading and broke them. He thought about enlisting—about the Spanish legion—about a profession. He chafed against his captivity, and cursed the idleness which had caused it. Helen said he was breaking his heart, and was sad to see his prostration. As soon as they could afford it, he should go abroad—he should go to London—he should be freed from the dull society of two poor women. It *was* dull—very, certainly. The tender widow's habitual melancholy seemed to deepen into a sadder gloom; and Laura saw with alarm that the dear friend became every year more languid and weary, and that her pale cheek grew more wan.
>
> (*Pendennis*, vol. 1, chap. 21)

Pen's unfocused restlessness emerges in the rapid sequence of his pretentious activities and insubstantial daydreams. The emphasis is on his impatient feelings and fantasies, not on any serious attempt to think over his situation. When he thinks "about enlisting," the telltale construction of the gerund shows his avoidance of the more purposeful movement from subject to verb in a completely formed idea. Significantly, his escapist thoughts about the Spanish legion are more specific than his vague notion of finding "a profession." He curses his idleness instead of confronting it. The quick movement away from Pendennis to Helen and then to Laura, who registers Helen's sorrow through its outward signs, is also something that happens often in Thackeray. His narrative passages remind the reader that several perspectives exist and that many characters are likely to be involved in what one character sees as his own exclusive problem.

George Eliot's characters, though they are often as skillful as Thackeray's at egoistic blindness, are made more capable of analytical reflection. This is not to argue that their thinking is always more illuminating—Casaubon's reflections on his marriage may be articulate, but they do not yield valuable insights—but rather, that the mode of thought George Eliot presents differs from that found in Thackeray. Both authors create characters of limited understanding—the mental lives of Hetty Sorrel and Rosey Mackenzie seem equally impoverished. But on the other end of the scale, George Eliot creates characters whose intellectual command of their circumstances far excels anything found in Thackeray. Even George Eliot's more limited characters, moreover, enjoy a greater harmony between intention and impulse than is common in Thackeray. Hetty Sorrel seeks her destiny in a way that Rosey Mackenzie does not. Becky Sharp's fusion of will and desire, conscious and unconscious self, would seem to be perfect, yet Thackeray momentarily suggests quite another perspective. When the narrator comments that "her success excited, elated, and then bored her" (*Vanity Fair*, vol. 2, chap. 16), he invites us to see Becky's resourceful career as a compulsive quest, a restless drive for conquest that can never be satisfied.

George Eliot is more concerned than Thackeray is to trace the interaction between irrational impulse and deliberate thought: certainly Lydgate's decision to marry Rosamond cannot be called well considered. But George Eliot enables her readers to experience the process through which this decision comes. She is interested in the way the self sets noble promptings against baser ones, the way character emerges in—and indeed is partially formed by—its struggles with temptation. Bulstrode's gradual immersion in duplicity and crime is laid out as an orderly progression, with several turning points when he could have resisted but instead allowed himself to drift into opportunities for unscrupulous gain. Lydgate's gradual subjugation by Rosamond is explained as the victory of his sympathetic warmth and acquiescent passivity over his exasperated anger and resentment. Dorothea's decision to speak with Rosamond about Lydgate's difficulties results from the triumph of her habit of compassionate involvement over her momentary experience of jealous contempt. Although George Eliot's novels dramatize the complexity of the emotional forces influencing moments of significant choice and view with compassion those which are resolved ignobly or unwisely, they make it clear that the responsibility for the decision rests with the character who makes it and that other possibilities were open.

The characterization in Thackeray's novels, on the other hand, rarely allows the reader to experience directly the process by which characters arrive at decisions; they tend to be presented as faits accomplis. Pendennis's resolve to see no more of Fanny Bolton crystallizes suddenly around a memory stirred by the "sabbath evening, as the church bells were ringing"; and the reader learns fully of this abrupt and simple subjective process not at the moment of its occurrence, when Pen rushes away from Fanny in confusion, but afterwards, when he defends himself to Bows: "I thought of my own home, and of women angelically pure and good, who dwell there; and I was running hither, as I met you, that I might avoid the danger which besets me" (*Pennennis*, vol. 2, chap. 11). Esmond's decision to make no claim on the Castlewood property and title also comes instantaneously, in the irrevocable form of a deathbed pledge, and again there are only terse summaries of the internal struggle his generosity costs him: "He had had good cause for doubt and dismay; for mental anguish as well as resolution" (*Henry Esmond*, vol. 1, chap. 14). "Should he bring down shame and perplexity upon all those beings to whom he was attached by so many tender ties of affection and gratitude? . . . He had debated this matter in his conscience, whilst his poor lord was making his dying confession. On one side were ambition, temptation, justice even; but love, gratitude, and fidelity, pleaded on the other. And when the struggle was over in Harry's mind, a glow of righteous happiness filled it" (*Henry Esmond*, vol. 2, chap. 1). These neatly balanced abstractions are the most intimate view Esmond permits of one of his life's most significant commitments, yet other characters in Thackeray make decisions equally momentous with even less elaboration of the subjective processes behind them. When the wreckage of Barnes's marriage persuades Ethel Newcome to abandon her worldly aspirations, the reader is not invited to participate sympathetically as she weighs priorities or lives through emotional turmoil: the decision is made quickly, simply, and outside the novel.

A specific comparison of characters at moments of crucial decision sharply focuses the differences between the two authors. The style of the process by which Lydgate commits himself to maintaining a sympathetic rapport with Rosamond contrasts markedly with the style of Lady Castlewood's decision not to marry Esmond:

> He went out of the house, but as his blood cooled he felt that the chief result of the discussion was a deposit of dread within him at the idea of opening with his wife in future subjects which might again urge him to violent speech. It was as if a fracture in delicate crystal had begun, and he was afraid of any movement that might make it fatal. His marriage would be a mere piece of bitter irony if they could not go on loving each other. He had long ago made up his mind to what he thought was her negative character—her want of sensibility, which showed itself in disregard both of his specific wishes and of his general aims. The first great disappointment had been borne: the tender devotedness and docile adoration of the ideal wife must be renounced, and life must be taken up on a lower stage of expectation, as it is by men who have lost their limbs. But the real wife had not only her claims, she had still a hold on his heart, and it was his intense desire that the hold should remain strong. In marriage, the certainty, "She will never love me much," is easier to bear than the fear, "I shall love her no more." Hence, after that outburst, his

inward effort was entirely to excuse her, and to blame the hard
circumstances which were partly his fault. He tried that evening,
by petting her, to heal the wound he had made in the morning,
and it was not in Rosamond's nature to be repellent or sulky; indeed, she welcomed the signs that her husband loved her and
was under control. But this was something quite distinct from
loving *him*.

(George Eliot, Middlemarch, chap. 64)

Although the language in this passage fully articulates the extent of Lydgate's
suffering, it evolves an orderly response to his emotional collision with Rosamond. Lydgate first identifies and registers his most profound reaction to
the scene, evaluating the probable consequences of any future clashes. He
reviews his previous experience of disappointment, of which the disillusionment occasioned by this quarrel is a graver continuation. He acknowledges
both the present state of his affection and the desirability of maintaining it,
and he resolves on the mode of conduct to pursue. Lydgate's struggle with
conflicting feelings is made very clear, but the reader experiences this troubled
interlude as a process which can be intelligibly ordered and rationally explained. The very vocabulary supports this impression: "the chief result,"
"he had long ago made up his mind," "the ideal wife must be renounced,"
"certainty . . . is easier to bear than . . . fear," "hence . . . his inward effort."

Of course, the degree of conscious control in Lydgate's thinking is not
exaggerated. He continues to blind himself to the full extent of Rosamond's
deficiencies, and he refuses to understand that his marriage is already a piece
of bitter irony. His perception of Rosamond's want of sensibility depends
on her failure to adopt his concerns; the egocentric bias of his perceptions
persists. There is also a touch of melodramatic self-pity in the simile involving lost limbs. But even with a character like Lydgate, whose understanding
is flawed, George Eliot depicts a reflective mode of thinking in which
chronological and causal relationships remain clear and in which rational
judgment informs the process of drawing conclusions and formulating
resolutions.

Rachel Esmond's agitated speech to Henry creates a quite different
impression:

"Hush!" she said again, and raised her hand up to his lip. "I have
been your nurse. You could not see me, Harry, when you were
in the small-pox, and I came and sat by you. Ah! I prayed that
I might die, but it would have been in sin, Henry. Oh, it is horrid
to look back to that time. It is over now and past, and it has been
forgiven me. When you need me again, I will come ever so far.

When your heart is wounded, then come to me, my dear. Be silent! let me say all. You never loved me, dear Henry—no, you do not now, and I thank heaven for it. I used to watch you, and knew by a thousand signs that it was so. Do you remember how glad you were to go away to college? 'Twas I sent you. I told my papa that, and Mr. Atterbury too, when I spoke to him in London. And they both gave me absolution—both—and they are godly men, having authority to bind and to loose. And they forgave me, as my dear lord forgave me before he went to heaven."

(*Henry Esmond*, vol. 2, chap. 6)

Although Rachel, like Lydgate, is clearly struggling with conflicting feelings, hers are neither so directly nor so completely identified. She has two strong reasons for refusing Esmond—her fear that he doesn't love her and her wish to absolve herself of guilt for her past love by denying her present feeling. Her speeches to Esmond in the scene from which this passage is taken half identify these reasons, but in a fragmented way and never with complete explicitness. True to Thackeray's form, Rachel emphasizes roles ("I have been your nurse," " 'Twas I sent you" to college, "they both gave me absolution") and facts (Harry's smallpox, his departure for college) which imply the complex emotions she will not articulate openly. Her curious digression to Harry's illness (why should being his nurse prevent her from marrying him?) cannot be understood unless the reader remembers her sudden jealousy when his infection reveals his attentions to Nancy Sievewright. The reader must also recall her speech to Esmond in prison: "Why did you not die when you had the small-pox—and I came myself and watched you, and you didn't know me in your delirium—and you called out for me, though I was there at your side?" (*Henry Esmond*, vol. 2, chap. 1), a speech which shows her treasuring, but not acknowledging, a sign that Henry does love her.

When Rachel asserts that she wanted to die, but "it would have been in sin," she is developing her earlier statement that "I would love you still—yes, there is no sin in such a love as mine now." These cryptic remarks hint at the erotic emphasis in her love but stop characteristically short of outright confession. And the suppression of rational connections in her speech further enhances the impression, so prevalent in Thackeray, of passion stifled and denied before it can develop. Whereas George Eliot's reconstruction of Lydgate's thoughts and feelings emphasizes the way one is joined to the next, Thackeray's presentation of Lady Castlewood deliberately severs such links. It is through the barest nuances of vocabulary and emphasis that Thackeray defines some of the most important currents in her feelings. Her statement that the "horrid time" is now "over . . . and past, and it has been forgiven me" discloses, but only indirectly, one of the central elements in her decision to refuse Esmond: her determination to extricate herself entirely from her complicated and painful feelings about her marriage and the man who tempted her adulterous love. Something "over and past" and clearly "horrid" is easier to come to terms with than something immediate, continuing, tempting as well as tormenting. Rachel prefers to be "forgiven" and to cling to a maternal definition of her love, but her emphatic, extravagant language measures the desperation in this effort.

Subtle linguistic details suggest the outlines of complex psychological processes throughout Rachel's speech. The extent of her wish to shape reality to her own emotional needs, for example, is suggested in her eagerness to "say all," meaning both everything that is on her mind and also everything that can ever be said about her relationship with Esmond, excluding any interpretations from his point of view. Her effort to take over all interpretations of his emotional state accounts for the absoluteness of her statement that "you never loved me" and that "a thousand signs" showed it. (In fact, she offers only one not very compelling piece of evidence, Esmond's eagerness for college.) The strenuousness of this attempt to manage her wayward passion for Esmond, to package and seal it forever as dignified maternal solicitude, shows in the ritualistic, indeed, formulaic quality of her final sentences where the repeated insistence on absolution and forgiveness—"they both gave me absolution—both," "having authority to bind and to loose," "they forgave me," "my dear lord forgave me"—suggests warding off evil with magical incantations. The true confusion of her feelings, however, emerges in her inability to settle on the precise arrangement she wishes for their relationship. First adopting the generous position that "when you need me again, I will come ever so far," she then shifts to a more gratifying arrangement in which Esmond seeks her out: "When your heart is wounded, then come to me, my dear." This passage does not create the same impression of emotions nearly out of control that comes earlier in the reconciliation scene. Like Lydgate, Rachel has made a decision and she adheres to it tenaciously. But the passionate commentary which punctuates her factual summaries (wishing to die, thanking Heaven that Henry doesn't love her, craving absolution), the rush of brief, simply constructed sentences, the conspicuous omission of connections when connections are needed, suggest that the details of her speech mean more than she will say, perhaps more than she can say.

George Eliot's way of depicting character, then, gives far more prominence to rational reflection and conscious control than Thackeray's. It is perhaps impossible to separate character altogether from the narrative voice which presents it; and George Eliot's narrative voice, which renders thoughts and actions so thoroughly intelligible, embodies the possibilities for under-standing and sympathy towards which her best characters move. At the same time, its commitment to the endeavor for comprehensive insight supplies the reader with a hortatory example, summoning her or him to strive after similar-ly luminous interpretations. Indeed, in the more thoughtful of her characters and in her lucid narrative presence, George Eliot may overemphasize in-telligibility and coherence, presenting an idealized version of human thought, a hopeful proclamation of its finest potentialities.

Thackeray, on the other hand, is more inclined to present the mind as it would function without the intervention of shapely rationality. His nar-rative perspective is more likely to immerse the reader in an abundance of emotional, physical, and factual details. He recreates the immediacies of sub-jective experience, the way circumstances, perceptions, feelings, fantasies jostle against each other in a single moment of awareness.

From time to time, of course, a narrative voice does step in with inter-pretations and analyses, perspectives that do not belong to a particular character. When little George leaves Amelia for his grandfather Osborne's house, Amelia attempts to convince herself that his egoistic prattle expresses genuine devotion, but the narrative comment makes clear her wish to be mis-led: "The poor mother was fain to content herself with these selfish demonstrations of attachment, and tried to convince herself how sincerely her son loved her" (*Vanity Fair*, vol. 2, chap. 15). Such remarks, however, tend to be fugitive; the commentary moves quickly to another perspective, another incident, another character, another feeling. Although, like George Eliot's narrative commentary, such passages hold out the possibility of in-terpretation, this kind of mental activity is far less available to Thackeray's characters. Understanding and insight are possible in the world of Thackeray's fiction, but they are unlikely to prevail. Thackery does not provide his readers with models of sustained intellectual analysis; rather, he offers juxtaposi-tions which, though they may stimulate reflection, do not embody it.

Thackeray's fiction is especially concerned with the wild and various forces of human irrationality: fantasies, illusions, longings, compulsions. Emotions as he depicts them have an obstreperous energy which has little to do with conscious notions of desirable behavior. Sometimes this is a mat-ter of humor and delight. In *Pendennis* it is hilarious when decorously respect-able characters erupt in fierce passion, as when Helen and Dr. Portman, confronting what they think is Pen's guilty involvement with the Fotheringay, tremble, turn pale, fling themselves, cry out, roar, growl, shriek, and gasp, all in the space of two pages (*Pendennis*, vol. 1, chap. 6). But by the time of *Henry Esmond* and *The Newcomes*, the discrepancy between social sur-face and passionate inner self is a matter for sorrowful regret. The tension between conscious will and unruly impulse is differently defined in different characters: Lord Castlewood's conscious self, for example, watches dismayed and helpless as irresistible compulsions lead to ruin (*Henry Esmond*, vol. 1, chaps. 12, 13, 14); in Lady Castlewood, the balance is reversed — consciously, she works to assert complete control over her deepest longings, denying and repressing them but driving herself to emotional exhaustion and nearly hysterical desperation. Beatrix Esmond shows both tendencies: her conscious self is at the mercy of a compulsive quest for triumph, for conquest of ever more splendid suitors and of the worldly wealth and power they represent, yet it is too successful in overruling another desperate desire, a longing for a lover who could somehow release in her a flood of passionate feeling (*Henry Esmond*, vol. 3, chap. 7). Yet whatever the difference in the pattern, the impression of unresolvable conflict is the same. Because the style of Thackeray's characterization conveys with such moving intensity these frustrated encounters between the self and passionate impulse, his most interesting fiction makes the process of moral judgment a complicated one. The determination to arrive at verdicts is shaken by the terrible sense of loss and destruction which permeates so much of his writing. Although he makes it very clear that his characters deceive, flatter, and indulge themselves, his novels so question the possibility of any reasonable accommodation between profound feeling and the controlling intelligence which attempts to shape it to social roles and requirements that critical judgment is supplanted by a more ambiguous mood of rueful contemplation.

PETER  K.  GARRETT

# Thackeray: Seeing Double

To begin with beginnings was appropriate for dealing with Dickens, since the openings of his novels perform so dramatically the formal gesture of juxtaposing the diverse elements his multiple narratives combine. For Thackeray it might be more appropriate to begin with his endings, which tend to dramatize not the inclusive power of narrative but its arbitrariness and inadequacy. Contemplating the New Palace of Westminster, Thackeray "declared he saw no reason why it stopped; it ended nowhere, and might just as well have gone on to Chelsea." Some contemporary critics perceived the same formal problem in Thackeray's own works: "His conception of a story . . . is incomplete. There is no reason why he should begin where he does, no reason why he should end at all (W. C. Roscoe). Modern readers are more likely to praise the realism of such "incompleteness," but this revaluation of what is perceived as formal looseness fails to confront the more general problem of form in Thackeray. We shall be concerned at several points with moments in his novels that blur the outlines of narrative form: uncertain or multiple beginnings, displaced or muffled climaxes, inconclusive or ironically conventional endings; but these are only more dramatic instances of the way forms ranging from conventions of social behavior to underlying conceptual structures of thought are continually placed in question by Thackeray's fiction.

Thackeray and Dickens share a strong sense of conventional patterns, types, and forms, but Dickens's symbolic imagination tends to work through inherited forms like the mystery plot, intensifying and reinterpreting them,

From *The Victorian Multiplot Novel: Studies in Dialogical Form.* © 1980 by Yale University. Yale University Press, 1980.

while Thackeray works against them, resisting their arbitrariness and attempting to displace and discredit them in his effort to reveal a truth they obscure. This process can be more fully observed in Thackeray's development through the early burlesques and parodies, but for our purposes we can begin to define his conception of form and distinguish it from Dickens's by considering the early scene in *Pendennis* where the young hero for the first time attends a play and sees "the Fotheringay," the actress with whom he becomes infatuated. Thackeray suspends the narrative at the moment of her first entrance to comment on the sentimental drama by Kotzebue in which she appears:

> Those who know the play of the "Stranger" are aware that the remarks made by the various characters are not valuable in themselves, either for their sound sense, their novelty of observation, or their poetic fancy.
>
> Nobody ever talked so. If we meet idiots in life, as will happen, it is a great mercy that they do not use such absurdly fine words. The Stranger's talk is sham, like the book he reads, and the hair he wears, and the diamond ring he makes play with— but, in the midst of the balderdash, there runs that reality of love, children, and forgiveness of wrong, which will be listened to wherever it is preached, and sets all the world sympathising.
>
> (Chap. 4)

We can compare this passage with Dickens's comments on the stylized conventions of melodrama in chapter 17 of *Oliver Twist*. Both passages dwell fondly on the absurd unreality of popular drama; both claim that such contrived spectacles nevertheless offer access to an important truth. But for Dickens that truth is manifested through the form of melodramatic artifice, with its pattern of extreme contrasts, while for Thackeray the form of "fine words" and theatrical illusion is simply false: "sham," "balderdash." The truth, or "reality" which is somehow "in the midst" of these shams without being contaminated by them is a truth of inner feeling, the generous sentiment which responds to the display of "love, children, and forgiveness of wrong." Thackeray's art, by implication, will reject the falsified speech and behavior of sentimental drama, just as it rejects those of "silver fork" or "Newgate" novels, but its positive efforts will be aimed at communicating the truth of feeling and at tracing the relation between that inner truth and the false forms which distort it.

To regard this brief passage in isolation as a declaration of artistic principles may seem to assign Thackeray an aesthetic which is sentimental in its uncritical acceptance of generalized stock responses and confused in its failure to recognize, as Dickens does, the connection between form and significance.

The passage, however, is not an independent assertion but part of a scene, in which its generalizations perform the function of psychological analysis, helping to explain Pen's response to the play. The relation of commentary to action here, and the relation of this scene to the novel's larger context, can serve to illustrate more general principles of structure in Thackeray.

As Emily Costigan, as "Miss Fotheringay," enacts the role of Mrs. Haller, she demonstrates the power of the drama's "sham" to "set all the world sympathising." ("With what smothered sorrow, with what gushing pathos, Mrs. Haller delivered her part!") The multiplication of names here is significant: the actress, appearing under her stage name, plays the part of a character whose intense feelings she communicates without experiencing them herself. Pen falls in love with a double illusion. Not for one moment do we share his delusion; the groundlessness of his adolescent emotion is apparent even before the next chapter, "Mrs. Haller at Home," presents the "real" Emily in all her prosaic domesticity and complacent, amiable stupidity. But, as happens so often in Thackeray, the dichotomy of illusion and reality breaks down here. The passage on the "reality" which appears in the midst of *The Stranger*'s sham, as well as the generally sympathetic tone with which Pen's early follies are presented, prepare us to value the sincerity of his feelings and his capacity to experience them, to value feeling in itself, apart from its object. "To love foolishly is better than not to be able to love at all," the narrator comments later. "Some of us can't: and are proud of our impotence, too" (chap. 6). The point is subtly reinforced in the theatre scene when, as "Mrs. Haller" reaches the peak of pathos, "little Bows buried his face in his blue cotton handerkerchief, after crying out 'Bravo.' " Bows has "made her," "taken her in hand and taught her part after part" by drilling her in mechanical duplication of his example (chap. 6), yet he cannot help responding to the sham he has created.

Pen is also acting out a preestablished role. Awaking on the morning after the play, he is delighted to find that "he was as much in love as the best hero in the best romance he ever read" (chap. 4), for even before encountering Emily,

> Pen began to feel the necessity of a first love—of a consuming passion—of an object on which he could concentrate all those vague floating fancies under which he sweetly suffered—of a young lady to whom he could really make verses, and whom he could set up and adore, in place of those unsubstantial Ianthes and Zuleikas to whom he addressed the outpourings of his gushing muse.
>
> (Chap. 3)

And as we observe these interchanges of life and art, we should begin to recognize another level, on which Thackeray is contriving this charming fiction of youthful enthusiasm with which he strives to set us sympathizing.

*Pendennis* is the story not only of a young man's sentimental education but of the growth of a writer. Pen's career illustrates the development of the artist as his position converges with that of the authorial narrator, so that he can in turn become the narrative persona of later novels; but at the same time the story of his "fortunes and misfortunes" offers an implicit account of the motives and methods of narrative. Pen's progress moves through successive stages of error and illusion toward what is presented as eventual enlightenment, the choice of Laura and the domestic pieties she represents. But in an important sense the activity of the narrator moves in the opposite direction, recreating youthful illusions and celebrating the lost capacity to experience them. The principle of this substitution is indicated in a passage of narrative commentary that follows immediately after the conclusion of the Fotheringay episode and marks the beginning of Pen's next stage, his career at the university.

> Every man, however brief or inglorious may have been his academical career, must remember with kindness and tenderness the old University comrades and days. The young man's life is just beginning; the boy's leading-strings are cut, and he has all the novel delights and dignities of freedom. He has no idea of cares yet, or of bad health, or of roguery, or poverty, or tomorrow's disappointment. The play has not been acted so often as to make him tired. Though the after-drink, as we mechanically go on repeating it, is stale and bitter, how pure and brilliant was that first sparkling draught of pleasure!—How the boy rushes at the cup, and with what a wild eagerness he drains it! But old epicures who are cut off from the delights of the table, and are restricted to a poached egg and a glass of water, like to see people with good appetites; and, as the next best thing to being amused at a pantomime one's self is to see one's children enjoy it, I hope there may be no degree of age or experience to which mortal may attain, when he shall become such a glum philosopher, as not to be pleased by the sight of happy youth.
>
> (Chap. 17)

The most obvious implication here is the familiar image of Thackeray as the exponent of nostalgia ("Thackeray is the novelist of memory—of our memories as well as his own" [G. K. Chesterton, *The Victorian Age in Literature*]), but equally important is the way the passage indicates the function of narration, and the motive for the multiplication of narratives, in the reenactment through mediating surrogates of experience which is not (or no longer) directly accessible.

Following the original doubling of narrator and protagonist, the number of surrogates multiplies as the narrative progresses. In moving toward the position of the author, Pen serves this function for others, such as Warrington, and eventually arrives at a point where others must serve it for him. Thus, when he escorts Fanny at Vauxhall, he finds himself "pleased with her pleasure. . . . 'What would I not give for a little of this pleasure?' said the *blasé* young man" (chap. 46). At this stage, the narrative focus shifts to secondary figures who can provide substitutes for Pen's lost simplicity. Thus chapter 39, "Relates to Mr. Harry Foker's Affairs," focuses on the dissipated young brewer's heir at the point when all his precocious sophistication is swept away by his sudden infatuation with Blanche Amory. A similar shift after the evening at Vauxhall permits us to "peep into Fanny's bed" and "find the poor little maid tossing upon her mattress . . . and thinking over all the delights and events of that delightful, eventful night, and all the words, looks, and actions of Arthur, its splendid hero" (chap. 47).

As this passage suggests, there is an element of voyeurism in the effort to repossess these youthful experiences, but it is controlled by the distance Thackeray maintains, an effect that becomes clear when we fill in the ellipses: "Fanny's bed (which she shared in a cupboard, along with [her] two little sisters)"; "tossing upon her mattress, to the great disturbance of its other two occupants." The narrative is never completely dominated by Pen's or Fanny's or Foker's view of their experience, but is always colored by the benign irony of Thackeray's retrospection. Indeed, the whole pattern of doubling between character and narrator rests on the premise that experience can be understood only in retrospect, a truth which the characters' own experience repeatedly demonstrates. Thus the narrator comments on Pen's early life in London: "at this time of his life Mr. Pen beheld all sorts of places and men; and very likely did not know how much he enjoyed himself until long after, when balls gave him no pleasure, neither did farces make him laugh; nor . . ." etc. (chap. 36). After the convalescent Pen, Helen, and Laura have left Warrington alone in the chambers they have all shared, he immediately realizes "he had had the happiest days of his life . . . he knew it now they were just gone" (chap. 53). And later Laura realizes she has come to love Warrington only when he reveals the secret marriage that makes their love impossible (chap. 66).

Yet the clearer view of hindsight is always accompanied by regret for the lost possibilities it identifies; the narrative is marked by several extended passages of nostalgia for "the delightful capacity to enjoy" (chap. 30), or more generally for "old times . . . when people were young—when *most* people were young. Other people are young now, but we no more" (chap. 52). Even when change brings improvement, such as escape from illusion or obsession, it is still experienced as loss. Pen, realizing as he emerges from his illness that he no longer loves Fanny, is both relieved and ashamed: "It is pleasant, perhaps, but it is humiliating to own that you love no more" (chap. 53). The narrative takes the form of a generalized memory, preserving a link with the lost past, but while it reveals an underlying continuity through all the vicissitudes of life, it also reveals our isolation:

> Are you not awe-stricken, you, friendly reader, who, taking the page up for a moment's light reading, lay it down, perchance, for a graver reflection,—to think how you, you who have consummated your success or your disaster, may be holding marked station, or a hopeless and nameless place, in the crowd—who have passed through how many struggles of defeat, success, crime, remorse, to yourself only known!—who may have loved and grown cold, wept and laughed again, how often!—to think how you are the same *You*, whom in childhood you remember, before the voyage of life began! It has been prosperous, and you are riding into port, the people huzzaing and the guns saluting,—and the lucky captain bows from the ship's side, and there is a care under the star on his breast which nobody knows of: or you are wretched, and lashed, hopeless, to a solitary spar out at sea:—the sinking man and the successful one are thinking each about home, very likely, and remembering the time when they were children; alone on the hopeless spar, drowning out of sight; alone in the midst of the crowd applauding you.
>
> (Chap. 59)

The narrator's apostrophes assert the isolation and incommunicability of the self: "Ah, sir—a distinct universe walks about under your hat and under mine . . . you and I are but a pair of infinite isolations, with some fellow-islands a little more or less near to us" (chap. 16). But his narrative works against this condition. The retrospective account of typical early experience, the presentation of multiple surrogates, attempt to render simultaneously the perspectives which are in life successive and mutually exclusive stages of experience. This conflation of experience and subsequent understanding constitutes Thackeray's image of community, the shared fictive consciousness that joins the "distinct universes" of author and reader. It is clearly a community that does not and cannot correspond to any actual society but exists only within the narrative structure.

This fictive community of experience, the compound perspective which joins the unique and the typical, may be postulated as the goal of Thackeray's narrative, but the project and the means of fulfilling it repeatedly appear suspect. The corrupt Lord Steyne and his cronies throw an ironic light on the reenactment of youthful experience as they sit, appropriately, in a theatre box and discuss Major Pendennis's absence from town.

> "The secret is out," said Mr. Wenham, "there's a woman in the case."
>
> "Why, d—— it, Wenham, he's your age," said the gentleman behind the curtain.
>
> "Pour les âmes bien nées, l'amour ne compte pas le nombres des années," said Mr. Wenham, with a gallant air. "For my part, I hope to be a victim till I die, and to break my heart every year of my life." The meaning of which sentence was, "My lord, you need not talk: I'm three years younger than you, and twice as well *conservé*."
>
> "Wenham, you affect me," said the great man, with one of his usual oaths. "By —— you do. I like to see a fellow preserving all the illusions of youth up to our time of life—and keeping his heart warm as yours is. Hang it, sir,—it's a comfort to meet with such a generous, candid creature.—Who's that gal in the second row, with blue ribbons, third from the stage—fine gal. Yes, you and I are sentimentalists."
>
> (Chap. 14)

Closer to the novel's own procedure is the way Pen capitalizes on his first great love for the Fotheringay. At Oxbridge the story of his former passion and the verses which had expressed it contribute to his prestige: "There are few things which elevate a lad in the estimation of his brother boys, more than to have a character for a great and romantic passion" (chap. 18). Later he derives more substantial profit from the episode by reworking the manuscript in which he had recorded his experience into his "fashionable" novel, *Leaves from the Life-Book of Walter Lorraine*. Once the written record evokes only "the ghost of the dead feeling," it can be made into commerically successful literature, a process which seems to merit Warrington's scornful comment:

> "That's the way of poets," said Warrington. "They fall in love, jilt, or are jilted: they suffer and they cry out that they suffer more than any other mortals: and when they have experienced feelings enough they note them down in a book, and take the book to

market. All poets are humbugs; directly a man begins to sell his
feelings for money he's a humbug."

(Chap. 41)

But this is again an oversimplification, for even the "original" passion was
inspired and expressed by the conventional forms of romance. Nowhere can
we locate an unmediated source of feeling or value.

If truth cannot be established as an origin, it may be posited as a goal.
Thackeray attempts to oppose Pen's progressive emergence from illusion to
the continuing confusion of life and art represented by Blanche Amory, who
hovers between hypocrisy and self-deception, transposing her emotions into
her book of poems *Mes Larmes*, and attempting to act out its sentimental
fictions of her life. Thackeray passes a harsh final judgment on Blanche: "this
young lady was not able to carry out any emotion to the full; but had a sham
enthusiasm, a sham hatred, a sham love, a sham taste, a sham grief, each
of which flared and shone very vehemently for an instant, but subsided and
gave place to the next sham emotion" (chap. 73). Making Blanche represent
an irredeemable falsification of experience helps to advance both Pen's and
Thackeray's claims for a more honest art: "I ask you to believe that this person writing strives to tell the truth," he writes in his preface. "If there is not
that [the truth, or the striving?], there is nothing."

From the mingled "sham" and "reality" of *The Stranger* to the purely
"sham emotion" of Blanche Amory we have traced a circle where Thackeray
would have us find a more linear development. The issue here is not an interpretation of *Pendennis*, which has not been attempted, but the basic terms
in which Thackeray's fiction is defined, terms that lie closer to the surface
in this story of writers and actors than in any of his other novels. The problem of mediation, the ambiguous relation of feeling and the forms which
express it, of experience and the forms which represent it, is a central concern in all of Thackeray's work. His opposed narrative perspectives—the long
view of retrospection, of "philosophic" detachment and generalization, and
the view of the immediate experience, blind involvement and particularity—
these generate the structural dialogue of all his narratives, though in each
the relation between them is different. This type of compound perspective
is not inevitably linked to multiple narrative, but we can see in the multiplication of surrogates, in the effort to differentiate and oppose versions of a common theme or situation (e.g., Emily and Blanche: innocent disjunction vs.
compromised confusion of acting and feeling), and in the developmental
organization of these doubles and opposites to form a narrative argument,
the basis for a more fully articulated multiple narrative. It was, of course,
such a work which had preceded *Pendennis*.

*Vanity Fair* is a less intimate novel than Thackeray's later works. It does not ask us to become so closely and continuously involved in its characters' experiences as we do in those of Pendennis, Henry Esmond, or Clive and Ethel Newcome. Of all Thackeray's novels it best exemplifies that "panoramic method" which he represented for Percy Lubbock, the detached, broad survey of space and time that refuses to be confined to a single perspective or line of development, and of all his novels it most fully exploits the compositional possibilities of multiple narrative. In such a work there would seem to be little direct application for those preliminary notions of experience and its mediations we have derived from *Pendennis*. But in turning back to *Vanity Fair* we can recognize not only the same pattern of relationship between the narrator and his narrative but the same terms for representing it. Consider the late, minor scene which occurs during the excursion to Pumpernickel, where, the narrator informs us, "I first saw Colonel Dobbin and his party" at the table d'hôte of the Erbprinz Hotel. Later than evening, he sees them again:

> It was what they call a *gast-rolle* night at the Royal Grand Ducal Pumpernickelisch Hof,—or Court theatre: and Madame Schroeder Devrient, then in the bloom of her beauty and genius, performed the part of the heroine in the wonderful opera of Fidelio. From our places in the stalls we could see our four friends of the *table d'hôte*, in the loge which Schwendler of the Erbprinz kept for his best guests: and I could not help remarking the effect which the magnificent actress and music produced upon Mrs. Osborne, for so we had heard the stout gentleman in the mustachios call her. During the astonishing Chorus of the Prisoners over which the delightful voice of the actress rose and soared in the most ravishing harmony, the English lady's face wore such an expression of wonder and delight that it struck even little Fipps, the *blasé* attaché, who drawled out, as he fixed his glass upon her, "Gayd, it really does one good to see a woman caypable of that stayt of excaytement." And in the Prison Scene where Fidelio, rushing to her husband, cries "Nichts nichts mein Florestan," she fairly lost herself and covered her face with her handkerchief. Every woman in the house was snivelling at the time: but I suppose it was because it was predestined that I was to write this particular lady's memoirs, that I remarked her.
>
> (Chap. 62)

The immediate function of the scene is to illustrate this stage of Amelia's experience: "I like to dwell on this period of her life," the narrator has just explained, "and to think that she was cheerful and happy," and he goes on to remark of both Amelia and Dobbin, "perhaps it was the happiest time of both their lives indeed, if they did not know it—and who does? Which of us can point out and say that was the culmination—that was the summit of human joy?" The ability to perceive such a pattern is of course developed only in retrospect, but here Thackeray characteristically superimposes that more distant, superior vision on the immediate moment. This undramatic episode is the actual "culmination" for this couple, not, as required by conventional form, their later, tearful reunion on the pier at Ostend: "Here it is," the narrator ironically exclaims, "the summit, the end—the last page of the third volume" (chap. 67).

Amelia and Dobbin's idyll at Pumpernickel is thus set in the context of their previous trials and subsequent anticlimax, and it is here that "Thackeray" first encounters his characters and learns their story: "It was on this very tour that I, the present writer of a history of which every word is true, had the pleasure to see them first, and to make their acquaintance." The scene at the theatre, he affirms only half-jokingly, is thus located at the origin of the entire narrative, and we recognize that its pattern of doubled response is an emblem of mediated feeling, in which Amelia becomes the surrogate for more detached observers like the narrator.

If we consider the relation between Amelia and the writer of her "memoirs" which is presented here as the "original" relation between the narrator and characters of *Vanity Fair*, we postulate a narrative whose figures function first of all as registers of experience, instruments for establishing a characteristic relation to the world. This is admittedly an unfamiliar way of describing *Vanity Fair*. It seems more easily applicable to a novel by Henry James, where the characters' inner lives are much more fully developed and there is less discrepancy between their level of consciousness and the narrator's. But the paradox of a narrative which aims to recreate experience that is never directly available is, as our brief consideration of *Pendennis* has suggested, a major constituent of Thackeray's fiction. In *Vanity Fair*, where his irony more clearly reflects on his own authorial activity, we can explore that paradox further. At this point, let us simply note the implications of the theatre scene, which stresses the process of mediation and subordinates the questions of moral judgment that usually preoccupy critical discussion of the novel. We can return to the way the characters register experience after examining the novel's narrative perspectives and developmental structure.

The account of "Thackeray" as a friend of the characters and witness to their experiences is, of course, only one of many authorial images in *Vanity Fair* and stands opposed to the figure of the showman who manipulates his puppets while subjecting them to a constant stream of commentary.

Thackeray's shifting narrative stances serve the rhetorical purpose of controlling distance, but they also cast an ironic perspective on the act of narration itself, exposing the problematic process of mediation which conditions all knowledge and evaluation of the fictional world. The possibility of a multiple narrative rests, as we have seen in Dickens, on the convention of narrative omniscience, which permits the shift of focus between concurrent actions. Thackeray frequently exploits this power, as in the famous juxtaposition which concludes chapter 32: "Darkness came down on the field and city: and Amelia was praying for George, who was lying on his face, dead, with a bullet through his heart." The repeated presentation of simultaneous actions creates an awareness that any given event or sequence is only part of a larger pattern and creates an expectation that it will be correlated with others, an expectation on which the narrator can in turn play: "In the autumn evenings (when Rebecca was flaunting at Paris, the gayest among the gay conquerors there, and our Amelia, our dear wounded Amelia, ah! where was she?) Lady Jane would be sitting in Miss Crawley's drawing-room singing sweetly to her" (chap. 34).

Yet for all the novel's heavy reliance on this convention, the narrator repeatedly reminds us that it *is* a convention ("novelists have the privilege of knowing everything" [chap. 3]) and that his ability to reveal the separate, hidden lives of his characters depends on the assumption of a fictive role:

> I know where [Amelia] kept that packet she had—and can steal in and out of her chamber like Iachimo—like Iachimo? No—that is a bad part. I will only act Moonshine, and peep harmless into the bed where faith and beauty and innocence lie dreaming.
>
> (Chap. 12)

> If, a few pages back, the present writer claimed the privilege of peeping into Miss Amelia Sedley's bed-room, and understanding with the omniscience of the novelist all the gentle pains and passions which were tossing upon that innocent pillow, why should he not declare himself to be Rebecca's confidante too, master of her secrets, and seal-keeper of that young woman's conscience?
>
> (Chap. 15)

Furthermore, the claim to omniscience may just as easily be withdrawn, leaving the narrator uncertain ("My belief is . . ." [chap. 16]) or unable to decide on the correct version: "But who can tell you the real truth of the matter?" (chap. 2). Later, lacking entrée to the aristocratic world of Gaunt House, he must rely on the reports of "little Tom Eaves" (chap. 47), and eventually we are told that much of the novel has been derived from Tapeworm, the

Secretary of Legation at Pumpernickel, "who of course knew all the London gossip, and was besides a relative of Lady Gaunt," and who, in response to Dobbin's questions, "poured out into the astonished Major's ears such a history about Becky and her husband as astonished the querist, and supplied all the points of this narrative, for it was at that very table years ago that the present writer had the pleasure of hearing the tale" (chap. 66).

The doubtful authenticity of such information is matched by the doubtful authority of the narrator as moral commentator. The general moral perspective imposed by the title is enforced by numerous reflections on the vanity of the world and its distorted values, and "Thackeray" appears to strengthen his criticism by disowning any moral superiority, admitting his own implication in these errors: he is the preacher in cap and bells addressing his "brother wearers of motley." But the more he tries to define his position in relation to his story and audience, the more deeply compromised he becomes:

> I have heard a brother of the story-telling trade, at Naples, preaching to a pack of good-for-nothing honest lazy fellows by the sea-shore, work himself up into such a rage and passion with some of his villains whose wicked deeds he was describing and inventing, that the audience could not resist it, and they and the poet together would burst out into a roar of oaths and execrations against the fictitious monster of the tale, so that the hat went round, and the bajocchi tumbled into it, in the midst of a perfect storm of sympathy.
>
> At the little Paris theatres, on the other hand, you will not only hear the people yelling out, "*Ah gredin! Ah monstre!*" and cursing the tyrant of the play from the boxes; but the actors themselves positively refuse to play the wicked parts, such as those of *infâmes Anglais*, brutal Cossacks, and what not, and prefer to appear at a smaller salary, in their real characters as loyal Frenchmen. I set the two stories one against the other, so that you may see that it is not from mere mercenary motives that the present performer is desirous to show up and trounce his villains; but because he has a sincere hatred of them, which he cannot keep down, and which must find a vent in suitable abuse and bad language.
>
> I warn my "kyind friends," then, that I am going to tell a story of harrowing villany and complicated—but, as I trust, intensely interesting—crime. My rascals are no milk-and-water rascals, I promise you. When we come to the proper places we won't spare fine language—No, no! . . .

And, as we bring our characters forward, I will ask leave, as a man and a brother, not only to introduce them, but occasionally to step down from the platform, and talk about them: if they are good and kindly, to love them and shake them by the hand; if they are silly, to laugh at them confidentially in the reader's sleeve: if they are wicked and heartless, to abuse them in the strongest terms which politeness admits it.

Otherwise you might fancy it was I who was sneering at the practice of devotion, which Miss Sharp finds so ridiculous; that it was I who laughed good-humouredly at the reeling old Silenus of a baronet—whereas the laughter comes from one who has no reverence except for prosperity, and no eye for anything beyond success. Such people there are living and flourishing in the world—Faithless, Hopeless, Charityless: let us have at them, dear friends, with might and main. Some there are, and very successful too, mere quacks and fools: and it was to combat and expose such as those, no doubt, that Laughter was made.

(Chap. 8)

The two juxtaposed stories hardly demonstrate the narrator's high motives or moral rectitude. Instead, emerging from a confusion of fictive and "real characters," of commercial and religious values, the claim of "sincere hatred" for vice seems no less an assumed role than the expression at other points of cynical worldly wisdom, where " 'I' is . . . introduced to personify the world in general" (chap. 36). Irony infects every moral stance the narrator and his audience may adopt, whether he offers them the pleasures of righteous condemnation ("let us have at them") or of tolerant acquiescence: "It is all vanity, to be sure, but who will not own to liking a little of it?" (chap. 51).

As a result, every comment or interpretation which the narrator introduces can exert only conditional authority. His formulations raise but cannot resolve the novel's issues; they must be tested against the implications of the narrative as a whole. A brief example, in which Thackeray again sets two stories "one aginst the other" may be found in chapter 61, "In Which Two Light Are Put Out," presenting the deaths of the two old merchants, Sedley and Osborne. The chapter opens with the well-known meditation on the "second-floor arch," in which that detail of Victorian domestic architecture becomes "a memento of Life, Death, and Vanity," and these general reflections on the common fate soon modulate into more pointed remarks (with glances at the story of Dives and Lazarus) on the best state of mind and worldly condition in which to meet death: "Which, I wonder, brother reader, is the better lot, to die prosperous and famous, or poor and disappointed?" Sedley exemplifies the latter; having become reconciled to his daughter during his final illness, the old bankrupt dies a humble penitent.

The shift of focus to his prosperous enemy Osborne strengthens our expectation that the narrative will now fulfill the illustration of the narrator's general moral contrast:

> "You see," said old Osborne to George, "what comes of merit and industry, and judicious speculations, and that. Look at me and my banker's account. Look at your poor grandfather, Sedley, and his failure. And yet he was a better man than I was, this day twenty years—a better man I should say by ten thousand pound."

But in the following account of Osborne's last days, the simple opposition breaks down. He comes to recognize the virtues of Dobbin, whom he has scorned and avoided since George's marriage, and becomes reconciled with him: " 'Major D.,' Mr. Osborne said, looking hard at him, and turning very red too—'You did me a great injury [inducing George to marry Amelia]; but give me leave to tell you, you are an honest feller. There's my hand, sir.' " Through Dobbin's advocacy, he also becomes reconciled with Amelia and leaves her an annuity in his will. As this old tyrant softens and attempts to make restitution at the end, his story becomes more parallel than opposed to Sedley's. In this complication of the schematic opposition which the narrator has formulated we may find an effect of "realism" (life does not conform to abstract patterns), or we may see instead the substitution of one pattern for another, stressing our common humanity instead of separating sheep and goats. We may even consider this shift in purely formal terms as the modification of illustrative functions by plot functions, since Osborne's will not only provides for Amelia's independence but informs her of her great debt to Dobbin. In any case, the episode shows how the significance of Thackeray's narrative emerges only from the play of all its elements against each other, and it also illustrates the tendency which most often directs that play, the decomposition of stylized antitheses.

We can observe this process not only on the scale of circumscribed episodes but in the developmental structure of the entire novel, which is also, of course, essentially composed of two stories set against each other, the careers of Amelia and Becky. By this doubling Thackeray made *Vanity Fair* "A Novel without a Hero," not only in its ironic refusal to embody moral ideals (Pendennis, as his biographer repeatedly reminds us, is also "not a hero" in this sense), but more fundamentally in its lack of a center. Its meaning is produced by the relation between its narrative lines, and that relation is always changing, like the narrator's shifting roles and stances. The absence of a single compositional center or perspective thrusts the problem of formal and thematic coherence into unusual prominence, so that the question of whether and how the separate narratives are to be connected becomes an active concern for the reader as well as the author.

One principle which is offered as a possible basis of connection is that of cause and effect, but it is repeatedly offered only to be withdrawn. Becky and Amelia begin the novel together, converge at the time of their marriages, honeymoons, and the Belgian expedition, and meet once more near the end at Pumpernickel. These intersections, especially the last, are sufficiently contrived to suggest that much depends on them, but this is not the case. Becky, failing to capture Jos in the opening sequence, must go off to the Crawleys just as she would if the episode had never occurred. The possible effects of Becky's stealing George from Amelia are forestalled by his death in battle, and Amelia goes on to suppress her awareness of this betrayal, devoting her life to the cult of his memory just as she would have done if he had never been unfaithful. The final twist of inconsequence comes when Becky produces George's damning note to persuade Amelia to recall Dobbin—and learns she already has (chap. 67). Becky laughs in delight, as may we, for the joke is as much on the reader, who should have realized by this time that the significant relationship between the two heroines will not be one of cause and effect. The episodes in which they confront each other directly simply give more explicit and dramatic expression to the play of similarity and difference between them which is implicit throughout. We do not read *Vanity Fair* as we do Dickens's later novels to discover a network of hidden causal connections, nor as we do George Eliot's to trace the minute links of consequence as they are formed. Thackeray forces us to do much sooner what the others also eventually require, to make connections on a different level.

That effort is both incited and directed by the strongly marked parallels between the two narratives which repeatedly place their heroines in situations that demand comparison. From the opening, where we observe their different responses to leaving school, through their parallel courtships, double honeymoon, and their behavior as wives and mothers, up to their final reunions with long-time admirers, we constantly interpret them in terms of each other. The pattern of their relationship is, like those we have observed on a smaller scale, initially formulated as an antithesis which polarizes both values and qualities of character. The first important occasion for establishing this pattern as the dominant structural principle comes at the point where the two narratives first diverge. This occurs in chapter 7, when Becky must go off to the Crawleys; she and Amelia remain apart until, along with Rawdon and George, they meet again in chapter 14. In terms of proportion and emphasis, Becky dominates this section. She appears in five of the seven chapters, and although Thackeray devotes a considerable part of them to exposition on the Crawley family, much of this is conveyed through her irreverent letters, while the main action presents her successful strategems for establishing herself at Queen's Crawley, as she makes herself indispensable to Sir Pitt, flatters the older son, flirts with the younger, and finally becomes Miss Crawley's favorite.

When, in chapter 12, the narrator interrupts these lively developments "to inquire what has become of Miss Amelia," he must deliberately frustrate the narrative interest and momentum which have just been created. This tactic becomes the explicit issue on which the transition turns, as the narrator records the objections of a hypothetical reader: " 'We don't care a fig for her,' writes some unknown correspondent with a pretty little handwriting and a pink seal to her note. 'She is *fade* and insipid.' " Amelia's claim to attention is first made a question of sentimental masculine preference: she is an instance of "the kind, fresh, smiling, artless, tender little domestic goddess, whom men are inclined to worship" and other women depreciate. But a more important claim emerges as commentary gives way to narration, and the general tendency for a woman like Amelia "to be despised by her sex" is dramatized in the way she is patronized and slighted by the Osborne sisters (and neglected rather than worshipped by George). Her situation assumes a reciprocal relation to the one we have observed in the preceding chapters: the passivity and inexpressive sentiment which lead to her rejection in Russell Square are both the opposite and complement of those qualities which have enabled Becky to succeed at Queen's Crawley. The period during which they have been separated now appears as the "finishing" education of each in her distinguishing qualities: "We have talked of shift, self, and poverty, as those dismal instructors under whom poor Miss Becky Sharp got her education. Now, love was Miss Amelia Sedley's last tutoress, and it was amazing what progress our young lady made under that popular teacher."

This comparison indicates an underlying symmetry beneath the disproportion of narrative emphasis. Despite the fact that Amelia's is "not much of a life to describe" while she remains protected "in the paternal nest" and Becky is already "on her own wing," she is undergoing a parallel development. And the antithesis of "self" and "love" as their respective "instructors" further implies that she represents the positive pole of value: while Becky cultivates the arts of appearance and manipulation, the unprepossessing Amelia cultivates the inner truth of feeling. They are thus made to divide the field of feminine nature: "Some are made to scheme, and some to love." But again the antithesis is no sooner formulated than it begins to break down. In practice, Amelia's tuition in love consists of worshipping an idealized image of George and elaborating her feelings in long, often unanswered letters. If Becky deludes others, Amelia deludes herself; if Becky is self-seeking, Amelia is self-indulgent. We may favor one or the other, as the narrator does at different points, but Thackeray will never allow us to rest in a simple conception of the relation between them.

This process of construction and deconstruction, of formulating, breaking down, and reformulating binary oppositions, is carried on throughout the novel's development. It is elaborated in many subsidiary doublings, beginning with the opposition of the two Pinkerton sisters in the opening scene and continuing through numerous parallels and contrasts of character and situation. The local effects of these parallels are various and often quite complex, but their general tendency is toward the assimilation of differences, the merging of oppositions into equivalences. The convention of contrasting protagonists is traditionally the basis for a developmental structure which functions as argument, differentiating values by the outcome of the action, whether through poetic justice or its ironic inversion (to which Thackeray seems closer), the misfortunes of virtue and the prosperity of vice. But Thackeray blurs the pattern: both heroines experience prosperity and misfortune; both end in positions of secure respectability that do not provide complete happiness. Thackeray deliberately frustrates conventional expectations of a decisive and satisfying resolution: "I want to leave everybody dissatisfied and unhappy at the end of the story—we ought all to be with our own and all other stories."

Critical commentaries on Thackeray's parallelism typically retrace this movement of assimilation, beginning with contrasts and ending with equivalences. Kathleen Tillotson, after describing the more obvious contrasts between the two heroines' fortunes at different stages, observes that "there are also the subtler running contrasts of Becky's treatment of her son Rawdon, Amelia's of George: subtle because Thackeray is critical both of heartless neglect and passionate possessiveness. Or the likeness within difference of Amelia's stupid fidelity to her husband's memory, and Becky's stupid infidelity to Rawdon. Each is an egoist." And the two most detailed studies of the novel's parallels both conclude with a general impression of sameness: "These contrasts . . . create a sense of the limited possibilities of human existence" (Myron Taube), "the structure emphasizes that, in spite of the differences in men and their lives, all the inhabitants of Vanity Fair are ultimately circumscribed by an inescapable pattern of sameness" (Edgar F. Harden).

This would seem to be the conclusion of Thackeray's argument: all differences ultimately dissolve in the vision of common vanity, which includes author and reader as well as characters. It is a conclusion which may seem either profound or reductive, or which may seem rather to abandon all moral censure in favor of general compassion. In any case, it is, we must remember, specifically the perspective of the conclusion, the long view taken from the end: "Ah! *Vanitas Vanitatum!* Which of us is happy in this world? Which of us has his desire? or, having it, is satisfied?" But Thackeray mistrusts decisive conclusions, both of plot and argument, and this diminishing perspective, in which all the characters become puppets once more, is not the only one he offers. Against the long view of retrospection and disillusioned wisdom he sets the claim of the irreducible moment; against the simplifying conclusion he sets the greater complexity of his narrative process. Both perspectives are engaged at each point in the narrative, and it is only by considering in some detail the way they interact that we can fully recognize the subtlety he derives from his schematic patterns.

Let us return to the point where we began—where "Thackeray" claims he began—to the double spectacle in which characters, like Amelia at the opera, become both the object of observation and the medium of experience. Thackeray's use of the characters as registers of experience is organized by a characteristic dichotomy between modes of response, formulated in the comments which introduce the auction of Sedley's goods after his bankruptcy: "If there is any exhibition in all Vanity Fair which Satire and Sentiment can visit arm in arm together; where you light on the strangest contrasts laughable and tearful: where you may be gentle and pathetic, or savage and cynical with perfect propriety," it is at such assemblies (chap. 17). The basic principles of the novel as spectacle are here made remarkably explicit: its numerous contrasts are exhibited as objects of satire and sentiment, two modes which may on occasion appear together but which "propriety"—and the separation of plot-lines—usually keep apart. Becky functions as both object and agent of satire as she pursues her erratic career in the great world, while Amelia provides the sentimental interludes, offering an alternative or reproach in her domestic obscurity and suffering.

But these complementary stories are not only observed as spectacle. They also offer alternative modes of participation, the means of entering into the individual's perspective and provisionally adopting an active or passive stance toward the world of Vanity Fair, of imaginatively joining its strenuous game of power and position or of deliberately withdrawing with those who live on its margins and dedicate themselves to less glamorous pursuits. The teleology of the novel's argument may insist on the equivalent vanity of all the forms of life it presents, but at many points along the way to ultimate disillusionment we are invited to enter into the characters' sharply different experiences—in part for the very reason that they *are* only available in the passing moment: "What well-constituted mind, merely because it is transitory, dislikes roast-beef?" (chap. 51).

Participation in the adventures of Thackeray's active heroine comes fairly easily: "The famous little Becky Puppet has been pronounced to be uncommonly flexible in the joints, and lively on the wire." We can not only admire her unscrupulous agility but frequently side with her, since she is most often engaged in an uneven contest with the established powers of a corrupt society. She represents the claims of an amoral energy, of vitality, resilience, and wit. Most of all, she presents a brilliant performance, which we can both observe and join. Her sheer skill can at times command the admiration even of those she has duped: "What a splendid actress and manager!" thinks Steyne after learning how she has deceived him. "She is unsurpassable in lies" (chap. 52). Not that Becky's lies and selfishness are themselves admirable: she can never evade moral criticism for very long. But in those moments when the burden of judgment is removed from both character and reader, her power as a medium of experience is released. In such moments Becky's powers of invention offer not lies but creative fictions; her energy and resourcefulness in sustaining and varying her performance constitute a comic celebration of the power of art over life's accidents and inequities, as when her efforts to win favor with Lady Southdown by soliciting both religious and medical advice result in her being forced to take the countess's medicine.

> Lord Steyne, and her son in London, had many a laugh over the story, when Rawdon and his wife returned to their quarters in May Fair. Becky acted the whole scene for them. She put on a night-cap and gown. She preached a great sermon in the true serious manner: she lectured on the virtue of the medicine which she pretended to administer, with a gravity of imitation so perfect, that you would have thought it was the Countess' own Roman nose through which she snuffled. "Give us Lady Southdown and the black dose," was a constant cry among the folks in Becky's little drawing-room in May Fair. And for the first time in her life the Dowager Countess of Southdown was made amusing.
>
> (Chap. 41)

Thackeray's passive heroine can hardly exercise an equally powerful attraction: "the Amelia Doll . . . has had a smaller circle of admirers," but his tactic is, as we have seen, to claim a positive value for this apparent deficiency. Thus, in defending the shift from Becky's intrigues at Queen's Crawley to Amelia's quiet life at home, he links her capacity for feeling with her lack of obvious dramatic interest: "Poor little tender heart! and so it goes on hoping and beating, and longing and trusting. You see it is not much of a life to describe. There is not much of what you call incident in it . . . the life of a good young girl who is in the paternal nest as yet, can't have many of those thrilling incidents to which the heroine of romance commonly lays claim" (chap. 12). These comments recall the terms in which Thackeray has previous-

ly defended his own art, with a similar mock apology ("I know that the tune
I am piping is a very mild one") and opposition to more popular, factitious
modes: "We might have treated the subject in the genteel, or in the romantic, or in the facetious manner" (chap. 6), with parodic samples of each alternative. In advising his readers that they "must hope for no such romance,"
Thackeray claims for his work a negative, or relative, realism: its "truth"
is perceived through the displacement of falsifying conventions like the
heightened drama of romance—or like the acceptance of marriage as a conclusion ("As his hero and heroine pass the matrimonial barrier, the novelist
generally drops the curtain, as if the drama were over then" [chap. 26]). Just
as Thackeray the performer is linked with Becky, Thackeray the adherent
of unglamorous truth is linked with Amelia: her sensibility seems to offer
access to an inner truth which the false forms of Vanity Fair distort and
repress.

In terms of moral evaluation, the opposition of false wordly values to
the truth of the heart would establish Amelia as the novel's moral norm, an
interpretation which has the support of Thackeray's most distinguished
biographer:

> Life is redeemed for Thackeray only by affection, by love, by loyal-
> ty to the promptings of the heart. . . . Becky's career is admirably
> suited to illustrate the destructive operation of the standards of
> Vanity Fair, but Thackeray desired through Amelia's history to
> show what he would put in their place, the life of personal rela-
> tions, the loyalty and selflessness inspired by home affections. This
> recurring contrast was essential to his purpose.
>
> (Gordon N. Ray, *Thackeray: The Uses of Adversity*)

But we have already seen how "this recurring contrast" breaks down into
equivalence. Amelia's opposition to Becky offers not so much a standard of
judgment as an alternative mode of participation, a perception of Vanity Fair
through the experience of its victim, one who is thrust to its periphery by
the same forces that enable the more aggressive to move toward the center.
This complementarity may be rendered dramatically, as when Amelia silently
suffers while Becky charms George, or by structural implication, as when
through the central section of the novel, Becky's fortunes rise while Amelia's
descend; but it generally invites us to find in the account of Amelia's trials
what is absent from Becky's adventures, a depth of feeling which extracts
from the world's vanity not comedy but pathos.

Yet as the narrative moves toward Amelia in this search for inner "truth,"
we repeatedly find the way blocked. The narrator adopts a protective attitude toward her vulnerable sensibility and deliberately limits his omniscience

to shield her. Thus, when she seeks religious consolation for the distress of her early married life, the narrator ostentatiously draws the curtain: "Have we a right to repeat or overhear her prayers? These, brothers, are secrets, and out of the domain of Vanity Fair, in which our story lies" (chap. 26). The value of such feelings can apparently be preserved only by placing them beyond the range of observation: to present them directly would be an act of betrayal or violation: "Her sensibilities were so weak and tremulous, that perhaps they ought not to be talked about in a book" (chap. 38). To invoke qualities which can be properly represented only through their literal absence may seem a mere trick, creating an illusion of depth. We see an instance of such an effect in George Osborne's romantic manner:

> George had an air at once swaggering and melancholy, languid and fierce. He looked like a man who had passions, secrets, and private harrowing griefs and adventures. His voice was rich and deep. He would say it was a warm evening, or ask his partner to take an ice, with a tone as sad and confidential as if he were breaking her mother's death to her, or preluding a declaration of love.
>
> (Chap. 21)

There is a suspicious echo of this effect in the narrator's defense of his claim that Amelia's "simplicity and sweetness are quite impossible to describe in print. But who has not beheld these among women, and recognized the presence of all sorts of qualities in them, even though they say no more to you than they are engaged to dance the next quadrille, or that it is very hot weather?" (chap. 27). But this concerns only the realm of social appearance, however ingenuous, and is offered here in explanation of Amelia's immediate popularity with the young men of George's regiment: "Her simple artless behaviour, and modest kindness of demeanor, won all their unsophisticated hearts." Becky's public performances are deliberately contrived to suggest "the presence of all sorts of qualities" she does not in fact possess, to express emotions she does not feel. In perceiving her disingenuous behavior not just as false but as superbly artful, we indirectly grasp one of her most important qualities as a potential surrogate; correspondingly, we can perceive Amelia's "simple, artless behaviour" as an inadequate expression of the potential depth of feeling which may be realized through her mediation, requiring an imaginative effort to grasp what cannot be presented directly.

Thackeray conveys the sense of a more direct approach to states of intense feeling and at the same time indicates the necessity of preserving a distance from them by enacting the violation of Amelia's privacy through

the figures of Dobbin and Becky. Dobbin contrives to get a last glimpse of
her before the regiment leaves for battle.

> And presently Dobbin had the opportunity which his heart
> coveted, and he got sight of Amelia's face once more. But what
> a face it was! So white, so wild and despair-stricken, that the
> remembrance of it haunted him afterwards like a crime, and the
> sight smote him with inexpressible pangs of longing and pity.
>     She was wrapped in a white morning dress, her hair falling on
> her shoulders, and her large eyes fixed and without light. By way
> of helping on the preparations for the departure, and showing
> that she too could be useful at a moment so critical, this poor
> soul had taken up a sash of George's from the drawers whereon
> it lay, and followed him to and fro with the sash in her hand,
> looking on mutely as his packing proceeded. She came out and
> stood, leaning against the wall, holding this sash against her
> bosom, from which the heavy net of crimson dropped like a large
> stain of blood. Our gentle-hearted Captain felt a guilty shock as
> he looked at her. "Good God," thought he, "and is it grief like
> this I dared to pry into?" And there was no help: no means to
> soothe and comfort this helpless, speechless misery. He stood for
> a moment and looked at her, powerless and torn with pity, as
> a parent regards an infant in pain.
>
> (Chap. 30)

Later Becky also intrudes, enabling the narrator both to distinguish his own
greater restraint and to reinforce his claim for the deeper reality of private
emotion hidden by the spectacle of dramatic public events:

> Until this dauntless worldling came in and broke the spell, and
> lifted the latch, we too have forborne to enter into that sad
> chamber. How long had that poor girl been on her knees! what
> hours of speechless prayer and bitter prostration she had passed
> there! The war-chroniclers who write brilliant stories of fight and
> triumph scarcely tell us of these. These are too mean parts of the
> pageant: and you don't hear widows' cries or mothers' sobs in
> the great Chorus of Victory. And yet when was the time, that
> such have not cried out: heart-broken, humble Protestants,
> unheard in the uproar of the triumph!
>
> (Chap. 31)

Since such moments do render a powerful sense of Amelia's "helpless, speechless misery," the narrator's claim that her inner qualities are "impossible to describe in print" or "secrets" that lie out of his domain must be recognized as part of Thackeray's strategy rather than literal statements of authorial policy. They serve to intensify awareness of what remains unspoken by an ostentatious reticence that finds its counterpart in the way the narrator draws attention to his decorous refusal to present Becky's more sordid adventures, paying ironic tribute to hypocritical social conventions governing what "ought not to be talked about in a book" (see especially the opening of chapter 64, with its extended simile on the siren's "hideous tail" hidden beneath the water).

In both cases, as on other occasions when we are reminded of the narrator's presence and functions, Thackeray is insisting on the inevitable process of mediation which precludes complete immediacy or direct knowledge. Amelia's role as the primary focus of sentiment does not give her a privileged place in the novel's scheme of values, nor does her tender sensibility represent a stable inner truth, since her emotions are nearly always implicated in errors of judgments and self-deception. But in using her trials to elicit a sense of pathos, Thackeray opens an alternative means of indirect participation in his fiction. From the detached, inclusive perspective of retrospective evaluation, his two main narratives may cancel each other out, but from the perspective of more intimate involvement, they augment and mediate each other. Their elaborate counterpoint extends the novel's range beyond satire or sentiment into effects of remarkable complexity.

Many of these effects: the interplay of similarity and difference, the expansive force of participation in opposed modes of experience, and the combination of "short" perspective that dwell on the quality of the moment with longer ones that set it in the context of narrative sequence—all may be observed in the brief span of two chapters, 50 and 51, which juxtapose important episodes in each of the two heroines' stories. The first presents Amelia's losing struggle against poverty and final surrender of Georgy to old Osborne; the second presents Becky's triumphant social success in the aristocratic world she has long sought to enter. The effect of their juxtaposition is not just another contrast but the most extreme contrast of the novel, the lowest point in one heroine's fortunes set against the highest in the other's. The pattern produces many obvious ironies bearing on life's injustice, the misfortunes of the humble and loving, the prosperity of the worldly and cynical, which are brought into sharp focus by the two heroines' respective attitudes toward their sons: for Amelia to give up hers is the greatest ordeal she has experienced since her husband's death, while Becky willingly lets hers be sent off to school as a step in her progressive intimacy with Lord Steyne. Other specific parallels between the two chapters elaborate the contrast. Amelia's efforts to make money include the painting of "a couple of begilt Bristol boards," producing "feeble works of art" which are rejected by the Fancy Repository and Brompton Emporium of Fine Arts, and she writes a pleading letter to Jos, "painting in terms of artless pathos" the family's condition. While this "poor simple lady, tender and weak" is vainly trying "to battle with the struggling, violent world," Becky succeeds through her skillful performances in both life and art, disarming and conquering those she meets and, at her peak of acclaim, actually performing in mime and song.

The contrast also serves as a restatement of the antithesis between the outward glitter and excitement of "the great world" and the inner realm of feeling and secret suffering. Becky's penetration "into the very centre of fashion" helps to reveal the hollowness of its glamor: "Her success excited, elated, and then bored her." Amelia's silent struggle appears as only a parenthesis in the account of Becky's conquests; the title of chapter 50, "Contains a Vulgar Incident," offers the characteristic mock apology for descending to such commonplace matters as domestic hardship and love. Again, the narrator insists on the recognition of hidden pathos, like the widows' cries and mothers' sobs drowned out by the chorus of victory after battle as the account of Amelia's painful separation from her son expands into generalization: "The child goes away smiling as the mother breaks her heart. By heavens it is pitiful, the bootless love of women for children in Vanity Fair."

But the juxtaposition of these two chapters also yields a much more profound effect of similarity between the sharply different experiences they present. I do not mean the sort of ironic parallel we might draw by standing back to observe, for instance, that Amelia's blind and overly possessive love for her son is as "vain" and mistaken as Becky's avid desire to enter the great world. I mean the opposite sort of connection which creates greater involvement rather than the reductive abstractness of the "long" view. The most surprising effect of these episodes is the way both momentarily escape from ironic comparison and allow us to participate in both Amelia's suffering and Becky's elation, to pass from one to the other with a sense of the underlying continuity, the shared intensity of these extremes that draws us more deeply into both experiences. Here the two heroines fully realize their capacity for mediation. Thackeray clearly indicates the element of hysterical excess in Amelia's devotion to her son ("Her heart and her treasure—her joy, hope, love, worship—her God, almost!"), but this does not qualify compassion for her misery. Becky's values are at least equally distorted; we are not asked to approve of her ambitions, but we are induced to participate in her triumph. The narrator has earlier remarked that Becky, "from her wit, talent, and energy, indeed merited a place of honour in Vanity Fair" (chap. 34), and here she gains that reward. Wit, talent, and energy can be appreciated for themselves, quite apart from their moral direction, and in Becky's artistic triumph at Gaunt House they appear in a moment of brilliant purity: "She had reached her culmination: her voice rose trilling and bright over the storm of applause: and soared as high and joyful as her triumph."

The bond of intensity between these reciprocating episodes, the double realization of the potential for participation through these characters, is crucial, but it is not the only factor working here. Thackeray still preserves the distance entailed by narrative mediation, a distance which the reader can only try to cross. In presenting Amelia's suffering, the narrator displays the same reticence we have observed earlier: "She could say nothing more, and walked away silently to her room. Let us close it upon her prayers and her sorrow. I think we had better speak little about so much love and grief." The quality of her experience must, to an important extent, be grasped indirectly, as in the description of the way she leaves Georgy alone with his aunt: "She was trying the separation:—as that poor gentle Lady Jane Grey felt the edge of the axe that was to come down and sever her slender life." Thackeray cited this image in a letter as an example of the way pathos should be "indicated rather than expressed. . . . I say that is a fine image whoever wrote it . . . that is greatly pathetic I think: it leaves you to make your own sad pictures." Inducing this sort of participation is the method of both episodes. Neither offers the illusion of an objective spectacle, and the restriction imposed by the narrator's tact on his presentation of Amelia's suffering is matched by the restrictions supposedly imposed on his knowledge of Gaunt House by his position as "an uninitiated man [who] cannot take upon himself to pourtray the great world accurately."

Beyond the factor of narrative mediation, there is the added complication of temporal perspective: both episodes are organized by an opposition between the suspended moment and the continuing sequence. Amelia's protracted struggle and painful act of renunciation are momentous from her own perspective, but Thackeray also sets them in a larger context by including other points of view and continuing the narrative past the separation. Georgy welcomes the change and adapts to it readily; for him, and for the Osbornes, whose side is also sympathetically presented, it is not a loss but a renewal. Like the juxtaposition with Becky's successes in the following chapter, these contrasts intensify the pathos of Amelia's situation, but they also offer alternative perspectives on the same event and allow us to see it as part of a continuing, manifold sequence and not just as an isolated crisis. Becky's triumph is more emphatically framed by commentary and narrative that indicate its transience. It is the narrator's retrospective knowledge that authorizes us to suspend judgment in order to participate in the quality of her experience: "let us make the best of Becky's aristocratic pleasures . . . for these too, like all other mortal delights, were but transitory." The reader is explicitly warned, as the narrator begins his account of the climactic evening at Gaunt House, that "it will be among the very last of the fashionable entertainments to which it will be our fortune to conduct him." Thus a double perspective plays upon Becky's supreme moment: it is "her culmination," both a point of intensity whose quality may be valued for its own sake and the peak of a development which now leads downward.

The title of chapter 51 suggests a double perspective in evaluative as well as temporal terms: "In Which a Charade is Acted Which May or May Not Puzzle the Reader." The longer narrative perspective sheds an ironic light on the roles Becky plays. She achieves her culmination as "the most *ravissante* little Marquise in the world"; even at the peak she can only masquerade as one of the aristocracy. While this charade confines to a circumscribed fiction the role she hopes to play in reality, the other, in which Becky appears as Clytemnestra (for the first time), projects a possibility she may actually realize, a possibility which is underscored by Steyne's aside: "By ——, she'd do it too." Just as the last pages of the previous chapter move on to place its focal event in the context of continuing action, so here Thackeray concludes by giving the narrative a sharp downward turn with Rawdon's arrest for debt as he leaves Gaunt House. The reader may or may not be momentarily puzzled, but it soon becomes clear that this is part of another charade. The conspiracy of Clytemnestra and Aegisthus is replaced by that of Becky and Lord Steyne, and as fiction is transposed from art to life, moral judgment becomes necessary once more. The next intense experience in which we shall be invited to participate will be Rawdon's when he returns home to discover his wife and her patron alone together. But the satisfaction offered by that famous moment of moral retribution will in turn give way to new complications that qualify its claims as the narrative progresses.

This rhythm of approach and withdrawal, setting the arresting interest of the individual and the immediate against the longer perspectives of generality and retrospection, is always at work in Thackeray's narrative, and in the end it is always the longer perspectives which prevail. A concise paradigm may be seen at the end of *Pendennis*, when the hero excitedly returns to Laura with the news that they are now free to marry. Thackeray forces us to pause on the threshold as Pen rushes in to tell her: "May we follow him? The great moments of life are but moments like the others. Your doom is spoken in a word or two. A single look from the eyes; a mere pressure of the hand, may decide it; or of the lips, though they cannot speak" (chap. 74). The narrative passes over the scene and then circles back to it, as if it had already taken place, displacing the moment of culmination in order to reaffirm the longer, leveling view and mediating its emotional intensity. In *Vanity Fair*, the end also imposes uniformity: the weak and the strong, the selfish and the generous, the clever and the foolish appear equally implicated in vanity, equally secure and dissatisfied, equally to be pitied and dismissed: "Come children, let us shut up the box and the puppets, for our play is played out." The final stress on common vanity may be seen as the conclusion of the novel's moral argument, but it can also be seen as a return to the basis of its logic. Its elaborate, restless play on patterns of difference and similarity, exaggerating oppositions in order to collapse them, never allowing the reader a single, stable perspective or standard, this method too rests on *vanitas*, or emptiness, the emptiness which underlies the production of meaning from sheer difference. This ultimate groundlessness makes the novel both reductive and open: if *Vanity Fair* forces us to recognize that all its moments are but moments like the others, each yielding to the next, it also induces us to participate in an expansive process that can have no logical conclusions.

Whether or not *Vanity Fair* is Thackeray's greatest novel, it is certainly the one in which he most fully exploits the dialogical possibilities of multiple narrative. Later works show clear advances in some respects but regression in others. The convention of morally contrasted heroines, for instance, reappears in the opposition of Blanche and Laura in *Pendennis*, of Beatrix and Rachel in *Esmond*, and gives way to a single, divided heroine with Ethel in *The Newcomes*. In this sequence one can observe the evolution of greater complexity in characterization, but there is also a simplification of developmental structure as Thackeray directs his hero toward the definitive rejection of the "bad" heroine and choice of the "good," or, in the case of Ethel, presents the unconditional victory of the good side of her character. Thackeray's allegorical design for the cover of the original parts of *Pendennis* shows his hero ambivalently poised between the two heroines and their opposed attractions, worldly rewards and domestic pieties. But in the end Pen must choose, and, as if to validate this simplification, Thackeray redrew the design for the frontispiece of the book to show his right-minded hero moving in the direction of Laura, home, and duty. Both *Pendennis* and *Esmond* fix the hero's final position with a late scene of revelation that exposes and condemns the false heroine. Pen's discovery of Blanche with Harry Foker (chap. 73) is primarily comic and merely frees him to carry out the choice of Laura he has already made, but Esmond's discovery of Beatrix with the Pretender supposedly produces a sudden and permanent disenchantment: "The roses had shuddered out of her cheeks; her eyes were glaring; she looked quite old. . . . And as he looked at her he wondered that he could ever have loved her. His love of ten years was over" (vol. 3, chap. 13).

These scenes invite comparison with Rawdon's discovery of Becky and Lord Steyne, a moment of equally stark exposure. But in *Vanity Fair* the apparently decisive revelation dissolves into new complexities, not just through the narrator's ambiguous question, "Was she guilty or not?" (chap. 53), but through the inclusion of more than one point of view. For Rawdon the discovery of Becky's treachery is clear and decisive, but Becky also experiences her own discovery: "She stood there trembling before him. She admired her husband, strong, brave, and victorious." Her belated recognition of strength, moral as well as physical, in the man she has foolishly underestimated is the obverse of his belated disillusionment; Thackeray's counterpoint yields a subtle irony: "At the moment—the only moment—of appreciation, she loses Rawdon" (Barbara Hardy). Becky stands exposed, but not, like Blanche and Beatrix, in order to be summarily dismissed; Thackeray is as much concerned to explore the quality of her experience in defeat as in triumph and to contemplate the emptiness with which it confronts her: "All her lies and schemes, all her selfishness and her wiles, all her wit and genius had come to this bankruptcy." Most important, the scene comes after only three-fourths of the narrative, not at the very end. Rawdon goes on to compromise his position by accepting the appointment Becky's schemes have secured; Becky goes on from this reversal to gain her eventual reward, a booth of her own in Vanity Fair. Thackeray refuses to endorse a simple, decisive resolution.

These differences between *Vanity Fair* and Thackeray's next two novels are closely related to his change of structural principles. The decision to center the narratives of *Pendennis* and *Esmond* in their heroes' careers prevents him from giving independent development to the alternative possibilities represented by his contrasing heroines. But at the same time the later novels explore other forms of doubleness—and duplicity. *Esmond* is, in fact, an impressive example of the way a double logic can work in a single-focus narrative; like *Great Expectations*, it condenses opposed meanings that might have been articulated separately. The narrative is generated by the initial doubling of Esmond in his twin roles of protagonist and narrator of his story, a division which is stressed by the detached, impersonal manner of his "memoirs," in which he generally refers to himself in the third person. But this doubling of the younger, often deluded, experiencing self and the older, supposedly enlightened, narrating self is common to the autobiographical form and is only the most obvious division. A more important split arises from Esmond's questionable reliability. As several recent critics have shown, it is possible to find in his story quite a different meaning from the one he ascribes to it. Where Esmond presents the account of a development through successive stages of error to eventual wisdom, we can see the cyclical repetitions of oedipal fixation; where he presents an image of modest, self-abnegating virtue, we can see the self-aggrandizing pride of a man who has substituted himself for the series of idols he previously worshipped; where he claims to have achieved lucid retrospective detachment, we can see self-perpetuating blindness. As in the opposition of Amelia and Becky, we can make no final choice between these opposed versions, but neither can we entertain both at once. Alternating between them, we stage our own dialogue of perspectives.

In *The Newcomes* Thackeray returned to the use of multiple narrative. Its slow, expansive account of "the world, and a respectable family living in it" (chap. 38) makes extensive use of shifting narrative focus to present the numerous coexisting microcosms that together constitute a broad social panorama. Thematically, however, the multiplication of situations and narratives has a restrictive rather than expansive effect, for its major use is to stress the repetition of the same patterns from one world or generation to another, most importantly the pattern of arranged marriages in which love is sacrificed for wealth or social position. As argument, these parallels contribute to the novel's bitter critique of worldly, "respectable" values, but they also become the occasion for self-conscious reflections on the production of fiction by recreating archetypal patterns. Thackeray's general term for such patterns is "fable," and the novel is framed by opening and concluding sections that directly relate it to the traditional moral apologue. The "Overture" begins with a brilliant pastiche of beast fables that anticipates several themes. To the objections of "the critic" ("What a farrago of old fables is this! What a dressing up in new clothes!"), the narrator replies, "What stories are new? All types of all characters march through all fables: tremblers and boasters; victims and bullies; dupes and knaves," etc. But this insistence on the fictive, conventional basis of his work also supports its claim to significance, since life too is marked by the recurrence of familiar patterns: "There may be nothing new under and including the sun; but it looks fresh every morning, and we rise with it to toil, hope, scheme, laugh, struggle, love, suffer, until the night comes and quiet. And then will wake Morrow and the eyes that look on it; and so *da capo*."

In this stress on repetition we can again see Thackeray imposing the long perspective, in which similarity overwhelms difference. But in *The Newcomes* this perspective is complicated by a method which carries over from *Esmond* some of the problems of mediation that arise from the use of a character as narrator, since the novel is told by Pendennis. Pen (the scribe) is often little more than a transparent authorial persona, but since he is not entitled to conventional omniscience, his narrative is marked by several explanatory asides on the sources of his knowledge that put his authority in question. Some of these appear only as rationalizations for his access to other characters' thoughts: "What young Clive's private cares were I knew not as yet in those days . . . it was only in the intimacy of future life that some of these pains were revealed to me" (chap. 35). But this perspective from the "future" involves limitations as well as privileges. The long view of retrospection offers the possibility of greater knowledge and judicious detachment: "This narrative . . . is written maturely and at ease, long after the voyage is over whereof it recounts the adventures and perils." But it also relies on conjecture and invention: "The public must once for all be warned that the author's individual fancy very likely supplies much of the narrative; and that he forms it as best he may, out of the stray papers, conversations reported to him, and his knowledge, right or wrong, of the characters of the persons engaged" (chap. 24). Pen justifies his method by analogy with those of historians, archeologists, and paleontologists: "As Professor Owen or Agassiz takes a fragment of a bone, and builds an enormous forgotten monster out of it . . . so the novelist puts this and that together" (chap. 47). The fictional narrator claims scientific validity for a narrative that has already been characterized as old fables dressed up in new clothes.

Thackeray frequently plays on this paradox, introducing analogies between his characters and the figures of fable. Ethel, for instance, is the princess courted by three suitors, Kew, Farintosh, and Clive, and manipulated by Lady Kew, the old witch or bad fairy who was not invited to the christening. But the parallels are also ironic, since the narrative does not fulfill the ideal moral norms of fable: the good suffer and the wicked go unpunished. The incomplete applicability of archetypal patterns matches the incomplete knowledge of the "historian"; the apparent contradiction between "scientific" and "fabulous" narration is resolved in their common fictiveness. Both rely on models or heuristic fictions; both can yield only partial and hypothetical knowledge, never direct possession of the particular and immediate.

In Pen's reconstruction of the past Thackeray expresses the aspiration toward complete repossession of experience; each recovered fragment gives hope of total knowledge:

> In the faded ink on the yellow paper that may have crossed and recrossed oceans, that has lain locked in chests for years, and buried under piles of family archives, while your friends have been dying and your head has grown white—who has not disinterred mementoes like these—from which the past smiles at you so sadly, shimmering out of Hades an instant but to sink back again into the cold shades, perhaps with a faint faint sound as of a remembered tone—a ghostly echo of a once familiar laughter? I was looking, of late, at a wall in the Naples Museum, whereon a boy of Herculaneum eighteen hundred years ago had scratched

with a nail the figure of a soldier. I could fancy the child turning
round and smiling on me after having done his etching. Which
of us that is thirty years old has not had his Pompeii? Deep under
ashes lies the Life of Youth, the careless Sport, the Pleasure and
Passion, the darling joy. You open an old letter-box and look at
your own childish scrawls, or your mother's letters to you when
you were at school; and excavate your heart. Oh me for the day
when the whole city shall be bare and the chambers unroofed—
and every cranny visible to the Light above, from the Forum to
the Lupanar!

(Chap. 28)

The conceit of excavation results in a remarkable parallel to Dickens's project
of removing the house-tops and revealing the pattern of social interconnec-
tions. Here the synoptic vision proposes a total, spatial apprehension of time,
but the archeological imagery suggests that such omniscience is possible only
when the buildings are no longer inhabited, when life has departed. These
suggestions are confirmed by the effect of this passage in context. It interrupts an account of the brief period of idyllic happiness Clive and Ethel enjoy
together in Baden. Since they are the hero and heroine, whose union is blocked
by all the worldly values the novel condemns, its logic would seem to direct
us toward sympathetic participation in their experience of intimacy here, but
instead of dwelling expansively on this moment, the novel sets it at a great
distance. The very expression of desire to recapture the past serves to make
it more remote; their happiness appears only through their surviving letters
found "among Colonel Newcome's papers to which the family biographer
has had subsequent access," reduced to the traces of "faded ink on the yellow
paper."

The novel itself is such a trace. Its hypothetical reconstructions and
rehearsals of old fables can represent experience only as tokens of its absence,
making the individual an instance of the typical, the moment a reenactment
of the perpetual. Thackeray insists on the mediation that qualifies the
authority of his long perspectives by keeping his patterns incomplete, as he
does at the novel's end by his suspended resolution. After preparing for the
final union of his hero and heroine, first by reforming Ethel and preventing
her marriage to Farintosh, then by rescuing Clive from his mistaken marriage by killing off Rosey, Thackeray refuses at the last minute to follow
through with a conventional happy ending. Instead, Pen's narrative stops
with the death of Colonel Newcome, and "Thackeray" himself appears to
deliver the epilogue: "As I write the last line with a rather sad heart, Pendennis and Laura and Ethel and Clive fade away into Fable-land." He professes

sympathy with the reader's frustrated desire for a satisfying conclusion and, surveying the fragmentary evidence which the text provides, offers his own conjecture: "My belief then is, that in Fable-land somewhere Ethel and Clive are living most comfortably together." Finally, abandoning even plausible reconstruction, he surrenders his fiction to the reader's sentimental preferences:

> Anything you like happens in Fable-land. Wicked folks die *à propos* (for instance, that death of Lady Kew was most artful, for if she had not died, don't you see that Ethel would have married Lord Farintosh the next week?)—annoying folk are got out of the way; the poor are rewarded—the upstarts are set down in Fable-land—the frog bursts with wicked rage, the fox is caught in his trap, the lamb is rescued from the wolf, and so forth, just in the nick of time. And the poet of Fable-land rewards and punishes absolutely.

This mock concession recalls the ironic conclusion of *Vanity Fair*, with its subversion of the happy ending and final stress on fictiveness. But here the effect is not one of diminution and dismissal; the characters do not dwindle into puppets but recede beyond our range of observation, preserving their independence from the "author."

We can derive from this epilogue an effect of "realism" by emphasizing Thackeray's negation of sentimental conventions, confirming the ironic conviction that poetic justice prevails only in fables, not in life, and that *The Newcomes* is really an antifable. But an alternative reading is equally possible, for the epilogue, confirming the promise of the "Overture," locates the entire fictional world in "Fable-land," where "anything you like happens." What has already happened there is thus the result of authorial wish, in this case directed toward the frustration rather than the fulfillment of young love and idealism, the persistent pattern of the parallel narratives. From this perspective it becomes clear that unhappy endings are no more "realistic" than happy ones, though either may fulfill or violate the logic of the preceding narrative. Thackeray leaves the pattern of his narrative incomplete, but this is actually consistent with its logic, since it has repeatedly qualified the authority of its patterns and questioned the validity of its own procedures. Setting one incomplete pattern against another, suspending his narrative between "the world" and "Fable-land," Thackeray preserves the doubleness of his vision.

MARIA DiBATTISTA

# The Triumph of Clytemnestra:
# The Charades in Vanity Fair

When Thackeray remarked that "the unwritten part of books . . . would be the most interesting," he meant, among other things, that the art of implication is the most subtle of authorial decorums. At no time in *Vanity Fair* is that art practiced so well as when Thackeray retires from the stage as "Manager" of his comic history and allows Becky Sharp to enact the tragic charade "The Triumph of Clytemnestra." It is a singular performance, played "with such ghastly truth" that it leaves the spectators speechless with fright and admiration. The scandalous identification of Becky, the novel's mock-heroic adventuress, with the heroic figure of the most majestic female dissembler in the chronicles of myth and history marks the culmination of Becky's career in the world of vanity. Implied in her "comic" rise from articled pupil to lady of fashion is the terrible project of Clytemnestra to revenge herself against a power both envied and resented.

The silent truth of Becky's "character" is reemphasized in her second major appearance as Clytemnestra. Her reassumption of Clytemnestra's demonic identity in the novel's penultimate illustration haunts the reader's imagination by ominously suggesting an ongoing campaign of vengeance, an undiminished talent for subterfuge, and, of course, the ghastly literalization of what in Becky's moment of triumph was represented as an "innocent" charade. In a murderous pantomime, a terrorized Jos Sedley pleads with the "Good Samaritan," Colonel Dobbin, to deliver him from the demonic schemer, while an inspired Becky balefully looks on from behind a curtain,

From *PMLA* 95, no. 5 (October 1980). © 1980 by the Modern Language Association of America.

seemingly awaiting the propitious moment to strike. The illustration presents an "interesting" (in Thackeray's sense) explanation of Sedley's suspicious death, for there is, in fact, no corresponding evidence in the written text to corroborate the visual testimony against Becky. The details of the illustration—and they are designedly indistinct—alone prove incriminating. Becky is Clytemnestra primarily in her *attitude*, in the aggressive and threatening stance she assumes toward her potential victim. Her hand, the agent of her murderous intention, is blurred in shadow, allowing just the suggestion of a poised weapon. The caption identifies Becky with Clytemnestra; the illustration insists on dark equivocations, on a shady and shadowy reality. The only verdict that can be rendered is Rawdon's anguished but legally dubious earlier judgment on Becky's seemingly treacherous conduct: "If she's not guilty, . . . she's as bad as guilty."

Thackeray claimed that behind all his personifications "there lies a dark moral, I hope" (*Papers*). But the meditative Thackerayan "I" who at times almost abuses his authorial license to intrude on the narrative with moral commentary remains conspicuously silent on the psychological, ethical, and social significance of Becky's impersonation of Clytemnestra and on the "dark moral" explicated through feminine retaliatory or "opportunistic" violence. He communicates Becky's affinity to Clytemnestra exclusively through the media of charade and illustration. In her two appearances as the murderous queen, Becky becomes pure icon, an unspeakable and speechless image of demonic womanhood. The garrulous narrator's uncharacteristic reticence in the presence of this icon has never been adequately remarked, much less explained. Thackeray refuses to make the obvious connection between Cytemnestra's rebellion against the warrior culture that authorizes the sacrifice of her child, Iphigenia, and his own extensive critique of the attitudes toward women and childen in the bourgeois, jingoistic, mercantile culture of nineteenth-century England. He never interprets the material of the charade and illustration as a didactic allegory of the multiple vanities of familial, social, and political ambitions. Nor does he elaborate the myth of Clytemnestra into a cautionary tale or homiletic parable. He merely displaces it into a network of images that compose, in Dorothy Van Ghent's words, "the face of a gorgon of destiny."

Van Ghent skillfully traces the cultural derangements adumbrated in the novel's theme of "the fathers" to a classical and Freudian intuition of "the monstrous nature of man." Selecting for comment the "incidental" image of the chronometer "surmounted by a cheerful brass group of the sacrifice of Iphigenia" that summons the Osborne clan to its evening ritual meal, she remarks:

The depths which are suggested by this picture, but quite as if accidentally, are the depths of Greek tragedy and, still further back, of Freud's dim, sub-human, imagined "primitive horde": the "dark leader" with his "hushed female company," and the ridiculous but furious Victorian clock "cheerfully" symbolizing the whole.

I would not argue with Van Ghent's view of Becky Sharp as the condensation of the "imperatively aggressive" and "insanely euphoric" attitudes prevailing in the morally sick civilization represented in *Vanity Fair*. I would only expand consideration of Thackeray's appropriation of classical material to interpret this pervasive cultural pathology. This essay first considers the charades that dramatize the dark classical moral represented in Thackeray's historical fabling and then examines his motive for innuendo, his reasons for submerging his classical and Freudian intuitions of cultural pathology in the depths of his picture of Vanity Fair.

II

It is part of the controlling conceit of Thackeray's novel to present history as an extended sequence of performances ("puppet shows") enacting a moral so dark that to illuminate it fully might be politically or spiritually perilous. Thackeray literalizes his controlling metaphor in the chapter "in which a charade is acted which may or may not puzzle the reader." But the apparent decision to clarify his metaphor is cunningly compromised by the riddling nature of the charades.

As a form of verbal "play," charades are designedly opaque. They attempt to communicate a hidden meaning, usually symbolized by a single word that assumes fetishistic properties because its meaning and form are shrouded in an often guilty secrecy. In charades the word is divided into its constituent sounds—the words within the word—and each component is dramatized. The audience, reader, or spectator must then recombine these "floating signifiers" to discover the whole word, whose original and primary significance is again dramatized at the end of the charade in the tableau of the Whole. Although charades appear to play freely with meaning, their "real" meaning is predetermined in a word that cannot be replaced by, or mistaken for, another word. In the best charades, those combining verbal wit with social or emotional "fact," the secret word representing the Whole denominates not only a sum greater than its constituent parts but the exact reverse of those parts. Such a feat of verbal reversal and transformation is illustrated in Jane Austen's *Emma* by Mr. Elton's charade for "courtship" or in Charlotte Brontë's *Jane Eyre* by the charades for "Bridewell," puzzled out by Rochester's fashionable guests. Brontë's charades, like Thackeray's, are particularly cunning in communicating their ghastly truth. As ironic word-plays, the charades reveal the private and unsuspected torment of Rochester and his mad, imprisoned wife, Bertha Mason, through publicly enacting the word's two syllables, in tableaux that seem especially grim given the innocent surfaces of "Bride" and "well."

Charades, then, are never totally gratuitous forms of entertainment. They constitute a mode of verbal double-dealing that involves and often implicates the actors or spectators—sometimes both—in the social or psychological reality dramatized. Charades are dumb shows "to catch the conscience of the king" by playing out a deliberately concealed evil, an ignored social danger, or an obscure external menace or private horror. The incriminating potential of charades is emphasized by the disguises and roles adopted by the concealing-revealing performers who enact them. Thus Thackeray identifies the characters in the first series of charades—Colonel Crawley as Agamemnon, Becky as Clytemnestra—but their social identity dissolves, although not completely, into the drama they enact without being technically guilty. Characters thus assume roles in a play whose meaning is made transparent *through* them but is not necessarily made transparent *to* them. Their assigned roles are charged with a characteristic Thackerayan innuendo and equivocation; to repeat the judgment of Colonel Crawley, these performers, if not guilty, are as bad as guilty. And the same may be said of those in complicity with them—the audience of the charades.

It is the emotionally felt presumption of personal or cultural guilt that pervades and shadows the apparently "innocent" entertainments at *Vanity Fair*'s Gaunt House. The charades begin with an oriental tableau depicting a Turkish dignitary and voluptuary examining the "wares" of an Eastern slave trade. Despite the exotic decor evoking an alien, barbaric milieu, the initial moments of this charade announce a universal, not a historically localized, cultural pathology: sexual bondage, enslavement, exploitation, and victimization. As a Nubian slave makes his obeisant salaams to "my lord the Aga," the fashionable audience responds with a "thrill of terror and delight," a spontaneous demonstration of feeling that betrays an "exquisite" and volatile sexual fantasy of demonic virility that lies perilously close to the surface of the audience's "civilized" consciousness.

The icons of sexual imperialism that abound in this charade implicate the spectator-audience in the guilt, not of association, but of attitude, as Becky's second appearance as Clytemnestra suggests. Thus the Nubian slave's obeisant salaams to the Kislar Aga eerily recall and comment on the attitude of the idolatrous and slavish Amelia, who, on her wedding night, prostrates herself before her master, George Osborne. And the audience's "thrill of terror and delight" echoes George's own exquisite sensation as he gazes on the "slave before him in that simple yielding faithful creature" and feels his soul thrill within him, the "Sultan's thrill" in sexual mastery and "the knowledge of his complete power." In exposing the secret fantasies of sexual appropriation masquerading as "lawful matrimonial pleasures," Thackeray attempts his subtlest, perhaps most damaging penetration into the dark and tumultuous instincts underlying the civilized structures of sexual conduct and the social institution of marriage.

The aestheticizing of these sadomasochistic yearnings is represented in the ensuing sequence of the tableau when the entreaties of the beautiful slave girl asking to be returned to her Circassian lover are contemplated as composing an attitude of "beautiful despair." The "obdurate Hassan" only laughs at her sentimental notion of the Circassian bridegroom, mocking the slave girl's "Arcadian Simplicity" in believing that love, not power, determines the destiny of women in the markets of Vanity Fair. The tableau, which contrasts the "genteel" fictions of disinterested love with the sexual imperialism of a rich and decadent culture, is resolved through a sudden and completely illusory deus ex machina. The repressed takes its revenge on the oppressor, as the Kislar Aga, the black eunuch of the oriental harem, brings in a letter, a ghastly joy transfiguring his face. In an ecstasy of revenge, "grinning horribly," and ignoring the Pasha's cry for mercy, the Kislar Aga pulls out a bowstring. The denouement of this revenger's tragedy is eclipsed in a sudden and decorous blackout that hides the "dark deed" from public view.

The orientalism of this charade may shield the audience from the dramatic immediacy of the eunuch's murderous revenge. Yet it also provides more than a distancing backdrop against which all contagious fantasies can be played out without fear of censure. The oriental setting accumulates into itself all Thackeray's previous suggestions in the novel that beneath England's treatment of women—hypostasized in the Victorian cult of angelic womanhood—abides an unregenerate barbarity, a "Turkish" lust for mastery: "We are Turks with the affections of our women," the narrator had earlier remarked of the "poor little martyr" Amelia, "and have made them subscribe to our doctrine too." Through Amelia, the angelic figure of self-sacrificing, self-effacing womanhood whose "gentle little heart" obeys "not unwillingly" such despotic doctrines, Thackeray is forced to examine the psychology of female martyrdom. The slave girl in the charades is only a public symbol of Amelia's private enslavement to a whole system of cultural imperatives. When the narrator attempts to "peer into those dark places where the torture is administered" to such willing victims, he sees a sight so pitiable and incriminating that he breaks out into a hysterical apostrophe to subjugated women that combines compassion for their plight with relief at his own masculine exemption from their "long and ignoble bondage":

> O you poor women! O you poor secret martyrs and victims, whose life is a torture, who are stretched on racks in your bedrooms, and who lay your heads down on the block daily at the drawing-room table; every man who watches your pains, or peers into those dark places where the torture is administered to you, must pity you—and—and thank God that he has a beard.

It is clear that Thackeray harbors no *intrinsic* respect for "the romance and the sentiment of sacrifice" as an expressive vehicle of heroic womanhood, for it is precisely such idealizations that secure Amelia's bondage. The narrator's voyeuristic penetration into the dark chambers of the feminine psyche that house such sentiments unmans him, and he retreats, in a kind of willing "blackout" of his aroused consciousness, from the pitiable spectacle by recalling, uneasily and rather comically, the sexual symbol of his difference and his exemption from such torture—his beard. Such unnerving glimpses of secret martyrdom, unwitnessed victimization, and "Gothic" savagery are appropriated by the first component of the charade word—"Aga," a cultural symbol of sexual barbarity infecting private life and expanded into public and political forms.

The second charade retains the Eastern background, but the suggestion of violence has been suppressed and transformed into a peaceful tableau. The eunuch has resigned himself to impotent passivity, and Zuleikah, the despairing pastoral lover, is now perfectly reconciled to her victimizer, the Hassan. There is hardly any action in the scene. Instead, interest centers on the imposing figure of an enormous Egyptian head, from which issues a comic song composed by Mr. Wagg. The dominating figure alludes to the Ethiopian king Memnon. According to Lamprière's *Bibliotheca Classica*, Thackeray's favorite source for classical material, Memnon's heroic death was commemorated by an enormous statue that possessed "the wonderful property of uttering a melodious sound every day, at sun-rising, like that which is heard at the breaking of the string of a harp when it is wound up." The statue and the legend it symbolizes emphasize the metamorphic properties of violence. Memnon was killed in combat with Achilles in defense of Priam's Troy. His mother, Aurora, was so disconsolate at the death of her son that she pleaded with Zeus to grant her sacrificed child an honor that might immortalize him. Zeus complied, and from the funeral pyre of Memnon there arose a flight of birds, the Memnonides. The myth is composed of several motifs involving scenes of violent, yet ultimately stabilizing metamorphosis: the metamorphosis of Memnon's bloody death into the seasonal return of the

Memnonides in ritual commemoration of the Ethiopian monarch; the transformation of violence into an artifact of civilization; the translation of grief into art, suffering into song. It is this final transformation that is emphasized in the "singing head" of the charade.

The peaceful harmony of this tableau vivant soon proves illusory, however, as the pacific and comic song issuing from the death's-head modulates into the unexpectedly dissonant and sublime chords of "the awful music of Don Juan." Like Agamemnon, Don Juan represents a type of sexually imperial masculinity with an immoderate appetite for power, and the strains from the opera provide a rhetorically musical bridge connecting the archaic bloodlusts of a barbaric civilization (the "subject" of the charades) with the sexual vendettas disrupting a more contemporary aristocratic milieu (the social "subject" of *Vanity Fair*). In the Mozartian opera of seduction and betrayal, of sexual transgression and retribution in the name of family honor or divine vengeance, Thackeray sees the same cultural ethos working out its evil destiny: a corrupt ideology of sexual imperialism underlying the myth of love in the Western world. The last of Thackeray's historical charades reveals the secret identity and cultural primacy of his central figure of virility- Agamemnon, a curious compound of heroic and barbaric manhood: an "Aga," a figure of sexual barbarism; a "Memnon," a figure of cultural authority and prestige. With mordant irony, Thackeray bestows on Agamemnon the epithet *anax andron*, the kingly man who will soon pay for the excesses of his manhood and of his kingship. In a sweeping and majestic gesture of feminine revenge, Clytemnestra, alias Becky Crawley, steals the dagger from the hesitant Aegisthus to complete the retribution, but here again the outcome is overcome by darkness.

The scene of the second series of charades moves to more familiar territory, as if to escape the malignancy and potency of the oriental and classical material dramatized in the first sequence. Thackeray's setting is now Fieldingesque, evoking the atmosphere of low-life farce and the memory of an earlier England where evil took the benign form of rascality. The first tableau of the second series depicts a comic "night" scene in a country house. The action is desultory: two bagmen play a game of cribbage, a chambermaid warms up the beds and wards off the bagmen's advances. The scene ends to the dreamy cadences of "Dormez, dormez, chers Amours." If the virulent "Amantium Irae" is exposed and released in the Cytemnestra-Agamemnon charade, here the strain is transposed and modulated into sweeter amatory tones anticipating the love lyric, "The Rose upon My Balcony," that concludes the entertainments.

But the submerged motif of sexual horror reasserts itself in the second tableau of the new series. The scene remains the same, but the insignia of the house is now revealed to be the Steyne arms, the chivalric "coronets and carved heraldry" that Thackeray has already described as bearing "the dark mark of fate and doom." Thus even though the scene resembles the merry comings and goings of *Tom Jones*'s Upton Inn ("inn," of course, is the syllable dramatized in this tableau), the Steyne arms visually suggest an invisible, internal, and still potent fatality at work, recalling Thackeray's earlier hint that a sexual curse haunts the Steyne house:

> It was the mysterious taint of the blood: the poor mother had brought it from her own ancient race. The evil had broken out once or twice in the father's family, long before Lady Steyne's sins had begun, or her fasts and tears and penances had been offered in their expiation.

An Aeschylean brooding over the fall of the great house informs Thackeray's account of evil communicating itself through the mysterious "stain" or taint of blood brought from an ancient race, an ancestral evil that hangs over Gaunt House as a dark reminder of the time "when the pride of the race was struck down as the firstborn of Pharaoh." The original sin embodies in the fatal union of the Steynes becomes the focus of the deepest progenitive anxieties about familial succession, patrimony, and the decline and eclipse of the aristocracy as a historical heritage. The charades' suppressed Ovidian theme of metamorphosis and their Aeschylean vision of sexual fate and familial doom combine to revive the repressed but never forgotten memory of unexpiated and unexpiable sins that will be violently avenged. Ominous hints of an avenging agent and future retribution are conveyed in the final "rustle" of movement at the end of the "inn" charade. As the curtain is drawn, a mysterious, though eminent, guest is being announced, perhaps an Orestes bent on revenge or, as Thackeray intimates, a Ulysses preparing for another kind of bloody homecoming. Christian hopes in the efficacy of penance (the expiatory prayers of Lady Steyne) are eclipsed by the urgency and power of these classical foreshadowings of an inevitable historical reckoning. They are only revived, belatedly, in the mark of Cain that Lord Steyne, after his failed attempt to appease Rawdon and exculpate himself, bears as the "scar" inflicted by Colonel Crawley, the avenging returned husband, in the melodramatic scene that marks the catastrophe of Becky and Steyne's illicit liaison.

In the final syllable of the second series of charades, anxieties about an impending cultural crisis provoked by the domestic tragedies and hypocrisies of a decaying aristocracy are concentrated into an image of imperial (political) fear. The final tableau shows a ship foundering in unruly seas, despite the heartening medley of "Rule Britannia." The spectacle of the imperiled ship of state, conventional symbol of maritime England, speaks to the most frightening nightmare haunting the British political mind. As the music of the tableau "rises up to the wildest pitch of stormy excitement," discharging itself in "gale," the source of the audience's uneasy, turbulent emotion (the specter of political unrest and unrule) is mollified by the transfiguration of Becky into Philomele. The charade completes its word: Philomele, "the night-in-gale."

The pairing of Clytemnestra and Philomele in the character of Becky Sharp is neither fortuitous nor incongruous. Philomele's story, like Clytemnestra's, constitutes an elaborate narration of sexual deception, brutality, violation of sacred familial bonds, and violent reprisal. Philomele is also a figure of outraged womanhood, literally concealed and silenced by her sexual seducer and tormentor, Tereus, king of Thrace, husband to Philomele's sister, Procne. Tereus's crimes against Philomele, whom he imprisons and mutilates by cutting out her tongue, are, like Agamemnon's, doubly grave, being the sins of both king and husband. Philomele, deprived of a voice to protest her ravishment, communicates the chronicle of her sufferings through art—the tapestry she weaves to tell of the sins of the fathers, the living fabric of primal wrongs. Like the scenes that evoke her presence, Philomele's speechless art reenacts the hidden outrage and silently protests against the oppressor's power. It is Procne who reads the tale and, like Clytemnestra, disguises her resentments while plotting her treacherous revenge. During the Bacchic orgies she murders her son Itys and serves him to the brutal and brutalizing Tereus in a grisly feast. When Tereus learns of this cannibalistic and retributive rite, his rage is predictably extreme, but his murderous designs against Philomele and Procne are forestalled by his own transformation into a hoopoe, Philomele's into a nightingale, Procne's into a swallow, and Itys's into a pheasant.

These grim classical legends of metamorphosis, fatal sexual unions, incestuous intrigue, familial cannibalism, sacrificed children, and female retaliation mirror and complement Agamemnon and Clytemnestra's family tragedy and, of course, all the incestuous, spiritually cannibalizing relationships in *Vanity Fair*. Thackeray seems to be following the late, Ovidian version of the myth that makes Philomele the nightingale and Procne the swallow, perhaps because the Ovidian reinterpretation attributes both pathos and the power of representation to the mute, raped sister rather than to the betrayed and betraying wife. The Ovidian version allows Thackeray to suggest the essential doubleness of Becky as a figure of cultural evil, representing a Clytemnestra and a Philomele, the ravisher and the ravished, the unscrupulous avenger and the plaintive victim. Thackeray's double image of female fatality culminates in the much remarked description of Becky as a siren of magical powers who lures men to their watery graves. (Clytemnestra simply lures Agamemnon to his bath to kill him.) The Becky-siren, "singing and smiling, coaxing and cajoling," conceals from view a "monster's hideous tail, . . . writing and twirling, diabolically hideous and slimy." The snake-siren image reveals more about the narrator's erotic imagination than it does about Becky's fatal sexuality, betraying as it does the sexual disgust and fear lurking beneath the "perfectly genteel and inoffensive manner" in which he relates her fiendish (Bohemian) adventures. If Becky is a monster with a remarkable and growing "taste for disrespectability," she is no *lusus naturae*, no freak of nature, but a freak of the culture whose model of angelic womanhood elevates the religious over the erotic instinct. Becky's "disreputable" character represents the potential for a demonic and malevolent female sexuality in contrast to the respectable but no less selfish "love" of her true opposite and double, Amelia, the martyr to the Victorian feminine ideal who dedicates her life to the "corpse" of her love.

## III

It was George Eliot who reminded us, citing the authority of Herodotus, that the woman question is not an extraneous or a peripheral factor in the historical analysis of change but a "fit beginning." Like Eliot's *Middlemarch*, *Vanity Fair* centers on the lot of women in its description of the origins of cultural crisis and its prophetic assessments of the possibilities for meaningful change. When Thackeray decides to forgo a military history celebrating England's heroic manhood during the Napoleonic era for a comic history chronicling the amatory and financial fortunes of female "non-combatants" and the men who love them, his decision is neither historically frivolous nor inconsequential. The stories of Becky Sharp and Amelia Sedley expand into paradigmatic fables paralleling and reflecting "those mutations which ages produce in empires, cities, and boroughs," mutations that are recorded in the migration of power from the landed gentry to an ascendant middle class with a ready-money, credit economy.

In the declining aristocracy (whose historical eclipse Thackeray dramatizes by the deep degeneracy of Sir Pitt Crawley presiding over the "rotten borough" of Queen's Crawley, by the cynicism of Lord Steyne, and by the "Dowagerism" reigning in Great Gaunt Street and in the rising merchant classes (which he treats satirically), Thackeray perceives, but cannot totally disavow, the same corrupt and corrupting sexual ideology, the wholesale "selling" and emotional victimization of women to ensure the traditional primacy and the economic power of an imperiled social caste. Marriage thus becomes the instrument of social and political ambitions, and all sexual attitudes serve to rationalize even as they dissimulate this fundamental, sexually "politic" economy.

Thackeray's formal appropriation of the Clytemnestra myth in the novel serves as a psychological and *historical* commentary on the unexamined delusions of the Victorian's sexual ideology. To identify Becky as Clytemnestra is not merely to invoke a psychological explanation for Becky's "natural" wickedness but to suggest that in the conduct of life the public and the private, the national and the domestic remain inseparable. Attitudes toward women, marriage, sex, because they are present at the very formation and foundation of a cultural order, constitute the primary basis of cultural and social stability. Ideology is all of a piece, so that the private tyrannies authorized by familial self-interest do not confine themselves to the domestic sphere but invariably and inevitably radiate to infect a society's conception of itself and to motivate the most decisive of national actions.

Becky Sharp is a representative figure whose social ambitions reflect the internal crisis of oppressed womanhood and the external menace of a "French" radicalism comically treated in the "bel esprit" of Miss Crawley, who passionately embraces Voltaire and Rousseau and talks "most energetically of the rights of women." Becky's radicalism is more subversive and disarming. Her mother was a Frenchwoman, and Becky's morals seem indebted to the darker elements in French novels. In the denigration and humiliation of women, Thackeray discerns a universal principle of violation that provides the logic of his domestic comedy and informs his intuition, pristinely classical in its pessimism, of the cycle of reprisal that underlies and determines all historical events. In one of the novel's few sustained moments of seriousness, the narrator comments on the historically decisive battle of Waterloo, a comment that is hauntingly applicable to the outrages committed and authorized by the bitter necessities of war for which Clytemnestra courts revenge in the *Agamemnon*:

> you and I, who were children when the great battle was won and lost, are never tired of hearing and recounting the history of that famous action. Its remembrance rankles still in the bosoms of millions of the countrymen of those brave men who lost the day. They pant for an opportunity of revenging that humiliation; and if a contest, ending in a victory on their part, should ensue, elating them in their turn, and leaving its cursed legacy of hatred and rage behind to us, there is no end to the so-called glory and shame, and to the alternations of successful and unsuccessful murder, in which two high-spirited nations might engage. Centuries hence, we Frenchmen and Englishmen might be boasting and killing each other still, carrying out bravely the Devil's Code of honour.

Shame and glory are the values endemic to a classical ethos, and their legacy is a cursed heritage of hatred and rage, the alternations of successful and unsuccessful murder. In contemplating the sweeping panorama of historical change and struggle, Thackeray discerns an endlessly repeatable cycle of victimization and revenge. Nor is this legacy confined to intercultural, international conflict. The organizing conceit of his novel centers on the interpenetrating metaphors of military and amatory campaigns to secure "positions," establish power, defend hegemony. And the deep interdependence, even identity, between acts of love and war, caricatured in the illustration depicting the comic *mésalliance* of Venus preparing the armor of Mars, penetrates far into the rhetoric of the novel's social and political satire. Through the controlling image of embattled relations, Thackeray suggests that tyrannies and servilities corrupting the foundation of social life eventually infect the entire cultural order. The mutually reinforcing projects of sexual and political revenge are symbolized in the Iphigenia chronometer, whose steady and remorseless ticking signals an ongoing, if unsuspected, cycle of aggression and retaliation. Becky's second appearance as Clytemnestra keeps this classical concept of familial, racial, and national fatality alive. It suggests that the "strife" between men and women, between the outraged female and the kingly male, is a strife not confined to private realms but, as Clytemnestra warns the chorus in the *Agamemnon*, a "conflict born out of ancient bitterness . . . pondered deep in time."

Thackeray's classicism in *Vanity Fair*, then, validates rather than contradicts the novel's critical realism and its narrative objective: "to expose," as Lukács rightly argues, "contemporary apologetics" (*The Historical Novel*). The mythological material that supports the novel's cultural interpretation and social criticism both reflects and anticipates the resurgent "paganism" whose "dark morals" will dominate the historical imagination of the second half of the nineteenth century. In this sense, *Vanity Fair* is an intriguing transitional text between the self-confident neoclassical novels of Fielding, who could develop potentially contagious Oedipal material within a transforming Christian vision of providentially ordered history, and the bitter, darkly pagan Aeschylean tragedies of Thomas Hardy. As the last two major illustrations of *Vanity Fair* testify, depicting the double face of Becky Sharp as Clytemnestra and as an ironic exemplum of "Virtue Rewarded," there exists an uneasy and problematic alliance between Thackeray's classical intuitions of cultural disorder and the Christian vision implied by his novel's ironic appropriation of its allegorical original, *Pilgrim's Progress*. The charades, the "play" within the larger historical performance enacted in the novel, are representative of Thackeray's dilemma and his proposed solution: through their *formal* opacity and equivocation, they suggest that the meaning of historical act or cultural "attitude" must be supplied, puzzled out by the spectator or reader. Thackeray deliberately displaces meaning into the external and alienating realm of impersonation, symbolic identification, and illustration, where it is subject to multiple, often faulty interpretations, even though, as the charades tell us, only one conclusion is right and inevitable.

The generic imperative of the charades is never to expose reality in the direct light of complete representation. It is this imperative that shadows and perhaps explains Thackeray's reluctance as a narrator to interpret the central classical myths of the novel and to expose Becky as guilty or innocent of certain sexual or social crimes. Thackeray's reticence in dealing explicitly with these issues may have something to do with the moral climate of his time, but his carefully chosen moments of silence originate, I would suggest, in a kind of ritual reluctance and fear at unveiling the deeper mysteries or hidden laws governing the fate of any society. Vanity, for Thackeray as for the Preacher, is the false idol of the unregenerate historical world, its dark divinity incarnated in the "Imperial Master," the "Magnificent Idea," the "August Presence" of the king who rules. As Thackeray prepares to initiate his readers into what he had earlier called the "mystical language" of vanity and to usher them into the very penetralia of mystery—the entertainments that provide the "high world" of fashion and power with its social rituals—he tellingly invokes the tutelary myth of Semele:

> They say the honest newspaper-fellow who sits in the hall and takes down the names of the great ones who are admitted to the feasts, dies after a little time. He can't survive the glare of fashion long. It scorches him up, as the presence of Jupiter in full dress wasted that poor imprudent Semele—a giddy moth of a creature who ruined herself by venturing out of her natural atmosphere. Her myth ought to be taken to heart amongst the Tyburnians, the Belgravians,—her story, and perhaps Becky's too.

Thackeray's attempt to allegorize the story of Semele into a comic parable of social vanity and class "imprudence," like his Clytemnestra charade, is only partially successful in concealing the generative meaning of the myth. Semele, a mortal, gains knowledge of divine and immutable form at the expense of her life; her story, and Becky's too, constitutes a cautionary myth linking the *éclaircissement* of the knower with a destructive, if generative, violence that is essentially sexual. Thackeray's allusion to this myth of sexual violence and violation introduces a variation on the novelistic theme of unhappy unions, a theme previously limited to the comic treatment of *"mésalliance"*: the imprudent marriage of Amelia Sedley and George Osborne.

The myth of Semele establishes a correspondence between demystification and annihilation that is crucial in understanding Thackeray's own attitudes toward novelistic knowledge, especially narrative omniscience. Complete knowledge becomes at best an instrument of historical and personal devaluation, as when the narrator "enlightens" his readers that the relics sent to Miss Crawley to effect a reconciliation between Rawdon and his aunt were purchased from peddlers trafficking in the spoils of war. "The novelist," advises the narrator in sardonic tones, "who knows everything, knows this also." Here omniscience is in the service of Thackeray's "cynicism," but the narrator is merely laughing up the reader's sleeve. At worst, complete demystification constitutes what Ruskin, in his troubled response to *Vanity Fair*, calls "blasphemy"—in its scriptural sense of " 'Harmful Speaking'—not against God only, but against man, and against all the good works and purposes of Nature":

> The word is accurately opposed to "Euphemy," the right or well-speaking of God and His world; and the two modes of speech are those which, going out of the mouth, sanctify or defile the man.
>
> Going out of the mouth, that is to say, deliberately and of purpose. A French postillion's "Sacr-r-re"—loud, with the low "Nom de Dieu" following between his teeth, is not blasphemy, unless against his horse; but Mr. Thackeray's close of his Waterloo chapter in *Vanity Fair*, "And all night long Amelia was praying for George, who was lying on his face, dead, with a bullet through his heart" (sic), is blasphemy of the most fatal and subtle kind.

Ruskin's appropriation of the vocabulary of the sacred to interpret the "speech" of omniscient narration locates the source of sancity or defilement in the speaker, not in the reality of the thing spoken. Thackeray's blasphemy in the Waterloo chapter is authorized, however, by the conventions of realism that prescribe the unbiased chronicling of event unmediated by palliative illusion. But in the charades of *Vanity Fair*, in the question of Becky's guilty liaison with Lord Steyne, and in the suspicious death of Jos Sedley, Thackeray resorts neither to voiced blasphemy nor to its Ruskinian opposite, euphemy. Rather he resorts to blasphemy's negation: an equivocal and equivocating silence. His *ultimate* reluctance to expose the illusion of love and the myth of good works emanating from God, man, and nature leads him to abscond, like a tormented demiurge, from the scene of the performances, leaving the stage of his history free for his performers to act out blasphemy without speaking it.

Perhaps it is the story of Semele ("her story, and . . . Becky's too") that remains the fable Thackeray takes most to heart. As the myth suggests,

Thackeray's critical silences could betray an anxiety, religious or metaphysical, about the limits of the human power to know and to represent. It is an anxiety Thackeray covertly expresses in his life of Swift, where he sees in Swift's genius—a genius almost Zeus-like in its power "to flash upon falsehood and scorch it into perdition"—an awful and an evil spirit. Thackeray describes Swift in a passage that recalls Semele's imprudent exposure to the glare of a dazzling magnificence:

> In his old age, looking at the "Tale of a Tub," when he said, "Good God, what a genius I had when I wrote that book!" I think he was admiring, not the genius, but the consequences to which the genius had brought him—a vast genius, a magnificent genius, a genius wonderfully bright, and dazzling, and strong,—to seize, to know, to see, to flash upon falsehood and scorch it into perdition, to penetrate into the hidden motives, and expose the black thoughts of men,—an awful, an evil spirit.

What Thackeray seems to fear in the example of Swift's life and the methods of his art is the fate ordained for the evil genius capable of penetrating into hidden motives and exposing the black thoughts of men: the "maddened hurricane" of a tormented man who suffered "frightfully from the consciousness of his own scepticism" and who "bent his pride so far down as to put his apostasy out to hire." The subjectivism underlying Thackeray's belief that Swift's art was inspired by the misanthropic resentments of a failed opportunist may reflect Thackeray's own fear of spiritual bankruptcy, a fear dramatized in the cynical apostasy of the haunted Lord Steyne, over whose head hovers the Damoclean sword of madness. It is this fear that may explain Thackeray's moral and ideological ambivalence in *Vanity Fair*, an ambivalence Arnold Kettle has defined as the desire to "expose illusions and yet keep them" (*The Introduction to the English Novel*). Such ambivalence lies at the heart of Thackeray's "gentlemanly ideal," an ideal that endorses the class-bound ideology his satire exposes.

Thackeray himself defends the moral status of silence when he defines Amelia's reticence as "the timid denial of the unwelcome assertion of ruling folks, a tacit protestantism." In Thackeray's tacit protestantism, so different from the vocal and charged denunciations of Swift, he lays to rest his social and narrative anxieties and exorcises the Swiftian specter of prophetic madness. It is such tacit protestantism that characterizes the melancholic anomie of the novel's broken or inconclusive ending: "Come children, let us shut up the box and the puppets, for our play is played out."

Having opened up a Pandora's box of social and historical evils, Thackeray vainly tries to shut them up in the confines of his fictional puppet box, to "miniaturize" and thus minimize the implications of his fable. As a satirist and critical realist, Thackeray is hopelessly divided between his evil genius for penetration into the hidden motives and invisible laws governing human relations and his Steyne-like cynicism in exposing a reality at once spiritually vain and morally horrifying. Charlotte Brontë rightly saw that the satirist of *Vanity Fair* could lift "the mask from the face of the Pharisee" through the "Greek fire of his sarcasm," but she mistakenly placed the "levin-brand of denunciation" in the tradition of biblical prophecy. If *Vanity Fair* often speaks as "solemn as an oracle," its testimony does not resemble the "faithful counsel" of a Micaiah prophesying evil ("Preface to *Jane Eyre*, 2d ed., dedicated to Thackeray). When Thackeray speaks, he speaks like the impotent prophetess Cassandra, who, in chronicling the *Agamemnon's* dark drama of sexual vengeance, laments that "there is no god of healing in this story" (l. 1248).

JULIET McMASTER

# Funeral Baked Meats: Thackeray's Last Novel

The wedding of Philip Firmin and Charlotte Baynes is a very dismal affair. Although the Pendennis children, the bridesmaids, are rigged out in new dresses and bonnets for the occasion, "everybody else looked so quiet and demure, that when we went into the church, three or four street urchins knocking about the gate, said, 'Look at 'em. They're going to be 'ung.' And so the words are spoken, and the indissoluble knot is tied. Amen. For better, for worse." The reader is teasingly required to choose his interpretation— the decisive words that are spoken could be either the marriage service or the urchins' pronouncement, and the indissoluble knot could refer as readily to the noose as to holy wedlock. It is no surprise to hear that the celebration afterwards is not very merry: "The marriage table did coldly furnish forth a funeral kind of dinner." The incident and narration are typical of *The Adventures of Philip*, Thackeray's last novel, in the alignment of love with death, and in the portrayal of a social ritual that is grimly accompanied by the rattle of the bones.

*Philip* is in many ways a tired novel, a book of the declining years, as Thackeray himself and many readers have admitted. It is characterized by a low-pressure narrative, a hero we cannot sympathize with, reactionary social attitudes, lapses in inspiration. And yet it is also galvanized by an intense though intermittent energy, which erupts in the brawling violence of the protagonist, Philip, and in the irascibility and occasional panic of the narrator, Pendennis. At the literal level it is often languid, as we lounge in the Penden-

From *Studies in the Novel* 13, nos. 1/2 (Spring/Summer 1981). © 1981 by North Texas State University.

nis drawing room and listen to cozy snatches of domestic chat; fervid but
obtuse morality from Laura, whimsical and half-hearted self-defense from
Pen. But at the metaphoric level we have death, murder, violence, horror.
The combination is not always successful. But it can be deeply disturbing,
as the characters grope for life and health, and feel their capable strong hands
touching some ghastly memento mori; and it can be humorous, too,
Thackeray here having developed a taste for the macabre to match Dickens's.
Thackeray's last completed novel, in fact, has much in common with
Dickens's, *Our Mutual Friend*, in that both are almost obsessively concerned
with death.

The social vision in *Philip* is one of the respectable arrangements of society as forming a thin crust over the abyss. Death has of course always had
its prominent place in Thackeray's novels. His characters do their feverish
social climbing in the context of mortality: Becky's sparkling smile collapses
into the haggard grimace of guilt in her unguarded moments, Sedley and
Osborne and all their successes and failures are mown down in the same
chapter by time's fell hand, and Jos in Brussels performs his comic routine
with his valet with the present fear of death upon him. In *Philip* this vision
is intensified, and our sense of the fragility of the respectable facade becomes
keener, and the interest in the facade itself less, in proportion as what it fronts
becomes insistent. Thackeray discovers endless ways of envisaging the tidy
surface, the horror beneath.

The Twysdens, among the scores of social ménages that he creates in
his work, are especially remarkable for the distance between the pretension
and the reality. Becky and Rawdon in Curzon Street certainly put up a more
glittering front, but then they do not really fool or seriously try to fool anyone,
for everyone knows they are living on nothing a year and that the crash will
come sooner or later. But the Twysdens keep up an agonized and desperate
pretense—they starve themselves in private in order to throw lavish dinners,
and gush about love and duty while clawing for the highest bidder in the
marriage market. Their prestige is maintained at a ghastly expense, while
they shudder under scanty coverlids or before niggard fires. The grave yawns
under their paltry devices in economy: "My love, I have saved a halfpenny
out of Mary's beer. Isn't it time to dress for the duchess's; and don't you think
John might wear that livery of Thomas's who only had it a year, and died
of the smallpox?" The next livery for John will be his shroud. The running
head for this passage is "Thrift, thrift, Horatio." One would certainly expect funeral baked meats to be carefully preserved in that family. Indeed we
see Mrs. Twysden prudently looking forward to the marriage tables as she
leaves Philip alone with Agnes:

> Mamma, I say, has left the room at last, bowing with a perfect
> sweetness and calm grace and gravity; and she has slipped down
> the stairs . . . to the lower regions, and with perfect good breeding
> is torturing the butler on his bottle-rack—is squeezing the
> housekeeper in her jam-closet—is watching the three cold cutlets,
> shuddering in the larder behind the wires. . . . And meanwhile
> our girl and boy are prattling in the drawing room.

The billing and cooing go on over "the lower regions," a hell complete with
appropriate tortures for the domestic Ixion.

In the person of Mrs. Baynes, another matron who stretches every nerve
and sinew to maintain the family gentility, the strain is more apparent, and
the demon visibly snarls behind the social simper: "She would pay us the
most fulsome compliments with anger raging out of her eyes. . . . It was
'Oh, how kind you are to her, Mrs. Pendennis! How can I ever thank you
and Mr. P., I am sure'; and she looked as if she could poison both of us,
as she went away, curtsying and darting dreary parting smiles."

The smile that is a social mask to conceal sentiments anything but joyful
is vividly envisaged to the description of Dr. Firmin, another character who
conceals impending ruin behind a display of prosperity.

> By the way, that smile of Firmin's was a very queer contortion
> of the handsome features. As you came up to him, he would draw
> his lips over his teeth, causing his jaws to wrinkle (or dimple if
> you will) on either side. Meanwhile his eyes looked out from his
> face, quite melancholy and independent of the little transaction
> in which the mouth was engaged. Lips said, "I am a gentleman
> of fine manners and fascinating address, and I am supposed to
> be happy to see you. How do you do?" Dreary, sad, as into a
> great blank desert, looked the dark eyes.

That is one of the many powerful passages in *Philip*, and the doctor's smile
is another of the images of the thin veneer that is a front for desperation,
like the footman's livery contaminated by smallpox, or the lovers' courtship conducted over the hell of the servants' hall. It is quite characteristic
of the progress of the novel that the smile should presently be viewed as
detachable. Madame de Smolensk, running a genteel boardinghouse on the
brink of bankruptcy, always dresses elegantly for dinner among her boarders:
"the worthy woman took that smile out of some cunning box on her scanty
toilet-table—that smile which she wore all the evening along with the rest
of her toilette, and took out of her mouth when she went to bed, and to
think—to think how both ends were to be made to meet."

One of the successful comic sequences of the novel is that where General Baynes, wretchedly guilty at having agreed to break the match between Charlotte and Philip, becomes so hot-tempered in his own defense that when his old friend and then his brother-in-law point out his shabby conduct he feels obliged to challenge them, successively. As the retired military men, who for years have been relegated to domestic roles, square their stooped shoulders and talk of honor, recruiting seconds, and sending messages, according to the approved ritual, they are interrupted by the incursion of another ritual— the general's wife comes to see if they will join her table at whist. Another panicky smile must be summoned: "The bloodthirsty hypocrites instantly smoothed their ruffled brows and smiled on her with perfect courtesy." The stirring of murderous instincts in the genteel boardinghouse affords an occasion for a lot of well-managed comic business, as the boarders look on in shocked excitement, the wives join the row, and Philip, the young man at issue, dramatically bursts into the center of the action. The story at the literal level maintains the comedy and averts tragedy, for in the event "the fratricidal bullet" is not fired; but the violence is done at the metaphorical and psychological level. While Baynes is fighting off the monitors who keep reiterating the unwanted promptings of his own conscience, the narrator moves into a macabre psychological allegory:

> Baynes will out-bawl that prating monitor, [an incommodious conscience] and thrust that inconvenient preacher out of sight, out of hearing, drive him with angry words from our gate. Ah! in vain we expel him; and bid John say, not at home! There he is when we wake, sitting at our bed-foot. We throw him overboard for daring to put an oar in our boat. Whose ghastly head is that looking up from the water and swimming alongside us, row we never so swiftly? Fire at him. Brain him with an oar, one of you, and pull on! Flash goes the pistol. Surely that oar has stove the old skull in? See! there comes the awful companion popping up out of water again, and crying, "Remember, remember, I am here, I am here!"

This is the major sphere of action in *Philip*; the events of the story are jaded, unexciting, and often the narrator can hardly bother to narrate them. But the panic and hatred within, the irrational fantasies and suppressed desperation that find their strangled expression in gestures and images—this is the major stratum of interest, erupting recurrently into the cooler world of social accommodation.

The sense of impending explosion is strong at the outset of the novel, when Dr. Firmin's past sexual and financial sins rumble in the background and finally burst into light, to make his son possibly illegitimate and certainly penniless; no wonder Philip feels his home is mined, and claims, "I walk with a volcano under my feet, which may burst any day and annihilate me." The other main movements in the action similarly evoke the violent internal upheaval, the serene exterior. General Baynes benignly welcomes Philip as his daughter's suitor, because the marriage would usefully cancel his financial obligation to Philip; the narrator can see the implications of his benignity: Charlotte is to be "her father's ransom," and later the image of her as Iphigenia to her father's Agamemnon is developed. The cozy romantic arrangements are motivated by more than love. The Little Sister, too, adopts the seductive mannerisms of courtship in order to snare Tufton Hunt when she steals the forged bill from him. "'Law bless me, Mr. Hunt,' then says the artless creature, 'who ever would have thought of seeing *you*, I do declare!' And she makes a nice cheery little curtsy, and looks quite gay, pleased, and pretty; and so did Judith look gay, no doubt, and smile, and prattle before Holofernes."

The fascinating interplay between death and the niceties of social behavior at one point moves the narrator to speculate, "If a gentleman is sentenced to be hung, I wonder is it a matter of comfort to him or not to know beforehand the day of the operation?" Execution is a recurrent source of imagery. As nemesis encroaches, Dr. Firmin speculates on the form his "execution" is to take: "A day passes: no assassin darts at the doctor as he threads the dim opera-colonnade passage on his way to his club. A week goes by: no stiletto is plunged into his well-wadded breast as he steps from his carriage at some noble patient's door. Philip says he never knew his father more pleasant, easy, good-humoured, and affable than during this period." Agnes Twysden's marriage to Woolcomb is also an "execution." And Pendennis savors the neat justice of the fact that Dr. Guillotin himself was decapitated by his own efficient machine.

Mental discomfort is recurrently envisaged as physical pain. A hostile review of Pendennis's latest publication is elaborated as a flogging; Philip in his jealousy broods Othello-like on "daggers, ropes, and poisons, has it comes to this?"; Charlotte's parents in trying to separate her from Philip "stab her to the heart," and "stretched Philip on an infernal rack of torture." And Charlotte in turn tortures her rival in the affections of her children, the Little Sister: "Tortures I know she was suffering. Charlotte had been stabbing her. Women will use the edge sometimes, and drive the steel in." Some of this metaphorical violence, of course, is fairly routine inflated language, familiar enough in romance, and even here satirized in the posturings of the absconded swindler Dr. Firmin, whose letters enlarge on the agonies of exile and the thorns of life on which he bleeds. And some of the hyperbole is

deliberately deflated by the narrator's humorous tone, as when he finds
himself quite by mistake beginning to feel sorry for Mrs. Baynes: "If I con-
template that wretched old Niobe much longer, I shall begin to pity her. Away
softness! Take out thy arrows, the poisoned, the barbed, the rankling, and
prod me the old creature well, god of the silver bow!" But often there is an
almost hysteric intensity in the vision, that endues moments in *Philip* with
the chilling power of Gothic. Mrs. Baynes, the "cruel, shrivelled, bilious,
plain old woman," gathers something of the force of nightmare. "You should
have seen that fiend and her livid smile, as she was drilling her gimlets into
my heart," says Philip of his mother-in-law; "I can see her face now: her cruel
yellow face, and her sharp teeth, and her grey eyes." And the coolly callous
remark of Tufton Hunt, who proposes to blackmail the Doctor, has the fine
Thackerayan power of understatement: "I prescribe bleeding."

His wife has become so terrible to General Baynes that at night he hides
under the counterpane and "lies quite mum" for fear she should discover he
is awake and proceed to "torture" him. Contemplating such violence and
fear in apparently harmonious domestic relations, the narrator is moved to
wonder why more husbands do not resort to the bolster, like Othello, and
then comments on his comment, "Horrible cynicism! Yes—I know. These
propositions served raw are savage, and shock your sensibility; cooked with
a little piquant sauce, they are welcome at quite polite tables." The metaphor
is an appropriate one for *Philip*, which within the bounds of a fiction palatable
to the readership of the *Cornhill* still has as its staple the raw propositions
that, under the polite forms and energetically maintained surfaces, husbands
and wives torment each other, parents victimize their children, and people
lay traps and pounce on victims.

The culinary metaphor is one of many, for Thackeray develops the view
of human relations as carnivorous, as a system of people devouring people.
The image is not new in his work, but here it occurs with such frequency
as to be almost a theme in itself. Often the reference is jocular, as in the conversation about Pendennis and his mother in the opening pages:

> "My dear, if that child were hungry, you would chop off your
> head to make him broth," says the doctor, sipping his tea.
> "Potage à la bonne femme," says Mr. Pendennis. "Mother, we
> have it at the club. You would be done with milk, eggs, and a
> quantity of vegetables. You would be put to simmer for many
> hours in an earthen pan."

It is not mere joking. Helen Pendennis, as we remember from the earlier novel,
has as her family crest a pelican feeding her young with her blood, and maternal self-sacrifice is her métier. As Pen eats mother soup, Philip may dine off

minced wife. "If [that dish which you liked] consisted of minced Charlotte . . . you know she would cheerfully chop herself up, and have herself served with a litte cream-sauce and sippets of toast." Another item on the cannibal menu is hashed author: Mugford the editor "likes always to have at least one man served up and hashed small in the *Pall Mall Gazette*." When Philip understands his good fortune in having escaped marriage with Agnes Twysden, he sees her as anthropophagous: "I might have been like that fellow in the *Arabian Nights*, who married Amina—the respectable woman, who dined upon grains of rice, but supped upon cold dead body." Dr. Firmin is a father who feeds off his own offspring. His recurrent plunder, first of Philip's fortune and then of his income, is seen as a process of drawing blood. "My patriarch has tied me up, and had the knife in me repeatedly," says Philip. "He does not sacrifice me at one operation; but there will be a final one some day, and I shall bleed no more." Pendennis concurs that "that devouring dragon of a doctor had stomach enough for the blood of all of us." After he has cheated his son of his inheritance, the doctor spreads the rumor that it was the son who ruined his father. This second betrayal by which the father throws his son to the wolves is envisaged in elaborate detail:

> Have you never heard to what lengths some bankrupts will go? To appease the wolves who chase them in the winter forest, have you not read how some travellers will cast all their provisions out of the sledge? then, when all the provisions are gone, don't you know that they will fling out perhaps the sister, perhaps the mother, perhaps the baby, the little, dear, tender innocent? Don't you see him tumbling among the howling pack, and the wolves gnashing, gnawing, crashing, gobbling him up in the snow? Oh, horror—horror!

It is quite characteristic of Thackeray's habit of admitting in himself the sins he castigates in others that eventually he should see the writer as an ogre too. In that fascinatingly self-regarding passage in which he counts his words as he writes them, and calculates how much he will get paid for them, and how he can feed his family and servants on the proceeds, he eventually concludes, "Wife, children, guests, servants, charwoman, we are all actually making a meal off Philip Firmin's bones as it were."

In *Philip* Thackeray spreads wide what he says in more concentrated form in his Roundabout Paper on "Ogres," which he wrote in the course of the novel's serial run. Here at the outset the author himself is an ogre, hungrily approaching a topic for his monthly essay: "I came to my meal with an ogre-like appetite and gusto. Fee, faw, fum! Wife, where is that tender little Princekin? Have you trussed him, and did you stuff him nicely, and have

you taken care to baste him, and do him, not too brown, as I told you? Quick!
I am hungry!" (chap. 17). With similar gusto he expatiates on the social
behavior and domestic habits of ogres, creating a gruesome personnel of
Humguffins, and Rawheads, and tossing off grisly jokes: "And if Lady
Ogreham happens to die—I won't say to go the way of all flesh, that is too
revolting" (chap. 17). His main thesis is that "there is no greater mistake
than to suppose that ogres have ceased to exist. We all *know* ogres. Their
caverns are round us, and about us." He explains:

> I mean, madam, that in the company assembled in your genteel
> drawing-room, who bow here and there and smirk in white
> neckcloths, you receive men who elbow through life successfully
> enough but are ogres in private: men wicked, false, rapacious,
> flattering; cruel hectors at home; smiling courtiers abroad; caus-
> ing wives, children, servants, parents, to tremble before them, and
> smiling and bowing as they bid strangers welcome into their
> castles.
>
> (Chap. 17)

That is the vision of family and social relations in *Philip*, though there it is
worked out in realistic terms as well as at the more violent metaphorical level.
The really savage, pitiless people are those who should be your nearest and
dearest. It is within their own families that the ogres bare their sharpened
fangs. Philip is robbed by his father, and betrayed by his cousin-fiancée.
Charlotte is sacrificed and cheated by her mother. The two pathetic Misses
Boldero are left in pawn by their mother, who skips without notice from
Madame de Smolensk's boardinghouse, leaving her bills unpaid and her
daughter's dependent on the cheated landlady. The marriages too are ogrous.
There is more than a hint that Dr. Firmin effectually did away with Philip's
mother (who presumably went the way of all flesh); Mrs. Baynes terrorizes
her husband, Woolcomb beats his wife. Mrs. Twysden, as we have seen,
entertains guests who smirk in white neckcloths at the price of cheating and
victimizing her servants. These are the people who are smiling courtiers
abroad but ogres in private. "I say, there are men who have crunched the
bones of victim after victim; in whose closets lie skeletons picked frightfully
clean" (chap. 17). Dr. Firmin, of course, has skeletons both figurative and
literal on his premises, having a guilty past and an anatomical specimen, "a
dilapidated skeleton in a corner," which has been used for medical studies.

The vision of intimate relations as a process of devouring modulates from
the comic to the horrible. The two parents are the characters in whom
Thackeray best realizes the potential of his cannibal theme for an intense
balance between humor and horror. Dr. Firmin, with his flashing diamond

ring and his patent subterfuges, is manifestly a posturing humbug, whose portrait is sold for a few shillings to his creditors amidst roars of laughter. But even when his poses and his humbug are taken into account, he remains a figure of powerfully sinister proportions. Mrs. Baynes is an absurd snob, and Philip and Pendennis gleefully expose her boardinghouse pretensions. But she too is never finally put down, but, in being associated with Lady Macbeth and vampires, continues to inspire dread. As a farewell embrace to her daughter, we hear, she "put a lean, hungry face against Charlotte's lip." The grotesque vision of the ogre crunching bones has been pared down to the adjectives, "lean, hungry." But the image as vividly conveys greed and possessiveness unmitigated by gentleness or tolerance. There are ogres all round us.

Dr. Firmin is not only a devourer; in certain aspects he is Death incarnate. It is around him that Thackeray clusters his imagery of death most insistently. His residence is on Old Parr Street—"It *is* a funereal street, Old Parr Street, certainly; the carriages which drive there ought to have feathers on the roof, and the butlers who open the doors should wear weepers." In this gloomy setting, as symbolically laden as Spenser's Cave of Despair, he makes his house a museum of mementos mori, which include his own portrait:

> Over the sideboard was the doctor, in a black velvet coat and a fur collar, his hand on a skull, like Hamlet. Skulls of oxen, horned, with wreaths, formed the cheerful ornaments of the cornice. On the side-table glittered a pair of cups, given by grateful patients, looking like receptacles rather for funereal ashes than for festive flowers or wine. Brice, the butler, wore the gravity and costume of an undertaker.

And his surgery, once a dissecting room for medical students, is equipped with a special side door for "having *the bodies* in and out." Not only does Dr. Firmin handle skulls and possess skeletons, he is himself a kind of death's-head, having "very white false teeth, which perhaps were a little too large for his mouth, and these grinned in the gas-light very fiercely. On his cheeks were black whiskers, . . . and his bald head glittered like a billiard-ball." In certain lights, we were reminded, his eye sockets are mere shadowy hollows under his brow—an effect that Walker attempted to capture in his illustration for Number 5. His medical vocation, which one would expect to make him a healing and life-giving figure, in fact does the opposite, as his function of counting his patients' heartbeats acts rather like Death's hourglass in a Danse Macabre. He "hangs on to the nobility by the pulse," we hear, and he is thus depicted in the initial to the first chapter. In fact at the outset we hear how he neglects his son in his serious illness in order to minister to a

"grand dook." When Tufton Hunt sees Firmin's carriage in the unfashionable
district of Tottenham Court Road, where the doctor claims to have patients,
he produces one of his worn-out Latin tags: " 'Pallida mors aequo pede—
hey, doctor? . . .' 'aequo pede,' sighs the doctor, casting up his fine eyes to
the ceiling." There is the possibility for the double reading again. According
to one we are dealing with the affected humbug with his pretentious display
of schoolboy Latin quotations; according to the other we can see him as pallid
death himself, calling impartially on rich and poor. It is another of the features
of the Danse Macabre that the agile skeleton comes in many guises, and his
grinning teeth and bony shins may protrude from palmer's weeds or cardinal's
robes. The doctor's appurtenances, his watch and his diamond ring and his
scented handkerchief, and his habit of "smiling behind his teeth," affect one
like the disguises of Holbein's Death.

But although in Dr. Firmin we find an almost allegorical personification of death, he is only the most obvious manifestation in a novel that deals
in mortality at large. Pen and Philip meet at Grey Friars, now remembered
as a multiple graveyard ("I think in the time of the Plague great numbers
of people were buried there," and establish their adult relationship over the
loss of their mothers—"When Philip Firmin and I met again, there was crape
on both our hats." We have many glimpses of the chilling or welcome summons of death. Again Thackeray hovers between the horrible and the
facetious. Madame de Smolensk's clientèle, who are in all conscience a rather
ghoulish gathering, are once imagined as being augmented by a group of
Banquo-like revenants: "If twenty gibbering ghosts had come to the boardinghouse dinner, madame would have gone on carving her dishes, and smiling
and helping the live guests, the paying guests; leaving the dead guests to gib-
ber away and help themselves." Considering the assembly literally present
are by no means all paying guests, we find the figure is a little more than
hypothetical.

In Lord Ringwood we are shown a worldly old reprobate who is haunted
not so much by fear of his own death in the future as by the ghosts of his
dead past, including his own dead self. He dare not stay in his own town
mansion when he is in town (his irrational terror has a certain pathos, like
that of General Baynes, hiding under the counterpane from his wife), because
there he is haunted by the family portraits, "ghostly images of dead
Ringwoods—his dead son, who had died in his boyhood; his dead brother
attired in the uniform of his day; . . . Lord Ringwood's dead self, finally,
as he appeared still a young man, when Lawrence painted him . . . 'Ah! that's
the fellow I least like to look at,' the old man would say, scowling at the
picture." His death, when it occurs, is the occasion for the familiar display
of pomp and ceremony. We get the *Times* obituary verbatim, with its

solemnity about how "the Lord of many thousand acres, and according to report, of immense wealth, was dead." Golden lads and girls all must (it seems), as chimney sweepers, come to dust. The initial for that chapter, a skull with a coronet is a fit emblem for a large part of the novel. Indeed throughout the novel the chapter initials, which Thackeray continued to execute himself after he had delegated the full-page illustrations to Walker, provide a further set of variations on the theme of mortality.

The influence of Ringwood's death spreads to the Christmas pantomime, attended by the Pendennis family, and presently Pendennis is as gloomy as though he were at a burial. As narrator Pendennis is our vehicle for the consciousness of mortality. One memorable passage shows him as more than half in love with easeful death himself. He professes to be glad his youth is over, glad that the pains of life are nearer at their end than their beginning, glad he does not have to live through again the thousand ills that flesh is heir to:

> No. I do not want to go to school again. I do not want to hear Trotman's sermon over again. Take me out and finish me. Give me the cup of hemlock at once. Here's a health to you, my lads. . . . Ha! I feel the co-o-ld stealing, stealing upwards. Now it is in my ankles—no more gout in my foot: now my knees are numb. . . .
>
> What is this funeral chant, when the pipes should be playing gaily, as Love, and Youth, and Spring, and Joy are dancing under the windows?

It is a remarkable soliloquy, and representative again of the general tone and theme of *Philip*, which is half the time celebrating energy and vitality, and the other half giving way to the death wish; half the time studying the frantic struggle to maintain an appearance, the other half exposing beneath the fixed smile the grin of the death's-head. The narrative again becomes a funeral chant at the death of General Baynes, whose passing is the occasion for the narrator to picture again his own death, and this time the reader's too: "A drive to the cemetery, followed by a coach with four acquaintances dressed in decorous black, who separate and go to their homes or clubs, and wear your crape for a few days after—can most of us expect much more?" Writer, reader, pauper, hero, are all required to keep in mind "how lonely they are, and what a little dust will cover them."

Pendennis as the narrator is much more prominent in *Philip* than he was in the similar set-up in *The Newcomes*, where he was again the biographer of a younger friend from Grey Friars. In fact his increased prominence has been considered as one of the faults of the novel, since the unlimited license

he takes to launch into a Roundabout-Paper-like digression inevitably takes
its toll on the pace of the narrative. We have here a structure something like
that of *Tristram Shandy*, where the narrator ostensibly intends to write the
story of his Uncle Toby's amours, but is always writing about himself,
whether he is progressing in or digressing from his other narrative. "But the
story is not *de me*—it regards Philip," Pendennis is always obliged to remind
himself "I feel that I am wandering from Philip's adventures to his
biographer's," he apologizes again. In fact, of course, the Pendennis digression, like the Shandean one, is "digressive, and it is progressive too—and
at the same time," for Pen is as much Thackeray's (and his own) real subject
as Philip. This writer has long been aware that there is no such thing as an
objective history, and so long as a history must be subjective, it is just as
well that the reader should know something of whose subjectivity he is dealing with. Pendennis is explicit enough about the limitations of his point of
view to make it clear that the Jamesian critics would have little to teach him:
"People there are in our history who do not seem to me to have kindly hearts
at all; and yet, perhaps, if a biography could be written from their point of
view, some other novelist might show how Philip and *his* biographer were
a pair of selfish worldlings unworthy of credit: how Uncle and Aunt Twysden
were most exemplary people, and so forth." However, the narrator is ready
to accept the responsibility for his subjective account: "This I say—*Ego*—as
my friend's biographer," he announces boldly. It is worth examining a little
more the content of the subjectivity of the "friend's biographer."

Philip Firmin, clearly enough, is one of Thackeray's projections of
himself. If Henry Esmond was a "handsome likeness," a rather delicate, formal, and self-satisfied self-portrait, Philip is the big, shouldering, boisterous,
imprudent, undignified troublemaker part of Thackeray that John Carey has
called the Prodigal. The biographical parallels with Thackeray's own career
are clear enough, and have been pointed out by Ray and others. Philip is
described at the outset as "A brave, handsome, blundering, downright young
fellow, with broad shoulders, high spirits, and quite fresh blushes on his face,
with very good talents (though he has been woefully idle, and requested to
absent himself temporarily from his university), the possessor of a competent fortune and the heir of another": in all but the "handsome," he resembles
Thackeray at the same age. Then, again like Thackeray, he loses the fortunes, dabbles in law, becomes a hack writer, falls in love with a childlike
girl in the Paris of the reign of Louis Philippe and imprudently marries her,
and proceeds to try to support a growing family on the inadequate earnings
of his pen. Mrs. Baynes is Mrs. Shawe as Charlotte is Isabella. There are
recognizable points of detail too. Philip, disappointed of the side dishes at
Mugford's dinner when the celebrated Mr. Lyon sends word he is not com-

ing, is again Thackeray, who was deprived of ortolans when his hostess heard Dickens could not attend her dinner. And Mrs. Baynes reneges on the payment of her daughter's income as did Mrs. Shawe.

It is equally clear that Pendennis is also Thackeray. He also has been through the storms of youth that he witnesses in Philip—the imprudent early marriage, the writing for a living; and, barring the ever-clinging Laura, his professional and domestic situation is clearly enough identified with his author's. The authorial "I" often refers to the historical author rather than the fictional one. The first part of the Little Sister's history, we hear, "I myself printed some twenty years ago"—in fact of course Thackeray had not yet invented Pendennis in 1840, when he published *A Shabby Genteel Story*. In manner, too, he seems to have touched in details of the self-portrait. Ray describes, in the older Thackeray, the mixture between the rigid propriety of his bearing on formal occasions, and the great warmth and complete unreserve in convivial company and among children. "His manner is cold," says Mrs. Mugford of Pendennis, "not to say 'aughty. He seems to be laughing at people sometimes. . . . But he is a true friend, Mrs. Brandon says he is. And when you know him, his heart is good." There are other details: Pendennis, like Thackeray, was given an embroidered waistcoat which was so flamboyant he scarcely dared wear it; Pendennis, like Thackeray, agonizes over having made a fool of himself in delivering an after-dinner speech.

All of this has been often noticed and well enough documented— Thackeray evidently drew on elements of his own experience for both of his two main characters. But the special feature here, it seems to me, is that Pen is Thackeray the Older, looking at Philip, who is Thackeray the Younger. The self-consciousness here is so intense as to be something like Donne's "dialogue of one." Thackeray, braver than Lord Ringwood, is ready to look his "dead self" firmly in the eye, and come to terms with it—or at least to make the attempt.

It is beyond the scope of this paper to examine fully the implications of this narrative stance; but if we do see the novel as the late Thackeray's view of his early self, we have a means of accounting for some of the things in it that have bothered many readers. Pendennis's unfailing sympathy for his turbulent friend, whose failings he frequently acknowledges but never punishes, is readily understandable. He is not the one to bring down poetic justice on himself, although he tries to live up to his claim that in his account he has nothing extenuated, nor set down aught in malice.

Criticism of Thackeray has often focused on the change in him that seems to have occurred at about the time of *Vanity Fair*. Gordon Ray sees the change as beneficial, as an access of sympathy and humanity that enlarged the scope of his work and enabled him to enter the Age of Wisdom. Joseph Baker finds the change to be for the worse, *Philip* being a "recantation" of the admirable values embodied in *Vanity Fair*; and John Carey has recently argued for a Thackeray who, after the satiric triumphs of the early work, sold out to a flabby Victorian establishment. Thackeray's own view of the matter, if that is indeed what we have in *Philip*, is certainly of interest.

Pendennis is obviously both envious and faintly ashamed of Philip. He knows himself to be more talented and intelligent, as well as more successful, but he cannot help admiring the unfailing ability of the young man to live straightforwards, unreflectingly encountering his life and unselfconsciously responding to it. Philip is outspoken, knowing what he thinks and likes and dislikes, and pronouncing his convictions with force if not subtlety: when he reviews a work, he declares it is "written by the greatest genius, or the greatest numskull that the world now exhibits." As for his judgments of people, "In the man whom he hates he can see no good; and in his friend no fault." In the face of these extremes, Pendennis is rather apologetic about his qualified judgments, his tact, and his prudently equivocal pronouncements. He acknowledges in advance some of Carey's accusations, and parodies his own tactful compositions. There *was* a time, he says, in his youth, when he had been called "a dangerous man":

> Now, I am already to say that Nero was a monarch with many elegant accomplishments, and considerable natural amiability of disposition. I praise and admire success wherever I meet it. I make allowance for faults and shortcomings, especially in my superiors; and feel that, did we know all, we should judge them very differently. People don't believe me, perhaps, quite so much as formerly. But I don't offend: I trust I don't offend.

Such honest self-exposure, prompted by a scrutiny of the difference between the past and present selves, is a triumph of self-recognition. Pendennis's readiness to acknowledge the admixture of good even in villains—in another passage he defends Iago, Tartuffe, Macbeth, and Blifil, and suggests they have been maligned—is the mark of the creator of characters like Becky, Major Pendennis, Beatrix, and Dr. Firmin. Philip would not be capable of creating such complex amalgams of good and evil. But he might have written *Catherine*, the book intended to show that the defense of criminals is immoral.

Philip's independence of class is another characteristic that Pendennis cannot help admiring, being achingly dependent on it himself. "He is one of the half-dozen men I have seen in my life," records Pendennis, "upon whom rank made no impression." Philip, though he has a fine taste in wine, can drink beer cheerfully among Bohemian cronies when he has lost his money, and he can and does tell his great-uncle Lord Ringwood to go to hell—a gesture that sets Pendennis fairly trembling. On the other hand, though Philip is no snob, he is thoroughly arrogant. His independence is born of a habit of command that he retains even when he has not the money to maintain the status of an independent gentleman. He is no republican, as his patronage of the Little Sister and his resentment of Mugford's familiarities testify. The young Thackeray may have been an outspoken castigator of snobbery, but he too took his stand on being a gentleman. Pendennis's more reflective class-consciousness would at least have saved him from some of the unpleasant-ness that Philip causes—for instance in insulting the amiable Mrs. Ravenswing.

Philip, in this dialogue of one, makes some judgments on his biographer too: " 'You call me reckless, and prodigal, and idle, and all sorts of names, because I live in a single room, do as little work as I can, and go about with holes in my boots: and you flatter yourself you are prudent, because you have a genteel house, a grave flunkey out of livery, . . . to wait when you give your half dozen dreary dinner parties. Wretched man! You are a slave: not a man.' " Since Thackeray is the creator of both incarnations of himself, of both Philip's accusations and Pendennis's self-exposure, we can at least assume that he has grown in humility. Philip is not prone to self-analysis or self-accusation; it is Pendennis and Thackeray who can discover and con-template the image of their present self as slavish.

Pendennis's faculty for self-examination does not make him any the hap-pier. He is the writer of *Vanity Fair*, who aims at achieving an increase in consciousness, rather than an anaesthetizing entertainment: "This, dear friends and companions, is my amiable object—to walk with you through the Fair, to examine the shops and the shows there; and that we should all come home after the flare, and the noise, and the gaiety, and be perfectly miserable in private" (*Vanity Fair*, chap. 19). In *Philip*, as we have seen, it is not so much the external panorama we examine, the shops and the shows, as the internal prospect, the pain and the fury that is within and behind the show. Or rather, Philip watches the shops and the shows, Pendennis watches Philip, and Thackeray watches Pendennis watching Philip. We have here something like a Thackerayan version of *The Heart of Darkness*, with Philip as the young idealist Kurtz, Pen as the Kurtz who has seen "the horror"—and, perhaps, Thackeray as the Marlow whose experience and wisdom en-compass both.

It is Pendennis who, like Thackeray, has the haunting consciousness of mortality upon him; and perhaps that is partly why both seek out and ad-mire the chaotic energy and vitality of Philip. In a passage which Thackeray transcribed in a letter to the Baxters, thus accentuating its personal ring,

Pendennis writes, "indeed, it is rather absurd for elderly fingers to be still twanging Dan Cupid's toy bow and arrows. Yesterday is gone—yes, but very well remembered; and we think of it the more now we know that To-morrow is not going to bring us much." The portrait of the dead self is executed by the dying self.

But for all that, I would still say *Philip* is a very lively book, for a book about mortality.

GEORGE LEVINE

# Pendennis: *The Virtue of the Dilettante's Unbelief*

*The misfortune of dogmatic belief is that the first principle granted that the Book called the Bible is written under the direct dictation of God for instance—that the Catholic Church is under the direct dictation of God and solely communicated with him—that Quashimaboo is the direct appointed priest of God and so forth— pain, cruelty, persecution, separation of dear relatives, follow as a matter of course. . . . Every one of us in every fact, book, circumstance of life sees a different meaning and moral and so it must be about religion.*

—W. M. THACKERAY, Letter to His Mother

Despite their resistance to the threats of passion and their ironic and disenchanted acquiescence in things as they are, Thackeray's novels reimagine both literature and reality subversively. We have seen that his strategies of representation and elaborate, inconsistent, and perilous. The seductive world of things (which the Thackerayan narrator indulges cozily) disguises a latent hostility to human ideals; the digressive plots deflate all energies directed toward the extreme, the violent, or the ideal yet imply the impossibility of narrative control; the narrator himself cautiously encapsulates the romance of the past in the language of disenchantment or of a slightly sour sentimentality, as though the energies there have no further life. The multiplicity and disorder of Thackeray's worlds, finally, leave only the smallest space for belief; for the order belief might impose entails the violent obliteration of all that does not conform to it. While Thackeray resists his own suppressed energies of desire, which might manifest themselves in narratives that manipulate ex-

From *The Realistic Imagination: English Fiction from* Frankenstein *to* Lady Chatterley. © 1981 by the University of Chicago. University of Chicago Press, 1981.

perience through the constrictions of plot, he strains at the limits the novel form imposes in his effort to honor the variousness of a reality that will not submit to human shaping. "Every one of us in every fact, book, circumstance of life sees a different meaning and moral." Belief in the objective reality of that "meaning and moral" is more deadly than the aimless wanderings of disbelief.

Of course, even in the disruptiveness of form in his later novels, Thackeray never allowed himself fully to imagine a literature built from a world so chaotically solipsistic. He consistently wrote comedy, and if he risked in his casualness the fragmentation and pluralism his antidogmatism implied, he always tried to draw back. He took his fictions to the edges of a world that threatened always to dissolve into pointless and amoral multiplicity. His baggy monsters did indeed become monstrous in the solidity and density of their resistance to idealizing literary energies.

To sustain the possibilities of realistic comedy in a world so threateningly amorphous, Thackeray was forced to invent a new kind of protagonist. Arthur Pendennis belongs in the antiheroic tradition of Catherine Morland and even Edward Waverley; but he is not merely *not* a hero. He is a figure who is invented to avert the fanatic's catastrophe of defeated idealism (as, say, that of Scott's Balfour of Burley) and the moral catastrophe of aimlessness into which the rejection of the ideal might thrust him. Pen has no genuine alternative ideal, nor does his world. He is not only unheroic, then, but ironically disengaged from his own ambitions and imaginations of a self requiring satisfaction, and from the ordering norms of his society. His maneuverings for survival through the constrictions of narrative form and the exclusiveness of moral beliefs threaten to exclude him from any recognizable conventions of narrative form or social ordering. He is a protagonist whose self tends to flow with the flow of experience itself, without a fixed point, without even a morality.

This is obviously an extreme formulation for such an apparently banal, egocentric, and worldly figure as Pen, but it suggests how Thackeray's art points forward toward a modernist skepticism about self and narrative such as we find developing in James and Conrad. The extreme is only an exaggeration, not, I think, a falsification of the sort of figure Pen tends to be. In Thackeray, certainly, dogmatic morality is as dangerous as immorality, while selfishness is the norm in a world so solipsistically structured. The pure character is always suspect, threatening to become a wimpy and parasitical Amelia or a compliantly aggressive and dangerous Helen Pendennis (rather like Thackeray's own mother, Mrs. Carmichael-Smith, to whom he wrote often about the dangers of her piety and dogmatism). *Pendennis*, of course, in keeping with realism's need for compromise, attempts to place Pen somewhere between this extreme piety and the immorality of those late-Romantic sufferers from ennui and cynicism like Dickens's James Harthouse or George Eliot's more impressive Grandcourt.

Thackeray's novels are novels of defeat, of ambitions unfulfilled, of frustrations and losses in loving, desiring, idealizing. They can remain comedies only if they can locate protagonists who risk little in defeat because they have no assertive, dogmatic selves that require satisfaction. Contrast Mr. Bows, the loving, loveable, and defeated musician, with the successful novelist Pen. Pen is Thackeray's survivor, not the heroic figure, or the loving dreamer, or the idealist, but the one who resists commitment as long as possible, who understands, in the midst of commitment, the absurdity of it, who dallies with the most possibilities, and who makes the best terms with his own inevitable weaknesses and irrational desires. He can believe nothing intensely enough to attempt to impose it on others and is therefore no revolutionary against prevailing beliefs. After all, although these are as absurd as their alternatives, they at least provide convenient modes of ordering, and antagonism to them would simply cause unnecessary pain. The great art becomes knowing the conventions and using them.

In *Pendennis* Thackeray invents himself as this kind of dilettante, and finds that he does not altogether like what he creates. The novel tests and challenges Pen's education as it weans him from the ideal, and in another surrogate (whose life dramatizes the heavy price of *not* being like Pen), George Warrington, Thackeray lovingly articulates what he does not like about his Pen-self. He allows George to love Pen and to be very hard on him as well, suggesting once again his desire for the kind of innocence that might make belief in the heroic and ideal possible. George, we should remember, comes to like Pen when Pen is fresh from college and still innocent, still full of the energies of desire that his sophistication will shortly subvert. In any case, George knows the dangers of those energies and the necessity for compromise, which is embodied in his very relation to Pen and, one might conjecture, in Thackeray's relation to himself.

As Pen develops, he finds that what seemed to him of ultimate importance turns quickly into a joke, and he loses much of his capacity to take himself seriously. The narrative implies that something of his boyhood generosity of impulse remains with him into his most cynical moments, and he is allowed some relatively disinterested acts, which rescue him from marriage to Blanche Amory. The rescue gives the novel the happy ending the form requires, yet it leaves behind a world of lonely people. And the rescue itself is curiously, one would almost think, deliberately, unsatisfactory. The resolution is long prepared for, but once more, plot seems out of harmony with the narrative as a whole. For one thing, the narrative has made it clear that Pen does not really deserve Laura and that the proper marriage would have been between Laura and George. For another, Laura is perilously close to an ideal figure; only her vitality when she finds herself popular and attractive in the middle of the book suggests the possibilities of life beyond self-denial. Finally, Pen treats Laura's beliefs in justice, morality, truth, and the moral life with condescending affection and admiration. He knows that they do not match the knowledge of the world he has acquired from the major and through his own disenchantments.

Women provide that small space in his novels where Thackeray can locate the ideal and save his fictions from the sort of modernist dissolution such disenchanted awareness might entail. In this Thackeray reflects certain dominant conventions of Victorian culture, for despite his obvious sexual attraction to women and his tendency to idealize them, his is a misogynistic world. Women, in Thackeray, are capable of believing, but we can see—as do his characters—that this is because they are barred from the knowledge available to men. When, in fact, they are educated about the world, they rather quickly become threatening or villainous—like Becky, or Beatrix, or Blanche. Women are, or ought to be, the repository of feeling and purity, virtues men are too busy and practical to sustain, and they thus become a kind of escape, both for Pen and Thackeray. In women, they can indulge the sentimentality they cannot otherwise afford. For Pen, Laura becomes the substitute for the romance and ideals of his youth, in which he can no longer believe (she is, in fact, his mother's childhood gift to him, as Elizabeth is a gift to Victor Frankenstein). The "rescue" of Pen is only part of a narrative fantasy of the ideal that the full narrative does not endorse.

In creating himself in *Pendennis*, then, Thackeray is writing an ironic myth of a new kind of hero. Pen, of course, has the obligatory "mixed" nature of realistic protagonists. But he challenges, in his conception, not only the absurd excesses of romance and pastoral, but the ideals of domestic fiction itself. It goes almost without saying that "there are men better than he" (vol. 2, chap. 75). It follows that people distrust his marriage to Laura and have rather grim expectations of it. Innocuous as Pen may seem to be, Thackeray does recognize the morally dangerous implications of his way of life. We can understand more clearly where the danger lies if we see Pen as the first in a series of problematic figures in nineteenth-century narratives who acquire increasing importance through the century. Pen's combination of detachment, cynicism, laziness, self-indulgence, and aestheticism, along with his single real commitment to an almost ideal woman, is characteristic. Although they are all very different, such figures as Will Ladislaw, Ralph Touchett, and Martin Decoud can be seen as descendants of Pen. Each of them is a dilettante; each is importantly severed from his community and undefined. In their more or less ironic attentiveness to details of the life that moves past them, they see things differently and threateningly and like Pen tend to flow with the flow of experience, to be satisfied with the ironies and objects that life throws their way, except when they are attracted to women who might be seen as ideal.

But in mid-Victorian fiction it is surprising to find so detached, cynical, and compromised a figure as Pen so gently treated. One need think only of the immorality attributed to his cousins Henry Gowan in *Little Dorrit*, or Bertie Stanhope in *Barchester Towers*, to realize how subversive a conception Pen might be. Bertie and Henry are, after all, rather Pen-like figures seen from a more firmly moral perspective. Thackeray sees the potentialities of a Bertie in Pen but needs to judge him differently, for what might be thought of as a shameless laxity and selfishness might also be understood as a more honest and honorable way to deal with an experience that refuses to succumb to the ideal. Even Conrad has difficulty avoiding overt hostility to the dilettante figure, and his rhetoric about Decoud is contemptuous and angry. Thackeray, in keeping with his antidogmatism, is more merciful.

Pen's development as dilettante is connected with the novel's preoccupation with the problem of the presentation or re-presentation of feeling. The problem even becomes the central subject of a series of important dialogues between Thackeray's two surrogates—Pen and George Warrington. The novel is full of other people's writing, of real theatrical performances, and of the theatrics required by society. We have Blanche Amory's *Mes Larmes* and Pen's *Walter Lorraine*, and passionate and morally righteous editorials written in jail. We have the major's letters and performances. At the start we have the performances of the Fotheringay. Pen's second affair results from the performances of Blanche Amory. Amid all these performances, Pen must learn to distinguish good fictions from bad. Presumably, he must find also whatever direct, unmediated feeling may exist in his world, apparently located with Laura and Helen, who do not perform. Pen must learn to break through the layers of inauthentic, merely literary and social, representations of feeling. But the narrative as a whole ultimately makes it difficult to imagine that there is any such thing as unmediated feeling. Even Pen's most authentic passions seem to be shaped by literary conventions.

Pen's progress through the novel is marked by his developing capacity to distance or transform feeling through language. The major's brilliant early strategies lead the way, but Pen's first independent movement in that direction is not quite self-conscious. It comes early in the novel, after his affair with Emily is disrupted by the worldly-wise major. In a wonderful piece of false pastoral, Thackeray shows us a Pen already, if not quite consciously, acting the role of feeling. He fishes; he sits by a pond under a tree and com-

poses "a number of poems suitable in his circumstances—over which verses
he blushed in after days, wondering how he could ever have invented such
rubbish" (vol. 1, chap. 15). Here is an early example of the Thackerayan
narrator's refusal to allow the intensity of immediate experience to escape
the ironies of retrospect or worldly-wise distancing. The whole affair immediately becomes comedy. But this "rubbish" serves other purposes later.
He shows the poems to his contemporaries at college as a badge of his
manhood, and they all pronounce him a "tremendous fellow" (vol. 1, chap.
18). The tree under which the rubbish is written is invoked for future use.
"Under that very tree," the narrator warns us, Pen would shortly be carry-
ing on another love-correspondence with his second flame, Blanche. But he
does not say so, interrupting himself to note, "but we are advancing matters." All romance turns into slightly spurious literature.

More interestingly, the narrator treats Pen's writing of poetry as clear
evidence that he is already himself rather separate from the experience of love:

> Suffice it to say, he wrote poems and relieved himself very much.
> When a man's grief or passion is at this point, it may be loud,
> but it is not very severe. When a gentleman is cudgeling his brain
> to find any rhyme for sorrow, besides borrow and to-morrow,
> his woes are nearer at an end than he thinks for.
>
>                                            (Vol. 1, chap. 15)

The medium is itself a way to distance writer from feeling, and the primary
relation becomes not that between lover and beloved, but between lover and
poem. The writing of poetry is a kind of narcissism; the focus becomes the
writer's power to convince his audience and himself that he feels intensely
and loves deeply. When Pen achieves the sophistication of the narrator, he
will begin (as Thackeray's later novels testify) to write self-conscious and self-
deprecating novels that are insistently aware of the falsifications of language
and the vanity of writing. Both Thackeray and Pen know that writing is a
defense against what it purports to describe, or an ironic substitute for it.

In the debate between Pen and Warrington, the moral questions related
to these problems of writing are paramount. To write is to stand outside
of experience. Yet the moral energy of the Victorian tradition and Thackeray's
own sense of himself as moralist (manifested in some degree in Warrington)
require of the writer a fuller engagement than Pen could give. The narrator,
whose own detachment has been manifest, puts the question this way: "Which
is most reasonable, and does his duty best: he who stands aloof from the
struggle of life, calmly contemplating it, or he who descends to the ground
and takes his part in the contest?" (vol. 2, chap. 54). Thackeray's position

here is difficult to locate, for both Pen and Warrington speak with authority and, in all likelihood, for him. The writer must stand apart from the experience in order to write about it; yet the writer needs the experience before he *can* write about it. At one point, Warrington mocks Pen and poets in general, rather accurately describing the Pen we have just seen. "Poets," he says, "fall in love, jilt, or are jilted: they suffer and cry out that they suffer more than any other mortals: and when they have experienced feelings enough they note them down in a book" (vol. 2, chap. 41). At this stage, Pen wants to argue that poets can have more sensibility than most and still, like Shakespeare, write for money, but the question of the authenticity of the writer's experience will recur.

Later, convalescent from his illness after his affair with Fanny, Pen begins to transform that affair by subjecting it to distancing Thackerayan irony. The process already undergone with the Fotheringay now becomes more self-conscious: "He laughed at himself as he lay on his pillow, thinking of the second cure which has been effected upon him. He did not care the least about Fanny now: he wondered how he ever should have cared: and according to his custom made an autopsy of that dead passion, and anatomised his own defunct sensation for his poor little nurse" (vol. 2, chap. 57). Fanny becomes part of a usable past, a story to tell; ironically, it will be Warrington who tells it. For Warrington had led a Pen-like life until he married beneath his class, a Fanny-like girl, as Pen just escapes doing twice. In the inversions and doublings that mark Thackeray's unsystematic working out of his materials (Warrington himself says that "there was no one to save me as Major Pendennis saved Pen" [vol. 2, chap. 57]), Warrington is forced, because he is tied to an impossible wife, to choose the disengagement into which Pen drifts. Wishing not to be "out of the stream," Warrington can yet only *argue* for the value of being in it.

Warrington's story, as I have already suggested, reveals the other side of Pen's way of choosing: being "in the stream," acting on one's passions, is so dangerous that it can lead to a permanent paralysis. Pen survives because he is intrinsically less serious than Warrington and is therefore a quick pupil of the worldly major. Withdrawal from engagement—as Warrington's life dramatizes—leaves only the joys of vicarious feeling: Warrington eagerly tells Pen to go out and play the game. But Pen's sort of pleasure in the game derives from a kind of disenchanted detachment, a bemused and playful recognition that the actors make fools of themselves and that the stakes are really lower than they seem. The comic substance of the novel is in its indulgent play with the tokens—the dinners, the wines, the clothing, the titillations, the social maneuvering. For Warrington, however, even these things risk pain: "What was he about dancing attendance here? drinking in sweet pleasure at a risk he knows not of what after sadness, and regret, and lonely longing?" (vol. 2, chap. 56).

As the dialogues between Pen and Warrington suggest, Thackeray was divided about himself and about his art. In a late chapter he puts the divisions about dilettantish disengagement with clarity and force. Both characters speak in Thackeray's voice. Pen, in rejecting dogmatic belief, pleads for toleration, even of the decadent aristocrats Thackeray had so acerbically parodied earlier in his career and of the outmoded and narrow-minded institutions of the Church:

> "I would have toleration for these, as I would ask it for my own opinions; and if they are to die, I would rather they had a decent and natural than an abrupt and violent death. . . . I will not persecute. Make a faith or a dogma absolute, and persecution becomes a logical consequence. . . . Make dogma absolute, and to inflict or to suffer death becomes easy and necessary."
>
> (Vol. 2, chap. 61)

It is a conventional liberal argument, of course, but it is consistent with the thrust of Thackeray's realism. The ideal and the attempt to enact belief threaten a terrible violence. The narrative forms that embody the ideal, that enforce the demands of Number One, are violations of the very possibilities of human knowledge. Pen's politics and morality here seem to Warrington, as they would have seemed to many in Thackeray's audience, merely amoral. The profoundly skeptical realist vision moves inexorably in this direction, but Pen is articulating another sort of morality, an almost Arnoldian one of refusing action. It is akin to the conservative-reforming politics of George Eliot, the commitment to free expression of John Stuart Mill, the Victorian secular faith in the possibility of discovering the truth by reason, and averting premature action until then.

But the other Thackeray, as we find him in Warrington, has affinities with Carlyle, and to that very un-Arnoldian faith that the end of man is action. Warrington recognizes the difference between his enforced disengagement and Pen's deliberate choice of it. More important, he finds Pen's tolerance merely the reverse side of a radical skepticism:

> "A little while since, young one . . . you asked me why I remained out of the strife of the world, and looked on at the great labour of my neighbour without taking any part in the struggle. Why, what a mere *dilettante* you own yourself to be, in this confession of general scepticism, and what a listless spectator yourself! you are six-and-twenty years old, and as *blasé* as a rake of sixty.

> You neither hope much, nor care much, nor believe much. You
> doubt about other men as much as about yourself. Were it made
> of such *pococuranti* as you, the world would be intolerable; and
> I had rather live in a wilderness of monkeys and listen to their
> chatter, than in a company of men who denied everything."
>
> (Vol. 2, chap. 61)

Warrington not only urges engagement, but speaks in Carlyle's language,
reflecting Thackeray's early enthusiasm for Carlyle, and the conscience with
which he judged himself. His tirade here echoes the chapter "Gospel of Dilettantism" in *Past and Present*. For Carlyle, one of the marks of dilettantism
is "insincere speech," that is, speech that dissolves action rather than points
directly to it or precedes it. Carlyle's chapter concludes with a parable that
dramatizes the effect of such speech, the story of Moses and the dwellers
by the Dead Sea. These dwellers found "the whole universe now a most in-
disputable humbug," and they disregarded Moses's Heaven-sent words. The
result is that the dwellers were turned into apes, and "sit and chatter to this
hour." The wilderness of dilettantish monkeys Warrington prefers to the
world of men who deny everything is merely the true image of that world.
From Carlylean perspective, Pen's plea for tolerance is the refusal to
distinguish God's words from chatter. The problem is that in novels like
Thackeray's God's words are indistinguishable.

The whole dialogue (although like everything else in the novel, it is not
allowed to be as serious as the substance of it would seem to require) points
to the divisions not only in Thackeray's art, but in realism itself. The condition for writing novels, it would seem, is the condition of the disengaged
spectator. The moral price of Warrington's plea for authority, choice, and
engagement is, as we have seen, very heavy. Pen for his part, sees himself
only as a realist: "I do not condemn the men who killed Socrates and damned
Galileo, I say that they damned Galileo and killed Socrates" (vol. 2, chap.
61). Here is at least one Victorian writer whose ideal of truth turns out to
be at odds with Carlylean moral firmness; to Carlyle it would seem very much
like chattering. Yet when the narrator intrudes shortly after, he justifies the
presentation of Pen's amoral view obliquely, by writing in a very Pen-like
way. He will not endorse Pen's arguments, but in effect he uses them. He
is merely trying, he says, "to follow out in its progress the development of
the mind of a worldly and selfish, but not ungenerous or truth-avoiding man"
(vol. 2, chap. 61). As Thackeray knows, Pen might well have been consigned
to the chapter on the Dandaical Body in *Sartor Resartus*. The narrator,
however, pleads for tolerance of this "man and brother," a tolerance that
might be merely a disguise of not much caring.

But Pen cannot presume to judge since he does not presume to know, and it may be that the pain of discovering ignorance leads to a retreat from a dangerous caring. Like a young and cynical John Stuart Mill, Pen recognizes that all views are partial, but all views have a right to be presented. The function of his novel is then to record reality as truthfully as possible, incorporating as part of the reality the recognition of the limits of this possibility, and to withold firm unqualified judgments. Thackeray's attempts to resist, and through Warrington he does resist, the effects of what he ungenerously calls Pen's "general scepticism and sneering acquiescence." But the skepticism is ultimately endorsed by the very shape of the novel.

*Pendennis* seems to want to suggest that Pen's progress *is* a progress, that he grows and changes, so that his cynical arguments with Warrington are described as a "stage." But later on, the same narrator will argue that there are no real changes in character. In the midst of the argument with Warrington, the narrator intrudes in a very Warringtonian-Carlylean voice. He talks of Pen as being in a "lamentable stage." "To what," he asks, "does this scepticism lead?"

> It leads a man to a shameful loneliness and selfishness, so to speak—the more shameful, because it is so good-humoured and conscienceless and serene. Conscience! What is conscience? Why accept remorse? What is public or private faith? Mythuses alike enveloped in enormous tradition. If seeing and acknowledging the lies of the world, Arthur, as see them you can with only too fatal a clearness, you submit to them without any protest further than a laugh: if, plunged yourself in easy sensuality, you allow the whole wretched world to pass groaning by you unmoved: if the fight for the truth is taking place, and all men of honour are on the ground armed on the one side or the other, and you alone are to lie on your balcony and smoke your pipe out of the noise and the danger, you had better have died, or never have been at all, than such a sensual coward.
>
> (Vol. 2, chap. 61)

The rhetoric is inflated and uncharacteristic. It lacks the self-consciousness about rhetoric that Pen has been developing, and it is, finally, unconvincing: first, because Thackeray as satirist was precisely the figure who made no further protest than a laugh; second, because the act of writing is an act of withdrawal from any engagement but that of seeing clearly. Moreover, the growth of Pen beyond the position denounced here is dubious.

Indeed, even here, in answer to both Warrington and, one must presume, the narrator (the distinction breaks awkwardly down in the passage), Pen speaks with more authentic Thackerayan substance, if still in too inflated a style: "The truth, friend . . . where is the truth? Show it me?" The lesson of his own self-consciousness and of his own limitations is here: "I see the truth in that man, as I do in his brother, whose logic drives him to quite a different conclusion, and who, after having passed a life in vain endeavours to reconcile an irreconcilable book, flings it at last down in despair, and declares, with tearful eyes, and hands up to Heaven, his revolt and recantation. If the truth is with all these, why should I take side with any one of them." There is, of course, some casuistry here. But if Thackeray really (at least probably) agrees with Pen, he wants to break from the complications of knowledge to the authenticity of feeling. Pen's discovery of inauthenticity everywhere, of a world full of bad literature, has led him to this point. The very structure of the book, even to the point of the division implied by the two convincing protagonists, George and Pen, leaves Pen and Thackeray with no satisfying place to locate authenticity. If there be authentic feeling in the book and not merely literary and dramatic constructions, it is among the losers, and it can be destructive. Mr. Bows, like the gruffer and more important Warrington, loves and longs for love, moves through the novel with a sad integrity and is betrayed by both Emily and Fanny. He makes a private music to sustain him. Like Warrington he is excluded from the "stream," and as a result he is not so much compromised as defeated. He cannot turn his feelings into a public art, except as he teaches Emily Costigan to mime it. Yet Pen manages to create a successful art (though not, on the narrator's account, very good art) because the authentic feelings he had are transformed into the materials of his writing and in the very act of transforming them, he enacts their absence.

Still the narrator writes as though authentic feeling were somewhere to be found, and his strongest hostility is consequently reserved for Blanche, the purest feigner: "For this young lady was not able to carry out any emotion to the full; but had a sham enthusiasm, a sham hatred, a sham love, a sham taste, a sham grief, each of which flared and shone very vehemently for an instant, but subsided and gave place to the next sham emotion" (vol. 2, chap. 73). Thackeray's hostility to Blanche implies a longing for the feeling he cannot represent. The quest for the authenticity of feeling that will justify the engagement Warrington insists on (but cannot himself undertake) is almost universally frustrated in the book. Its negative structure short-circuits every action that has claims to authenticity, as well as many that do not. Pen does not marry Emily or Blanche; Bows does not marry Emily or Fanny; Warrington does not marry Laura; Pen's mother does not marry the man she loves. Finally, despite the narrator's insistence that Pen, in his moral paralysis, is going through a stage, Pen does not really change either. The

narrator makes a point of pausing to remind us, with a *vanitas vanitatum*,
that we are always what we were, but older (vol. 2, chap. 59).

In Pen, at least, this is confirmed, for his general skepticism remains
with him until the end. There is, for example, his well-known excursus
on "But":

> "But will come in spite of us. But is reflection. But is the scep-
> tic's familiar, with whom he has made a compact; and if he forgets
> it, and indulges in happy day-dreams, or building of air-castles,
> or listens to sweet music let us say, or to the bells ringing to church,
> But taps at the door and says, Master, I am here. You are my
> master; but I am yours. Go where you will you can't travel without
> me. I will whisper to you when you are on your knees at church.
> I will be at your marriage pillow. I will sit down at your table
> with your children. I will be behind your death-bed curtain. That
> is what But is," Pen said.
> "Pen, you frighten me," cried Laura.
>
> (Vol. 2, chap. 71)

"But" is a monster that will be with Pen on his wedding night, and it is the
monster that pervades this book of compromises and retreats. Pen's vision
has taken him through the traditional forms of representation, has allowed
him to become a successful writer, and to marry the rare "ideal" figure in
the novel. But "But" persists, and undercuts the ideal in the act of marriage
and, we presume, of love. For Pen it is a saving But. For Laura it is under-
standably frightening. For Thackeray, it is a burden he could not shake.

Pen survives his dilettantism without the sort of banishment and alienation that characterizes the dilettante figure in much later fiction. He neither
learns to work hard and reject the clever superficiality of his earlier days,
as we are to believe Will Ladislaw does in *Middlemarch*, nor allows his
cynicism to become suicidal, as it does for Decoud. Like Will, he is apparently
redeemed by the idealist woman he loves. His cynicism and his sentimentality exist side by side (as they apparently did for Thackeray himself), and he
accepts the limits of the world because, despite his self-consciousness about
the absurdity of it all, he enjoys it. Thackeray, finally, though he gives Pen
a certain integrity, never quite allows him to be serious enough either to feel
the full bitterness of his acquiescence (as Warrington has expressed it in his
invocation of the wilderness of monkeys) or to attempt to impose some kind
of ideal meaning on experience. His strategy is the strategy of toleration.

The more intense issues of Pen's life are carefully disguised by the narrative, which sticks with remarkable consistency to the rambling diffuseness,
deflation, and density of particulars that characterize the realistic mode.

The episode with Fanny, for example, might have provided the materials for naturalistic treatment, and the critical illness that Thackeray allows Pen (echoing, as we know, the critical illness into which he fell while writing the novel) suggests the intensity of the issue and the eagerness with which Thackeray wanted to avert its extreme implications. During the illness, . . . Pendennis loses the power to make determining choices. His decision to avoid Fanny, which provokes the illness, makes little difference until Helen and Fanny finally battle it out.

   The novel is even more devious in avoiding extremes in the sequence relating to Helen's banishment of Fanny, for there Pen comes as close as he is allowed to do to the sources of his anger. The loving Helen, sentimentalized down to her last breath, is shown to be dangerously protective and exclusive, as idealists must be in Thackeray's compromised world. Pen's hostility can have no outlet, but when it is about to explode, Laura warns him that the confrontation he seeks with his mother will kill her. The book does not make much of it, and of course she dies in a new loving embrace with Pen; but beneath the sentiment and the respectability there is an intense and violent hostility. Neither Pen nor the narrative can find a place for so aggressively loving a figure. In effect, Pen does kill her, but in doing so he repurchases his past and cloaks and distances the intensities he could not entirely avert.

   It is worth reminding ourselves that *Pendennis* was written in the midst of Thackeray's deep and thwarted love of Jane Brookfield. His relation to her may remind us of that of Warrington to Laura, but in any case he could not fully confront the feeling either in life or in the novel. The expression of the feeling would be the occasion of its death, and Thackeray could not have escaped recognizing the ironies implicit in his passion though, certainly, he did not want to subject it to irony. As John Dodds remarks about Thackeray's later letters to Jane, he wrote "as if he were maintaining at some cost the rather delicate poise of his ecstasy and were fearful lest the dream be broken." *Pendennis* might be taken as a means to preserve the dream. The heart-whole Warrington survives the heartbreak: our self-conscious narrator reminds us that the "malady is never fatal to a sound organ." And the not quite deserving Pen, the more completely autobiographical figure, gets the woman. In his precarious teetering between romance and cynicism, Pen thus embodies for Thackeray the nostalgia that sustains and protects the dream while never threatening it with engagement.

   He can be allowed the victory, precisely because he does not quite care enough. He is in the middling dilettantish state that newly embodies the realist's compromise—the quietly dishonest assumption that the real world is not rife with extremes as the norm leads directly to *Pendennis*, for Pen's education seems to teach him, first, that nobody ever dies of heartbreak; second, that taking oneself seriously is always at least mildly absurd; third, that everyone is out for number one—except Laura (while Thackeray knows that she is, too). He learns, too, that the world does not really make much sense and is entirely unmalleable under the pressures of dreams or desires, but that there is no necessity, simply because it is unjust, not to take pleasure in what is.

The self-consciousness and disenchantment that we see growing in Pen, in a novel full of realism's surfaces, digressions, and compromises, grow more and more deadly to Thackeray's art as Pen takes greater control of it. The mask of the prematurely old and thwarted wise man who prefers the memory of passion to passion itself, and thus can enjoy retrospectively the risks and the ludicrousness, will increasingly dismantle narrative. Though this reflects Thackeray's idiosyncratic preoccupation with the thwarting and the necessity of passion, it is also absolutely right for the mode of realism, a form in which time, not human choice, is likely to be decisive, in which all things clamor for their significance and, thus, in which anything can be a subject and must be deflated as a consequence.

If we think of Victorian realism as an exuberant clearing of the house of fiction of its absurdities and obsolete conventions in the interests of a clear-eyed and forceful assertion of the truth, we must remember how much it is also a literature of compromise. Its characteristic mortality is implicit not so much in Dickensian exposures of the violence and brutality of which our society is capable, as in a George Eliot-like dissolution of easy moral categories, a recognition of our own ordinary and compromised natures, a toleration of the failures and fallings-away of others. From what seemed to be a scathing and cynical judge of mankind's cruelty and pretensions, Thackeray becomes a saddened man who is content to observe others fail as he has done and finds his pleasures in the variousness and disorder of experience. The characteristic tone toward which we see young Pen moving is registered in a letter of Thackeray's quoted by John Dodds:

> As I go this journey, I remember other thoughts scattered along the journey 3 years ago: and griefs which used to make me wild and fierce, and which are now sweet and bearable. We get out of the stormy region of longing passion unfulfilled—we don't love any the less—please God—let the young folks step in and play the game of tears and hearts. We have played our game: and we have lost. And at 45 we smoke our pipes and clear the drawing room for the sports of the young ones.

This is the novel Thackeray wrote for himself. The protection of his dream of passion is the comfort of knowing that it is too late to fight for it. He makes himself the novelist of memory.

RICHARD W. ORAM

# "Just a Little Turn of the Circle": Time, Memory, and Repetition in Thackeray's Roundabout Papers

When he chose the title of *Roundabout Papers* for his familiar essays in the *Cornhill Magazine*, Thackeray humorously called attention to their looseness and informality. Perhaps because they do appear to be so artless, the Roundabouts (1860–63) have been virtually ignored by critics, who, if they make note of them at all, are usually content to praise their easy charm. Yet even the title of the series is less straightforward than it seems; almost certainly it alludes to Thackeray's cherished belief that time is "roundabout" or cyclical in shape. The novelist whose subject is "everybody's past" (G. K. Chesterton, *The Victorian Age in Literature*) turns out to be an important essayist of memory as well, and one worthy of being compared with Lamb. In general, those Roundabouts which are reminiscential or which expound Thackeray's philosophy of time are the best of an admittedly uneven series. Taken together, "Tunbridge Toys," "De Juventute," "On Some Carp at Sans Souci," and "De Finibus" constitute an autobiographical document of considerable psychological interest. Although these papers are often amusing, their purpose is the essentially serious one of other nineteenth-century autobiographies, which, according to Jerome Buckley, set out "to place the changeful self in the perspective of its origins and accordingly to realize a sense of stability in a turning world, and at best, the imperturbable strength of acceptance."

Thackeray's notion of the shape of time is movingly set forth in a letter of condolence he sent from his sickbed to a childhood friend, J. F. Boyes,

From *Studies in the Novel* 13, nos. 1/2 (Spring/Summer 1981). © 1981 by North Texas State University.

in March 1861. Thackeray writes of being stirred by the sight of some old schoolbooks in Boyes's house: "What a turn it gave me, when I went to see you, to recognize the old books. Thalaba, Martyr of Antioch and so on!— Those recollections were not dead, only sleeping—and so, pray God, nothing dies love least of all. . . . So we all hold on by love to the past, and by just a little turn of the circle, it becomes the future." In a postscript, he asserts that "the have been is eternal as well as the will be. We are not only elderly men, but young men, boys, children." Self-conscious as always, he realizes that he is trying to console himself as much as Boyes: "looking at this paper thinks I—it is all about myself and not about my old friends." Similarly, in the most personal Roundabouts Thackeray is really addressing himself; Lady Ritchie remarks that the *Roundabout Papers* "might serve for a diary" of her father's last years. These essays hold out the same message of hope contained in the letter to Boyes. As if to convince himself that time doubles back on itself—that all endings are also beginnings, in short—Thackeray dwells on recurrences, repetitions, and moments of double vision.

The writing of autobiography is often a therapeutic exercise, and by 1860, Thackeray was very much in need of the spiritual comfort that several of the Roundabouts supply. His health had been steadily deteriorating for some years; as far back as 1853, he confessed, "I don't think my course is to be a long one." Despite his elation over the success of the *Cornhill* (which meant that he had won a measure of financial security for his daughters), Thackeray was troubled by spells of depression and the feeling that he was "written out." This Thackerayan world-weariness is readily apparent in the uncharacteristically somber *Roundabout Paper* "On Letts's Diary" (January 1862). Like Lamb's "New Year's Day," the piece is a meditation on death occasioned by the arrival of a new year, although "Letts's Diary" lacks the optimistic conclusion of the Elia essay. The tone of Thackeray's rejoinder to the usual "holiday paper" is announced in the title, which contains a morbid pun that is explicated in the text ("A diary, Dies To die"). Mr. Roundabout, who is one of Thackeray's thinnest personae, reminds us that inexorable time takes away our friends, relatives, and rulers (the Prince Consort died just as "Letts's Diary" went to press). For once, he finds that reminiscence is an unsatisfactory anodyne for his pain. A reading of his 1861 diary briefly brings to mind a few happy dinners, but it mainly recalls the "agonies" Mr. Roundabout suffered when his guests sneered and the cook ruined the main course. Revisiting the "days marked with sadness" results in the renewal of suffering and brings little compensatory understanding. And so Mr. Roundabout is left with an acute premonition of his own mortality: "Quick, children, and sit at my feet: for they are cold: and it seems as if neither wine nor worsted will warm 'em."

"On Letts's Diary" seems to illustrate John Carey's contention that "[Thackeray] saw time as a destroyer. As ripener, or renewer, he scarcely gave it a glance." But even here, in his most melancholy frame of mind, Thackeray is aware that time can be both destroyer and creator. Although the 1861 diary is closed, a new one is opened, "and in our '62 diaries, I fear we may all of us make some the '61 entries." Thackeray is particularly sensitive to the seasonal rhythms, repetitions, and continuities which give shape to everybody's life: "Well, year after year the season comes. Come frost, come thaw, come snow, come rain, year after year my neighbour the parson has to make his sermon." Another excellent example of what Jean Sudrann has called Thackeray's "Janus-faced" view of time may be found in his holiday paper for 1861, "Round About the Christmas Tree." Mr. Roundabout moralizes on time, the great devourer of Christmas ornaments and toys; "Yet but a few days," he tells his young friend Bob, "and flakes of paint will have cracked off the fairy flower-bowers, and the revolving temples of adamantine lustre will be as shabby as the city of Pekin." Nonetheless, another cycle of seasons will soon begin again: "To-morrow the diffugient snows will give place to Spring; . . . trees will have an eruption of light green knobs; the whitebait season will bloom."

In other *Roundabout Papers*, Thackeray moves away from the gloom of "Letts's Diary" and toward a greater acceptance of our life in time. He reminds himself that while the time-conscious man is condemned to suffer from the knowledge of his own mortality, the contemplation of the past leads to the recognition that "nothing dies love least of all." In "On Some Carp at Sans Souci," one of the later Roundabouts, Thackeray explores what it would be like to live without a consciousness of duration, and hence without memory. He concludes that such an existence would be devoid of meaning. "On Some Carp" develops a favorite Thackerayan theme—the difficulty of knowing much about the inner life of other people—by focusing on Mr. Roundabout's conversation with Goody Two-Shoes, a nonagenarian from a London workhouse who has been invited to share a Christmas meal. Intrigued by her extreme old age, Mr. Roundabout questions her about the historical events she has witnessed. After bombarding her with names, dates, and figures, he finally breaks down in exasperation at her ignorance of history: "'What a wretched memory you have! What? haven't they a library, and the commonest books of reference at the old convent of Saint Lazarus, where you dwell?'" Goody merely responds with a blank look, a "'Ho! ho!' and a laugh like an old parrot," making his presumption look foolish.

Mr. Roundabout has failed to perceive that his personal perspective on time is utterly different from hers. Like Henry Esmond, he feels a compelling need to measure his experience with reference to historical events, whereas

Goody has never heard of *Wade's Chronology*. Mr. Roundabout, therefore, apprehends an immense gulf between himself and one whose existence has been as nasty, brutish, and long as that of the carp at Frederick the Great's Sans Souci: "Oh! what has been thy long life, old Goody, but a dole of bread and water and a perch on a cage; a dreary swim round and round a Lethe of a pond?" Because she exists in an eternal present, without consciousness of time's passage, she by implication lacks the consolations of memory (i.e., she lives in a "Lethe"). Mr. Roundabout asks his reader to put himself in her place: "would you like to have a remembrance of better early days, when you were young, and happy, and loving, perhaps; or would you prefer to have no past on which your mind could rest?" The question does not need to be answered directly, for we already know that Goody "lies awake a deal of the night, to be sure, not thinking of happy old times, for hers never were happy."

As Thackeray notes at the essay's conclusion, both he and Goody Two-Shoes share the common human burden of Care. While the old woman must face each day with a memory that is a *tabula rasa*, he finds solace and gives his life meaning by remembering. Near the end of "On Some Carp," he describes a profoundly affecting moment of recollection that convinces him that nothing is lost forever (*"non omnis moritur*," he insists elsewhere in the essay): "Yesterday, in the street, I saw a pair of eyes so like two which used to brighten at my coming once, that the whole past came back as I walked lonely, in the rush of the Strand, and I was young again in the midst of joys and sorrows, alike sweet and sad, alike sacred, and fondly remembered."

The *Roundabout Papers* are rich in these remarkable moments of double vision in which the past is not so much remembered as recaptured whole. Not surprisingly, then, the adjective "Proustian" is almost automatically invoked in critical discussions of Thackeray's "reminiscential vision." Rather than look forward to Proust, however, I prefer to stay within a nineteenth-century context by examining Wordsworth's influence on Thackeray's religion of memory. Though he found the poet's later works tedious (apparently he never read *The Prelude*), we know that the Immortality Ode was a special favorite of his. In an 1840 essay on Cruikshank, written when the author was depressed by his wife's illness and the progress of his career, Thackeray complains that he, like Wordsworth's child, feels the "vision splendid" of youth dying "into the light of common day." He sees himself as "wandering farther and farther from the beauty and freshness and from the kindly gushing springs of clear gladness that made all around us green in our youth." So Wordsworth had helped him, at thirty years of age, to articulate his sense of loss resulting from the passage of time. Presumably the last stanza of the "Immortality Ode" also permitted him to arrive at a solution to the philosophical problem he poses by reminding him that time gives back while it takes away and that "the thought of our past years . . . doth breed / Perpetual benediction."

"Tunbridge Toys" and "De Juventute" are the most Wordsworthian of the Roundabout essays because their principal subject is the persistence of the child in the man. In other words, as Thackeray wrote to Boyes a few months after finishing the pieces, "we are not only elderly men but young men, boys, children." There is some evidence that Thackeray felt obliged to reiterate that wisdom over and over because he did not entirely believe it. In her study of *Lovel the Widower* (1860), Ina Ferris argues that Thackeray projects some of his personal anxieties onto the novel's neurotic narrator, Mr. Batchelor. "Whereas memory discovered for Henry Esmond an order informing the discrete moments of his existence, so enabling him to affirm a continuous realization of the self," she observes, "Batchelor's memory reflects his own fragmentation." Although traces of Batchelor's self-doubts appear in the autobiographical Roundabouts, Thackeray manages to purge them and reasserts the continuity of the self over time.

The bittersweet essay "Tunbridge Toys" begins with the author's meditation on a silver pencil-case with a movable almanac which, as he notes with characteristic chronological precision, he bought from a schoolmate "in the month of June, thirty-seven years ago." Thackeray purchased it on credit and suffered "agonies" thereafter at being in debt for three-and-six. Later, his tutor gave him a sum to be refunded to his parents and a little spending money for himself, which enabled him to pay off the obligation. Left without money of his own for breakfast, Thackeray dipped into his parents' twenty-five shillings (but only after much soul-searching) and extracted four pence for food before he boarded the coach that would take him home for vacation.

There is a considerable amount of psychological perception in his account of this trivial affair. For one thing, Thackeray has a relativist's insight into the importance of the small torments of childhood. In his autobiographical essay "Such, Such Were the Joys," George Orwell asks his reader to "Look back into your own childhood and think of the nonsense you used to believe and the trivialities which could make you suffer." Moreover, Thackeray carefully observes how certain sensory impressions linked with moments of stress imbed themselves in the memory; he distinctly remembers the flavor of the "peculiar, muddy, not-sweet-enough, most fragrant coffee." The whole experience lingers on in the mind so vividly that he begins to relive rather than remember and almost unconsciously switches into the present tense ("I am very hungry . . . I pace the street . . . I turn into a court"). Even though the twelve-year-old's guilty feelings choked him all the way home, the painful experience has been transformed into something intensely valuable for the adult. Significantly, Thackeray ends his anecdote with his return home and his happy reintegration into the family: "I had confessed; I had been a prodigal; I had been taken back to my parents' arms again." The effect of the recollection, like the "maternal joy and caresses" which awaited him, is both reassuring and restorative.

In "De Juventute," the companion piece to "Tunbridge Toys," a trivial object—in this case, the coin with George IV on it depicted in the pictorial capital—once more triggers a flood of recollections. Mr. Roundabout is certain that any middle-aged reader can easily "conjure back his life" by gazing at the old coin. That very day, he had come across a schoolmate he had not seen in thirty years, yet boyhood days still seemed as close as ever: "[His] smile was just as broad, as bright, as jolly, as I remember it in the past— unforgotten, though not seen or thought of, for how many decades of years, and quite and instantly familiar, though so long out of sight." The central section of the essay, however, calls the immanence of the past into some question. Thackeray's themes are familiar Victorian ones: the accelerating rate of change and the enormous gap between the modern and "praerailroad" worlds. Luxuriating in the role of old fogy, Mr. Roundabout amusingly sums up the changes of three decades by pointing to the deplorable decline in the talents of actresses and opera singers since the days of Taglioni. His sense of being whisked away into the future gives rise to a brief crisis. For a moment, the continuity between the Thackeray of 1861 and his youthful self breaks down: "The vision has disappeared off the silver, the images of youth and the past are vanishing away. . . . It was only yesterday; but what a gulph between now and then!" We are reminded of Elia's exclamation in "New Year's Eve": "God help thee Elia, how art thou changed!" Thackeray's chronicle of the radical changes in English society and literature ends with a series of *ubi-sunts* ("Where are they now, those sealing-wax vendors?"). But in the last paragraph of "De Juventute" the gulf between past and present closes. Thackeray's sudden flash of insight makes time cycle back on itself:

> In the midst of a great peace and calm, the stars look out from the heavens. The silence is peopled with the past; sorrowful remorses for sins and shortcomings—memories of passionate joys and griefs rise out of their graves, both now alike calm and sad. Eyes, as I shut mine, look at me, that have long ceased to shine. . . . Here is night and rest. An awful sense of thanks makes the heart swell, and the head bow, as I pass to my room through the sleeping house, and feel as though a hushed blessing were upon it.

The pattern of the essay is itself circular; Thackeray's initial confidence that the past is always accessible has not only been restored but reinforced by the end of the piece.

The moment when the dead past is suddenly transformed into immediate experience in "De Juventute" is comparable to Wordsworth's "recollected hours that have the charm / Of visionary things" (*Prelude*, 1.632–33); in fact, the experience described in the essay's lyrical conclusion is a variety of what M. H. Abrams has called "the modern Moment," which is "frequently connected with the concept of freshness of sensation as well as with the discovery of the charismatic virtue of a trivial object or event, and [which] is expounded both in secular and religious frames of reference." Like Wordsworth, Thackeray often draws an explicit analogy between religion and remembrance. The epiphanies that conclude "De Juventute" and "Tunbridge Toys," for example, take place in a churchlike atmosphere of "great peace and calm" allowing the author to achieve an ideal state of wise passiveness. Remembrance becomes as spiritually uplifting as prayer and gives one "an awful sense of thanks." The religious language immediately brings to mind Esmond's famous comparison of the "flash of self-consciousness," when what is dead revives once more, and the resurrection of the soul. It has not been sufficiently stressed, I think, that Thackeray's construction of a secular faith offering salvation from within (i.e., through imaginative recollection) is a characteristically Romantic endeavor. Furthermore, Thackeray's affinities with the Romantic generation become even clearer if we recall that "all process, Romantic thinkers believed, moves forward and also rounds back (M. H. Abrams, *Natural Supernaturalism: Tradition and Revolution in Romantic Literature*)."

If time is indeed cyclical, then every ending is a beginning as well. This is the lesson of "De Finibus," Thackeray's inquiry into the meaning of his art. "De Finibus" is arguably the finest of the *Roundabout Papers* (it is also one of the longest) because it superbly displays a mind in dialogue with itself. Thackeray speaks with startling candor of his deepest temporal and artistic anxieties; he talks out his self-doubts and is thereby able to come to terms with them. Thackeray gradually moves toward an understanding of the redemptive powers of memory and the imagination. Thus the essay is an essential text for anyone who wishes to understand the Thackerayan turn of mind.

"De Finibus" was begun on the evening of July 3 1862, immediately after Thackeray completed *Philip*. When his thoughts turned to the philosophical significance of endings in works of literature, he must have recalled the last of the *Idler* essays, in which Dr. Johnson observes that "There are few things not purely evil, of which we can say, without some emotion of uneasiness, 'this is the last.' . . . This sacred horrour of the last is inseparable from a thinking being whose life is limited, and to whom death is dreadful." It happens that Thackeray opens "De Finibus" with a reference to Johnson's superstitious habit of touching every post—he even went back to touch those he missed—in Pall Mall. Thackeray himself admits that he is afflicted with a related "mania" (in ohter words, a fear of discontinuity):

> As soon as a piece of work is out of hand, and before going to sleep, I like to begin another: it may be to write only half a dozen lines: but that is something towards Number the Next. The printer's boy has not reached Green Arbour Court with the copy. Those people who were alive half an hour since, Pendennis, Clive Newcome, and (what do you call him? what was the name of the last hero? I remember now!) Philip Firmin have hardly drunk their glass of wine, and the mammas have only this minute got the children's cloaks on, and have been bowed out of my premises— and here I come back to the study again: *tamen usque recurro*.

Thackeray offers his distaste for partings as a rejoinder to critics who wonder why he is always repeating himself by "asking us to meet those Pendennises, Newcomes, and so forth." However much his characters have pestered him at odd hours during the composition of a novel, their creator is reluctant to let them go. The opening section of "De Finibus" concludes with a note of sadness, as Thackeray mourns the final departure of Philip Firmin, whom "the printer came and took . . . away with the last page of the proofs." For a moment, he imagines that he sees the "gray shade" of Philip, but the dark figure that enters his study at twilight is only his servant John.

    Knowing that he is near the "finis" of his own life, Thackeray attempts to assess the value of his books and "this story-telling business." in general. "De Finibus" dramatizes his ambivalence about being an artist. He grumbles that he has been plagued by a balky muse and even wonders if "novel-writers [are] at all entitled to strait-waistcoats." On the other hand, he acknowledges that literature is valuable insofar as it soothes and entertains. Therefore, it is entirely appropriate that Thackeray turns to literature for consolation. The second section of the essay (following the break in the text) opens with an allusion to one of his favorite pieces of German poetry—the "Dedication" to Goethe's *Faust*. Returning to complete his drama after many years, Goethe speaks sadly of the loss of former friends and readers. First remembrance brings pain ("Der Schmerz wird neu") before it finally permits one to achieve a quasi-mystical union with the past. In his trancelike state, writes Goethe, "Was ich besitze, seh ich wie im Weiten, / Und was verschwand, wird mir zu Wirklichkeiten" ("The dear shadows rise up around him, he says; he lives in the past again. It is to-day which appears vague and visionary" in Thackeray's paraphrase). The poem acts as a timely utterance at this point in the essay and helps allay Thackeray's fears about the finality of "finis." Goethe's assertion that the memory can make the past as real as the present obviously accords well with Thackeray's conception of time as circular.

Though the novelist is primarily an entertainer, he is sometimes a seer as well. In order to illustrate his own prognosticative powers, Thackeray tells an anecdote that demonstrates time's circularity. Long after *Pendennis* was finished, he had an encounter with a man in a pub who bore "the most remarkable resemblance" to the character of Captain Costigan: "Nothing shall convince me that I have not seen that man in the world of spirits. . . . I had had had cognizance of him before somehow. Who has not felt that little shock which arises when a person, a place, some words in a book (there is always a collocation) present themselves to you, and you know that you have before met the same person, words, scenes, and so forth?" The modern reader realizes at once that Thackeray is describing an experience of *déjà vu*, one of those instants when time appears to double back on itself. Moreover, Costigan's resurrection reminds Thackeray that fictional characters never really die; they live on in the imagination after the last page of the book has been turned. And so Phillip Firmin is as alive as Mignon, Ivanhoe, and Leatherstocking. Once more, Thackeray discovers that the imagination provides an escape from the horror of "finis."

Captain Costigan's reappearance "in the world of spirits" and numerous other references to psychic phenomena in the *Roundabout Papers* testify to Thackeray's interest in the spiritualist controversies of the 1850s and 1860s. Although this topic has unaccountably been ignored by his biographers, Katherine H. Porter devotes a brief chapter of her study of spiritualism in the Browning circle to Thackeray. Aptly characterizing him as a "puzzled onlooker," Porter documents his participation in several séances; on one occasion, the table-rapping of D. D. Home was so convincing that Thackeray was distraught for several days afterward (Through a Glass Darkly: Spiritualism in the Browning Circle). For the most part, however, he treats spiritualism facetiously in the Roundabouts. In the burlesque "Notch on the Axe," for example, a perplexed narrator is involved in all sorts of preposterous events after he meets the mysterious Mr. Pinto, who fought at the Coliseum and participated (in various incarnations) in two thousand years of history. "Dessein's" concerns Thackeray's chat with the ghosts of Laurence Sterne and Beau Brummel. But in "Notes of a Week's Holiday," he half-seriously develops an analogy between spirit-travel and his sense of living in two ages at once:

A man can be alive in 1860 and 1830 at the same time, don't you see? Bodily, I may be in 1860, inert, silent, torpid; but in the spirit I am walking about in 1828, let us say. . . . Have you read Mr. Dale Owen's *Footsteps on the Confines of Another World*?—(My dear sir, it will make your hair stand quite refreshingly on end.) In that work you will read that when gentleman's or ladies' spirits travel off a few score or thousand miles to visit a friend, their bodies lie quiet and in a torpid state in their beds or in their arm-chairs at home. So, in this way, I am absent. My soul whisks away thirty years back into the past.

It is easy to see why Thackeray at least toyed with believing that spirits can return from the beyond. Reincarnation and metempsychosis, after all, are entirely consonant with his conviction that all things recur over time.

In any event, Thackeray's skepticism made it difficult for him to accept unquestioningly either the hope of a second existence in the spirit-world or the Christian promise of immortality. Troubled by the realities of loss and change, he finds that memory and the imaginative faculties can make time turn back on itself; in sum, "nothing dies love least of all." Thackeray rediscovers the truth of that maxim in the last paragraph of "De Finibus." A "rereading" of one's past at first leads to ennui and finally to philosophic acceptance: "Oh, the sad old pages, the dull old pages! Oh, the cares, the *ennui*, the squabbles, the repetitions, the old conversations over and over again! But now and again a kind thought is recalled, and now and again a dear memory. Yet a few chapters more, and the last: after which, behold Finis itself come to an end, and the Infinite begun." Thackeray's decision to finish an essay on endings with the word "begun" was an inspired one; he leaves us with the suggestions that every exit is an entrance somewhere else.

J.  HILLIS  MILLER

# Henry Esmond:
## *Repetition and Irony*

Thackeray's *Henry Esmond* is such an intricate tissue of repetitions and repetitions within repetitions that it can illustrate most of the modes of repetition in realistic fiction. It is also an admirable illustration of a certain self-unraveling intrinsic to the use of repetition in a novel as a means of affirming meaning and of affirming the author's authority. One tropological name for this unraveling of meaning is "irony," the trope without *logos. Henry Esmond* is a masterwork of Victorian irony, or of irony as such.

How can the reader thread his way among the different forms of repetition in this novel? What governs them or organizes them into a single web with a presiding figure? *Henry Esmond* repeats in displaced form certain configurations of person and event in Thackeray's own life, his relations to his family, to Mrs. Brookfield. The novel is a way of working through that real life by a detour through a fiction which obscurely repeats it. Moreover, as Stephen Bann, in one of the best essays on *Henry Esmond*, has said, the novel repeats with a difference the conventions of eighteenth- and nineteenth-century fiction: Fielding's *Tom Jones,* Scott's *Quentin Durward*, or Dickens's *Oliver Twist. Henry Esmond* plays ironically against those conventions, especially against the conventions of one familiar English form of the bildungsroman, the story of the orphan or illegitimate child who learns about the world, discovers his parents, comes into his inheritance, and lives happily ever after.

*Henry Esmond*, in addition, is a "historical novel." It repeats in a fictional narration certain historical personages and events from the eighteenth

From *Fiction and Repetition: Seven English Novels.* © 1982 by J. Hillis Miller. Harvard University Press, 1982.

century: Addison, Steele, Marlborough, the failure of the Pretender to take
the throne, and so on. The novel in its first publication was a cunning replica
of an eighteenth-century memoir, with an epigraph in Latin, an epistle
dedicatory, and an elaborate title page. The style of Henry Esmond's "history
. . . written by himself" imitates eighteenth-century syntax and vocabulary,
as well as (in the first edition) spelling and typography, though not with entire consistency, as other critics have noted. Thackeray's own somewhat ugly
face continually peeps through the mask.

One of the primary pleasures of reading Thackeray is purely stylistic.
This pleasure is one of the effects of irony. It arises from the reader's sense
of a constant slight discrepancy between "Thackeray himself" and the voice
or tone he has momentarily adopted: Pendennis, Esmond, or the all-knowing
narrator of *Vanity Fair*. One evidence for this, and one of the greatest
"pleasures of the text" in *Henry Esmond*, is the subtle and unostentatious
way in which motifs, once introduced—the color red, for example, or Diana,
the moon—recur, cunningly woven into passages which remain, from Henry's
point of view, seemingly no more than accurate descriptions of what was
there to be seen. These repetitions reveal the presence of Thackeray himself,
the artificer who has made it all. "Thackeray himself," in fact, insofar as
the reader can know him in his writing, is this need to be himself by writing
himself as someone else. This means a failure ever to be unequivocally
"himself," since he remains always in expressions of himself in his writing
an imaginary someone else.

*Henry Esmond* in itself, putting aside its relation to Thackeray, is one
of the greatest of English novels of improvised or imaginary memory.
Thackeray imagines a character and then imagines a complete memory for
him. This memory has that structure of intensities and dimnesses, of inclu-
sions and hiatuses, which is characteristic, it may be, of some "real memories."
Within *Henry Esmond*, Henry, the first person "I" writing his memoirs in
his old age in Virginia, repeats his youthful self, displacing it and bringing
it close at the same time, by writing of that earlier self in the third person,
as a "he." That writing contains a repertoire of the forms of repetition
characteristic of realistic fiction, repetitions within the fiction and repetitions
by the fiction of things and texts outside. Of the former, the most striking
is the repetition by Henry of his love for Rachel in his love of Rachel's daughter
Beatrix. The novel joins Gérard de Nerval's *Sylvie*, Brontë's *Wuthering
Heights*, Hardy's *The Well-Beloved*, and Proust's *A la recherche du temps
perdu* in dramatizing a love which is passed from one generation to the next,
or from one replica to the next, multiplying its strength in the repetitions.
In all these novels, this dramatization is reinforced by a complex tissue of
recurring motifs and scenes within the text. Images of portraits, of light, of

sun and moon, of eyes, stars, jewels, and tapers, of red, the color of blood, recur throughout. Episode echoes episode. The meaning develops through these repetitions. In addition, *Henry Esmond*, like *The Well-Beloved* and like the other novels in this chain, is punctuated by allusions to previous texts—Biblical, classical, and vernacular. Henry's story repeats a long sequence of similar stories going back to antiquity and to the legendary prehistory of man. *The History of Henry Esmond, Esq.* incorporates or repeats the histories of Hamlet; of Oedipus and Aeneas; of Diana and Niobe; of Rachel, Jacob and Esau.

All these elements are the given materials for interpreting *Henry Esmond*. Most readers would agree that these modes of repetition are there in the novel, would agree more or less on what they are, and would agree that they offer important data for any reading of the novel. The disagreements would come at a higher level, at the level of the attempt to make a definite interpretation. . . . The basic problem in understanding any repetitive series is to identify its basis, its ground, the law it exemplifies. What is the center which controls the tangle of repetitions? Just this search for authority governs *Henry Esmond* thematically, in its organization as a fabric of words, and in its relation to the various things outside the text it echoes. Whatever thread the critic chooses converges on the question of authority. On the stylistic level, this question becomes a search for the form of language which will give Henry Esmond, writing in his old age, authoritative command over the whole panorama of his life as it stands before that total memory he boasts of having. What is the appropriate style in which to paint one's self-portrait accurately from the perspective of this total recall and so see oneself clearly? From the point of view not of the fictional Esmond but of the real Thackeray, the question is what form of fiction will give him authoritative indirect command over his own life. That life is obscurely represented in the novel. What mode of fiction will give an authentic purchase on reality? The critic of the novel faces a related question. What handle should the critic use to get hold of this novel, or, to vary the metaphor, what pathway should he follow to enter it so that he can reach its deepest recesses, find out the center of its labyrinth of echoing words? How can the critic speak authoritatively of it?

The system of thematic imagery, for example, which organizes in its recurrences this novel, is a traditional pattern of original light and reflected light, of golden sun and silver moon. The sun is the chief source of light. All other lights are secondary, pale reflections of that king and father light. The latter is an image of the transcendent and divine power. This system of imagery is introduced at the beginning of the novel, when Henry first encounters Rachel. She appears to him in the way Venus appeared to Aeneas, as a *Dea certe*: "Her golden hair was shining in the gold of the sun" (bk. 1, chap. 1). Later, the images are shifted to Beatrix, just as Henry's desire is displaced from mother to daughter: "Mrs. Beatrix could no more help using her eyes than the sun can help shining, and setting those it shines on a-burning" (bk. 2, chap. 15); "There were times when this creature was so handsome, that she seemed, as it were, like Venus revealing herself a goddess in a flash of brightness. She appeared so now; radiant, and with eyes bright with wonderful lustre" (bk. 3, chap. 9). On the other hand, Beatrix at another time is said to have been the moon, changeable and fickle, "crescent and brilliant," but shining with a borrowed light, and possessed of a "malicious joy" in causing harm (bk. 1, chap. 12). She reminded Henry then "of the famous antique statue of the huntress Diana—at one time haughty, rapid, imperious, with eyes and arrows that dart and kill. Harry watched and wondered at this young creature, and likened her in his mind to Artemis with the ringing bow and shafts flashing death upon the children of Niobe; at another time she was coy and melting as Luna shining tenderly upon Endymion" (bk. 1, chap. 12). Which is she, sun or moon, and what does it mean to say that she is either?

Throughout the novel Rachel, Beatrix, and other characters are measured by their relations to this solar-lunar polarity. This often occurs in unostentatious ways. Lord Mohun's name, for example, echoes in its pronunciation the word "moon" and indicates his role as a false pretender to power over the members of Esmond's family. "Esmond" also echoes "moon." It ends in the syllable that means "moon" in German. Is this a senseless accident or does it have meaning? The question, throughout, is the following: Which character may be legitimately described as genuine gold, true sun? Who is possessor of intrinsic worth allowing him or her to rule as sovereign over the others? Who is qualified by divine right to serve as the model for others, as the source of their reflected light or transfused value?

If the reader turns to the political theme of the novel, the issue is the same one in displaced form. Thackeray has placed the story of his alter ego, "a handsome likeness of an ugly son of yours," as he wrote to his mother, in the period of political turmoil in England in the late seventeenth and early eighteenth centuries. During this period there was a multiple shift in dynasties, from the Stuarts to the House of Orange, then to the Hanoverian kings. The political question during all that time was a double one: What is the true source of kingship, and how, having established that, can one distinguish the true from the false pretenders to sovereignty? The clearest statement in *Henry Esmond* of the alternatives comes when Henry is about to lose his Stuart allegiance, his faith in the Pretender, and his belief in divine right at the same moment that he loses his infatuation with Beatrix. The political drama of the book is Henry's shift from the Stuarts to a "Whig" liberalism, "the manly creed . . . that scouts the old doctrine of right divine, that boldly declares that Parliament and people consecrate the Sovereign, not bishops, nor genealogies, nor oils, nor coronations" (bk. 3, chap. 9). Thackeray, we know, had read carefully Macaulay's *History of England.* His novel reaffirms Macaulay's Whig interpretation of English history. For Macaulay the bloodless revolution of 1688 was the decisive event making modern "democratic" England possible.

If Henry's love for Beatrix parallels his belief in the Pretender, the family level of the novel parallels both the political level and the level of material motifs. On the family level too the search is for a true source of authority. It too is a question of legitimacy. Who is the genuine heir to the Castlewood title and by what right does he hold that title? How can Henry take his rightful place in the genealogical line? The novel traces the clear design of what Freud calls a "family romance," an Oedipal story in which the son replaces the father and takes the father's place in the mother's bed. The pattern is all the clearer for being repeated in different forms and in different generations. *Henry Esmond* expresses with great power a tangle of family feelings, for example the mixture of filial devotion, brotherly love, religious worship, and veiled sexual desire in Henry's love for Rachel: "No voice so sweet," as he says, when they are reconciled after the estrangement caused by his participation in the duel that kills Rachel's husband, "as that of his beloved mistress, who had been sister, mother, goddess to him during his youth—goddess now no more, for he knew of her weaknesses; and by thought, by suffering, and that experience it brings, was older now than she; but more fondly cherished as woman perhaps than ever she had been adored as divinity . . . And as a brother folds a sister to his heart; and as a mother cleaves to her son's breast— so for a few moments Esmond's beloved mistress came to him and blessed him" (bk. 2, chap. 6).

By what right and by whose authority does Henry marry his "mother" and displace his "father"? Henry begins by seeking paternal or maternal authority in others. He ends by taking sovereignty upon himself, as the husband of Rachel and as the absolute ruler of his little kingdom of Castlewood in Virginia. The political and familial levels of the text converge when Frank Castlewood says of the Stuart Pretender, "He is not like a king: somehow, Harry, I fancy you are like a king" (bk. 3, chap. 9). If the political drama of the novel is Henry's shift from royalist to Whig, the family drama is his shift from "worship" of Rachel or Beatrix to allowing Rachel to worship him, after he has abdicated his rightful claim to be Viscount Castlewood in favor of Rachel's son Frank: " 'Don't raise me,' she said, in a wild way, to Esmond, who would have lifted her. 'Let me kneel—let me kneel, and—and—worship you' " (bk. 3, chap. 2).

To mention Oedipus is to introduce the final stratum of repetition in this novel—all its references to earlier texts. These references keep before the reader's mind the fact that *Henry Esmond* is only the latest link in a chain going back to *Oedipus Rex* and to certain Old Testament versions of the "family romance," for example the story of Jacob and Esau. Which of these stories has authority over the others? Which is the archetype on which all are modeled? Is it the Oedipus story, as Freud was later to argue, and as the crucial function of references to Oedipus in *Henry Esmond* would seem to argue was the case for Thackeray too? What would it mean, for this particular novel, or indeed generally, to say that Oedipus is the type of mankind, that Henry Esmond, without knowing it or wishing it, repeats the life story of Oedipus? What authority does this story have for Thackeray, and what does it have to say about the search for genuine authority?

To enter *Henry Esmond* by any of these routes is to confront ultimately the same question. What is the basis of legitimate sovereignty? To try to identify the answer the novel provides, it may be useful to take a somewhat circuitous route to the goal. This route goes by way of the identification of certain assumptions operative in all of Thackeray's work. Thackeray's starting place as a novelist is double: an assumption about styles of narration and an assumption about the human self whose vicissitudes are to be explored by way of imaginary replicas in those narrations. On this double presupposition all Thackeray's work as a novelist is superposed. These assumptions are exposed in two of his earliest works, published in *Punch*: *Novels by Eminent Hands* (originally *Punch's Prize Novelists*) (1844–45), and *The Book of Snobs* (1846–47).

*Novels by Eminent Hands* is a series of comic and maliciously accurate parodies of popular novelists of the day: Bulwer, Disraeli, G. P. R. James, Cooper, and so on. Along with Max Beerbohm's *A Christmas Garland* (1912) and Proust's *Pastiches et mélanges* (1919), they are the best such parodies in existence. Parody is a form of homage. It is also a form of literary criticism. In a master's "hands" it is one of the sharpest tools of insight and discrimination. The mode of parody is irony. By a slightly or grossly hyperbolic accentuation of stylistic features in the original, the parodist calls attention to those features and at the same time dismantles them by revealing their artificiality. Though the parodist may ridicule the style he parodies in the name of some proper style which he knows or for which he searches, his success as a parodist, as the parodies multiply, tends to suggest that there is no natural or "true" style. Any style, it would seem, can be undermined by parody. The parodist knows that a given story might be told in this style or in that style, though the style would determine to some degree the meaning the story would have. "Novels by Eminent Hands"—the title itself is a joke. It suggests that the novels were not written with the minds of their authors but were in their stylistic features produced unconsciously by craftsmen so trained in certain modes of narration that they are no longer the result of choice or thought. The books were written by hands working detached from bodies and brains, as the distinctive features of a man's handwriting or signature are not in his control.

This arbitrariness of the styles and conventions of narration remained one of Thackeray's constant assumptions. In the first edition of *Vanity Fair*, for example, in a passage often discussed, the narrator pauses at one point to say that the episode he is about to relate could be told in any one of a number of styles. He then proceeds to tell it first in the style of the "Silver Fork" novels, then in the style of the "Newgate" novels. Though these parodies were removed from subsequent editions of *Vanity Fair*, their corrosive implications remain latent within it. Once an author has reached the point of seeing any style of narration as artificial, it is difficult to return from that insight to claim, "I am now going to tell my story in the true, natural, unaffected style, without the falsification of any conventions." The parodist undermines his own enterprise. Whatever style he adopts is hollowed out by irony. He becomes his own parody, possessed only, in whatever mode he talks or writes, of the ventriloquist's gift for talking or writing as someone else.

This acute consciousness of the artifice in any literary language is evident also in Thackeray's habit, particularly in his early comic work, of adopting one pseudonym or another. Like Stendhal, Thackeray was a great inventor of pseudonyms and of the person and style to go with each invented name. At various times he wrote under the names of Theophile Wagstaff, Major Goliah Gahagan, Michael Angelo Titmarsh, George Savage Fitz-Boodle, Mr. Snob, and Mr. Charles James Yellowplush. The latter is an illiterate footman who in his turn adopts a nom de plume, a pseudonym within a pseudonym: C. Jeames de la Pluche. *Pendennis* is a first-person novel written as if by an imagined character, and later works like *The Newcomes* and *Philip* are presented as if written by Pendennis. Thackeray, it seems, had an aversion to writing in his own name. The implications of this penchant for pseudonymy are somewhat similar for Thackeray as for Stendhal. The man who takes a pseudonym, it may be assumed, has some doubt about who he is. He does not feel that he coincides wholly with himself, or with the given name and the patronymic which he wears before the world. He may find who he is by pretending to be someone else, by taking another name, another style, and wearing them as one wears a new suit of clothes on the assumption that "clothes make the man." The man who lives under a pseudonym, like the parodist, at once makes fun of the role he plays and at the same time uses it, he hopes, to express obliquely some aspect of himself, or perhaps to take on a self where there was none before if the name and habit should happen to stick. *Henry Esmond*, like *Pendennis*, or even like *Vanity Fair* (where Thackeray plays the role of the sad clown at the fair as well as of various other narrating personae), is continuous with the pseudonymous comic works. To the list of Thackeray's pseudonyms may be added Henry Esmond. Henry Esmond is a role Thackeray plays, a mask he wears, a name he goes by momentarily in the search by its detour to return to himself.

*The Book of Snobs* gives the other face of the double presupposition which underlies all Thackeray's work, or rather undermines it, since it is the presupposition of a lack of underlying support. It is two-faced also in being deceptive, duplicitous, like a double mask with no face behind it. *The Book of Snobs* is a series of sketches of various sorts of "snobs": military snobs, clerical snobs, university snobs, literary snobs, and so on. The full title of the book is *The Book of Snobs, By One of Themselves*. It takes a snob to know a snob. Just as the narrator of *Vanity Fair* does not exclude himself from the foolish vanity of the characters whose stories he tells, but is shown by the illustrator (Thackeray himself) in cap and bells looking with melancholy admiration at his own image in the mirror he holds in his hand, so no one can understand the mechanism of snobbery unless he is himself a snob. The deconstructive analysis of the mechanism of snobbery, such as the one performed by "Mr. Snob" in *The Book of Snobs*, does not liberate the analyzer from snobbery. It keeps him still implicated, since the analysis of snobbery in others, however clear-sighted and disillusioned, involves by that very fact the claim of superiority which is precisely one of the symptoms of snobbery. This double bind may not be by any means untied. To unknot it in one place makes a new knot somewhere else. On a large scale and in a more complex way, *Henry Esmond* is structured as just such another double bind, as I shall try to show. "You must not judge hastily or vulgarly of Snobs," says their anatomist: "to do so shows that you are yourself a Snob. I myself have been taken for one." In fact the first of the two papers on "Literary Snobs" has a picture to match the one in *Vanity Fair*. It is illustrated with a sketch by Thackeray showing the author as Mr. Punch, with a big nose and a Napoleon hat, carefully copying on a tablet on his lap his own reflection in a mirror.

*The Book of Snobs* shows Thackeray's extreme sensitivity to what in our day has been called "mediated desire," the psychological mechanism whereby desire is never direct but always routed through the desire of someone else whose authority authenticates my desire. If he or she finds something desirable it must be worth having, but without the help of another I cannot tell what I should want to have or to do. I desire only what is desirable to

others, or, in Thackeray's definition, "He who meanly admires mean things
is a Snob."

The universal domination of snobbery, in the society Thackeray
describes, follows from the absence of a true authority which can measure
things according to an absolute standard of desirability. Thackeray's
characters, as he says of those in *Vanity Fair*, are "a set of people living
without God in the world." That other person whose mean admirations I
meanly copy is put by me in the place of God in a world without God, or
in a world which has put itself outside God's help. It is impossible to know
from Thackeray's phrasing or indeed from his work in general which of these
quite different propositions he meant to affirm. Perhaps he meant to affirm
both at once in an oscillating indecision. This indecision is focused on the
word "without," which can mean either "outside of" or "entirely lacking."
Since no other person has the right or the substance to play god in a world
without God, mediated desire is always "mean," base and hypocritical, deceptive and self-deceptive. Its hollowness is proved, unhappily, more in possession than in unassuaged coveting. What I do not have and what others have
or find desirable I want, but when I finally get it, it instantly loses the golden
glow which had been reflected on it by the admiration of others. It or he
or she becomes revealed in all its meanness and drabness, its lack of intrinsic
value. This is Thackeray's melancholy or even "nihilistic" final wisdom. It
is nihilistic in the precise sense in which the word is defined, for example,
by Friedrich Nietzsche, as the devaluation of all values and their reduction
to nought, *nihil*, nothing.

The end of *Vanity Fair* provides the best and best-known formulation
of this sad insight. It is an insight which, characteristically, calls on the Bible
for its authority, according to that law whereby it is much easier to say
something really dark if I can blame it on someone else, particularly on
someone of acknowledged authority: "Ah! *Vanitas Vanitatum*! which of us
is happy in this world? Which of us has his desire? or, having it, is satisfied?"
*Henry Esmond* also exemplifies this melancholy wisdom, not only in the large-
scale story of Henry's disillusionment but in such episodes as the description
of the way Beatrix is admired by each court buck just because she is admired
by the others. In *Henry Esmond*, too, "There's some particular prize we all
of us value, and that every man of spirit will venture his life for" (bk. 3,
chap. 2), but this prize is, precisely, an *idol*, a thing of no intrinsic value
into which value has been projected: " 'tis I that have fixed the value of the
thing I would have, and know the price I would pay for it" (bk 3, chap. 2),
for, "Who, in the course of his life, hath not been so bewitched, and worshipped some idol or another?" (bk. 3, chap. 6). *Henry Esmond* too is based

on a mournful insight into the brevity and nullity of human life: "So night
and day pass away, and to-morrow comes, and our place knows us not"
(bk. 3, chap. 6).

Parody, pseudonymy, and snobbery are names of starting places for
Thackeray's work. He never abandons these or goes beyond them. They cannot in fact be gone beyond, since it is their nature to inhibit movement, except in place. Neither Thackeray nor his critic goes beyond the beginning;
they execute a circular trajectory returning to the starting point, perhaps with
better understanding of it, perhaps not. That remains to be seen.

I now turn to a description of the exact form that trajectory takes in
*Henry Esmond*. What makes the line the reader knows already. They are
the connections which can be made, the lines which can be drawn, intrinsic
and extrinsic, among the various repeating elements I have identified:
material motifs of sun, moon, blood, stars; the political theme of legitimacy;
familial patterns; literary allusions. Those lines differ, however, depending
on who draws them: Henry himself; "Thackeray," who stands as an ironic
shadow behind Henry; the critic who traces the line once more in one way
or another in his interpretation.

My image of the line is justified by Henry's use of it in his own language
about himself. Speaking, in anticipation, of Beatrix's thoughtless words to
her father about Lord Mohun, words which precipitate the duel in which
the father, Castlewood, is killed ("I think my Lord [Mohun] would rather
marry Mamma than marry me; and is waiting till you die to ask her";
bk 1, chap. 13) Henry says: "There is scarce any thoughtful man or woman,
I suppose, but can look back upon his course of past life, and remember some
point, trifling as it may have seemed at the time of occurrence, which has
nevertheless turned and altered his whole career" (bk. 1, chap. 12). Henry's
life is a course or career. It is a line which is marked by various crucial points
where the line turned. It also contains some gaps, sudden leaps which change
that life. These were breaks which made a hiatus in his life. Over these his
life jumped, and over them the retrospective narration must jump too in order
to trace out the whole line. Henry uses this figure of the gap to speak of
this year in prison for his participation in the duel in which Francis
Castlewood is killed:

> At certain periods of life we live years of emotion in a few weeks—
> and look back on those times, as on great gaps between the old
> life and the new. You do not know how much you suffer in those
> critical maladies of the heart, until the disease is over and you
> look back on it afterwards. During the time, the suffering is at
> least sufferable. The day passes in more or less of pain, and the

night wears away somehow. 'Tis only in after days that we see
what the danger has been—as a man out a-hunting or riding for
his life looks at a leap, and wonders how he should have survived
the taking of it.

(Bk. 2, chap. 1)

This drawing of a line between point and point to make a pattern may
be thought of, according to terms provided by the novel, either as the construction of a discursive memory or as the drawing of a true portrait. My
emblematic use of the portrait is justified by the many references to portraits
in the novel and by the symbolic value they are clearly meant to have. There
are, for example, several references to a portrait by Lely of the Dowager Lady
Isabella Castlewood as Diana, "in yellow satin, with a bow in her hand and
a crescent in her forehead; and dogs frisking about her" (bk. 2, chap. 3).
If Isabella, the wife of Henry's father, is Diana, so also is Beatrix repeatedly
called Diana. Beatrix repeats her aunt, in nature and in role. Each becomes,
or in Beatrix's case, almost becomes, a royal mistress, Isabella of Charles
II, Beatrix of that poor king, no king, James III, the luckless Stuart Pretender.

The first appearance of the motif of the portrait applies to Henry himself.
In the "Preface" by Henry's daughter Rachel Esmond Warrington, she writes:
"I wish I possessed the art of drawing (which my papa had in perfection),
so that I could leave to our descendants a portrait of one who was so good
and so respected." The first pages of Henry's narration turn on the distinction between the idealized Louis XIV or Queen Anne as portrayed masked
in grandeur by "the Muse of History" and the real king, "a little wrinkled
old man, pock-marked, and with a great periwig and red heels to make him
look tall," or the real Queen," a hot, red-faced woman, not in the least
resembling that statue of her which turns its stone back upon St. Paul's, and
faces the coaches struggling up Ludgate Hill" (bk. 1, Preface). Henry's implicit claim is that he has portrayed others accurately. Putting his art of
picturing under the aegis of the "familiar" history of "Mr. Hogarth and Mr.
Fielding" (bk. 1, Preface), he also claims that he has drawn that accurate
portrait of himself for which his daughter calls. He has "the art of drawing
. . . in perfection" with words as well as with the sketching pencil.

The reference to Hogarth and Fielding alerts the knowing reader to what
Thackeray's prototypes are for the technique of emblematic allusion he uses
throughout *Henry Esmond*. Thackeray, like Dickens, begins with the
eighteenth-century tradition of graphic and literary art as chief model for
a technique of ironic analogy, achieving complex resonance through uninter-
preted juxtaposition. An example is the scene in which Henry sees tiles of
Jacob cheating Esau of his birthright in the bagnio where Castlewood dies

from the wound he has received in the duel. A parallel is clearly intended, but Henry presents those tiles merely as vividly remembered fact. Such juxtapositions are a basic resource of Hogarth's art.

The means of Henry's supposedly accurate self-portrait is the putting together of such remembered images. Their validity lies in the fact that he remembers them. It is a basic presupposition of Henry's narrative of his life that he not only remembers it all but remembers it accurately. The novel is punctuated by the description of scenes, always involving images of light, which Henry claims are imprinted on his memory with extraordinary vividness and accuracy. These moments are the burning points of the narrative. They are its turning points too, bright spots of time between which the narrative is run, like the dots in the child's game which, connected by lines, reveal a pattern, a duck, a rabbit, or a face. To cite these passages seriatim once more (as they have often been cited in other essays discussing the theme of memory in *Henry Esmond*) is to indicate the key moments through which the narration is articulated as Henry "at the close of his life . . . sits and recalls in tranquility the happy and busy scenes of it" (bk. 1, chap. 7).

The phrasing in the last quotation indicates the Wordsworthian nature of Henry's enterprise. The emotions of the past are not felt at the time the narration is composed but are recollected in tranquility. They are created again in another form by the words of the narration. They are recreated in a way they never existed at the time, since they are given in recollection. They are also given in the light of Henry's mature demystified vision and in the light of his insight into the system of repetitions which makes his life a pattern, a portrait.

Each of these remembered images is double, even triple or quadruple. It is given as it was at the time or as Henry thinks it was at the time, bathed in the emotions of the time, according to that Wordsworthian definition of the poetic imagination as the creation, on the basis of a state of tranquility, of emotions appropriate to the images remembered. But how can one be sure that is in fact the way one felt at the time? Each image is also given in the secondary light of Henry's disillusioned interpretation of it, in his old age. The law of this double remembering is formulated in one place as follows: "'Tis not to be imagined that Harry Esmond had all this experience at this early stage of his life, whereof he is now writing the history—many things here noted were but known to him in later days. Almost everything Beatrix did or undid seemed good, or at least pardonable, to him then, and years afterwards" (bk. 1, chap. 12). The mark on the text of the discrepancy between the old Esmond and the young is the way he speaks of his young self in the third person, while he often uses "I" to speak of his old self in the present time of the writing down. The doubleness of all the remembered images lies in the gap between "he" and "I." Occasionally he uses "I" to speak of his young self, just as he occasionally drops into the present tense, the "historical present," for his narrative of past events, obliterating, for the moment, the distinction between past and present, "he" and "I." The effect of the historical present is hardly that of unmediated presentness. Its artifice calls attention to itself. It presents everything as image or phantasm, as an artifice of presentness brought back from the past by the words on the page, as a cinematic image is always present, though it is not to be mistaken for reality. The affirmed immediacy only increases the distance, the fictionalized effect:

> "How stupid your friend Mr. Steele becomes!" cries Miss Beatrix. "Epsom and Tunbridge! Will he never have done with Epsom and Tunbridge, and with beaux at church, and Jocastas and Lindamiras? Why does he not call women Nelly and Betty, as their godfathers and godmothers did for them in their baptism?"
>
> "Beatrix, Beatrix!" says her mother, "speak gravely of grave things."
>
>                                       (Bk. 3, chap. 3)

For the most part, Henry uses the past tense and the third person to tell his story. The effect of talking of one's past self in the third person, past tense, as a "he," is odd. It brings to the surface the fact that remembering is a kind of role-playing which hollows out the role that is played by repeating it with more or less irony. The present "I" plays the role of the past self who no longer exists. "He" is seen from the outside as another, but he can nevertheless, such is the power of memory, be played again, from the inside, with complete intimacy. We have in real life the kind of relation to our past selves, it may be, that a novelist writing as a third-person omniscient narrator has to his protagonist. By conflating the two modes here, the first-person autobiographical novel and third-person narration, Thackeray brings this similarity into the open. The "he" his "I" uses for young Henry is a sign for the difference and distance between the old Henry and the young. At the same time, it is an emblem of the way the novel is generated through Thackeray's performative act of playing the roles of both the young Henry and the old, both the "he" and the "I," in a phantasmal further doubling of that doubling.

If the phantom presence of Thackeray himself in each of the memory passages gives them a third level of significance, the fourth presence within them is the superimposition on each, as a kind of ghostly many-layered veil, of all the other similar passages. This occurs through the repetition in each of the same motifs. As each of these passages follows the last, they gradually accumulate into a resonating line of similar configurations, each echoing all the others and drawing its meaning from that echoing as much as from the intrinsic doubling of the combined perspectives of old Henry and young Henry which structures each taken separately. The meaning of this echoing is its affirmation that Henry's life hangs together. His life has meaning because the same elements recur in it and give it a total design justifying the drawing of a line connecting each part to all the others.

Here are the main members of the series, each with its quadruple perspective built into it. To cite them is to cite in miniature the whole book, since each concentrates in synecdochic focus one episode of Henry's life as he remembers it:

> To the very last hour of his life, Esmond remembered the lady as she then spoke and looked, the rings on her fair hands, the very scent of her robe, the beam of her eyes lighting up with surprise and kindness, her lips blooming in a smile, the sun making a golden halo round her hair.
>
> (Bk. 1, chap. 1)

> How those trivial incidents and words, the landscape and sunshine, and the group of people smiling and talking, remained fixed on the memory!
>
> (Bk. 1, chap. 1)

> Esmond long remembered how she looked and spoke, kneeling reverently before the sacred book, the sun shining upon her golden hair until it made a halo round about her.
>
> (Bk. 1, chap. 7)

> Indeed, he scarce seemed to see until she was gone; and then her image was impressed upon him, and remained for ever fixed upon his memory. He saw her retreating, the taper lighting up her marble face, her scarlet lip quivering, and her shining golden hair.
>
> (Bk. 1, chap. 8)

> And Harry remembered, all his life after, how he saw his mistress at the window looking out on him in a white robe, the little Beatrix's chestnut curls resting at her mother's side.
>
> (Bk. 1, chap. 9)

> He saw Lady Castlewood looking through the curtains of the great window of the drawing-room overhead, at my Lord as he stood regarding the fountain. There was in the court, a peculiar silence

somehow; and the scene remained long in Esmond's memory:—
the sky bright overhead; the buttresses of the building and the
sun-dial casting shadow over the gilt *memento mori* inscribed
underneath; the two dogs, a black greyhound and a spaniel nearly white, the one with his face up to the sun, and the other snuff-
ing amongst the grass and stones, and my Lord leaning over the
fountain, which was bubbling audibly. 'Tis strange how that
scene, and the sound of that fountain, remain fixed on the memory
of a man who was beheld a hundred sights of splendour, and
danger too, of which he has kept no account.

(Bk. 1, chap. 14)

Esmond went to the fire, and threw the paper into it. 'Twas a great
chimney with glazed Dutch tiles. How we remember such trifles
in such awful moments! . . . On the Dutch tiles at the bagnio was
a rude picture representing Jacob in hairy gloves, cheating Isaac
of Esau's birthright. The burning paper lighted it up.

(Bk. 1, chap. 14)

Her words as she spoke struck the chords of all his memory, and
the whole of his boyhood and youth passed within him.

(Bk. 2, chap. 1)

'Tis forty years since Mr. Esmond witnessed those scenes, but they
remain as fresh in his memory as on the day when first he saw
them as a young man.

(Bk. 2, chap. 5)

They walked out, hand-in-hand, through the old court, and to
the terrace-walk, where the grass was glistening with dew, and
the birds in the green woods above were singing their delicious
choruses under the blushing morning sky. How well all things
were remembered! The ancient towers and gables of the Hall
darkling against the east, the purple shadows on the green slopes,
the quaint devices and carvings of the dial, the forest-crowned
heights, the fair yellow plain cheerful with crops and corn, the
shining river rolling through it towards the pearly hills beyond;
all these were before us, along with a thousand beautiful memories
of our youth, beautiful and sad, but as real and vivid in our minds
as that fair and always-remembered scene our eyes beheld once
more. We forget nothing. The memory sleeps, but wakens again;
I often think how it shall be when, after the last sleep of death,

the *reveillée* shall arouse us for ever, and the past in one flash
of self-consciousness rush back, like the soul revivified.

(Bk. 3, chap. 7)

Esmond's narration presupposes and affirms a set of interrelated assumptions about memory. These assumptions form a system. Esmond's memory
is strongly affective. He remembers not only the scenes but the emotions he
believes he felt at that moment and which he feels again in reimagining the
scene as he writes it down. His memory is primarily visual, but it mingles
the other senses too in reinforcement of sight. He remembers the scent of
a robe, the sound of a fountain bubbling, though there are, in the passages
I have cited, no references to touch or to taste. In fact, Esmond's memory
(perhaps Thackeray's also) is not, like Proust's for example, strongly
gustatory, nor is it tactile. Esmond remembers seemingly "trivial" details with
extraordinary vividness. He says they are trivial, and that his memory has
"taken no account" of scenes far more important, but it is obvious that these
"trivial" details are significant, emblematic. They stand for the crucial relationships of his life, those to Rachel, those to Rachel's husband. In spite of
Henry's decade of infatuation with Beatrix and the elaborately circumstantial narration of his unhappy courtship of her, none of the passages I have
cited has to do centrally with Beatrix. Henry's "Fate," to use a word and
a concept which often recur in his self-interpretation, is ultimately to marry
Rachel and to live happily ever after. This is the significance of all these trivial
details and of the vividness with which they, out of all possible details, remain fixed in his memory. They were prophetic signs, prolepses of his ultimate
destiny.

Though Henry seems to be affirming here something like the Proustian
doctrine of the intermittences of the heart and of the heart's affective memory,
so that some things are remembered, but most forgotten, and memory is a
series of vivid bright spots with the darkness of irremediable forgetting between, in fact Thackeray's doctrine of memory here is quite different from
Proust's. Each trivial detail stands for a crucial moment in Esmond's relation to Rachel. Each is a pause in the forward movement of time, a missed
heartbeat, so to speak, which remains hovering, cut off from the flow of
before and after. Each is a static image, fixed on his memory, space here
for standing for time. The trivial detail, by a species of synecdoche, stands
for the whole scene and gives Henry access to it. The whole scene, in turn,
by another synecdoche, spatial panorama standing for temporal sequence,
gives him possession of all his life. Place is the repository of memory, of a
total memory which omits nothing and regathers all, with complete accuracy,
as the circumstantial narration of what comes between each of these scenes

and the next indicates. When Henry and Rachel walk out before Castlewood in the last of the passages I have quoted, they see not only all the details of the whole scene but, by means of them, all the details of the past: "all these were before us, along with a thousand beautiful memories of our youth, beautiful and sad, but as real and vivid in our minds as that fair and always-remembered scene our eyes beheld once more."

The latter passage indicates another important feature of Henry's memory and of these remembered scenes. Each stands by itself as a self-enclosed fixed image inscribed on the screen of Henry's total recall, each next to the others, like the pictures side by side in an Italian Renaissance fresco of scenes from a saint's life. At the same time, as the memories accumulate through time, each contains at the time it occurs echoes of the ones before. Henry's present memory is a memory of memories within a memory. It juxtaposes not only the present and a past time, but the past past times which were remembered when that past was present. Of each, except the first in the series, Henry could say what he says of the words of accusation Rachel speaks when she visits him in prison after the death of her husband. Each image is in resonance with all the others and calls them us, as "her words . . . struck all the chords of his memory, and the whole of his boyhood and youth passed within him." If Henry's memory is a spatial panorama of fixed pictures side by side, it is also a musical instrument with strings in tune at different pitches. To pluck one is to make them all vibrate.

Even the first encounter with Rachel is in more than one way a repetition. It is already a memory, jangling the strings of previous entities it echoes. Henry first sees Rachel (whose name is already a biblical reference) in the portrait gallery at Castlewood, where hangs the portrait of Rachel's predecessor, Isabella, as Diana the huntress. Henry sees Rachel as a duplication of another "Dea certe," Venus appearing to Aeneas, "remembering," as he says, even in the intensity of his immediate response to his first glimpse of Rachel, "the lines of the Aeneis which Mr. Holt had taught him" (bk. 1, chap. 7). No doubt, beyond that, as the echo of the *Aeneid* suggests, Henry's reaction to Rachel is spontaneously to treat her as a replacement for his real mother, Thomas Esmond's first Flemish wife. That real mother he does not remember at all ("for even his memory had no recollection of her"; bk. 2, chap. 13), and she is long dead when he visits her grave in Flanders. Rachel fills the void created by her loss. Moreover, the first encounter with Rachel already echoes Henry's first encounter with Isabella. The latter occurred earlier, but is given later, since Henry begins his narration with his first vision of Rachel, as though that were the true beginning of his life, the origin of the fateful line his life has followed. He then circles back to describe what had preceded that first encounter, the period of his life when he lived with his actual father, Thomas Castlewood, and was page to that father's wife Isabella. The first meeting with Isabella contains many of the same elements as the first meeting with Rachel. It is a grotesque artificial parody of that meeting. It occurred before but is presented after. This reversal obscures the fact that Henry's first meeting with Rachel is already a repetition, not a solid origin at all. What Isabella tries to be by painting herself, Rachel genuinely is. Or is she? Henry does not always think so. When he finally marries Rachel she, like everyone else except himself, has long since been bereft of divinity for him. The sun, the scent, the rings, eyes, the color gold, and the color red (lips in one case, petticoat, heels, and rouge in the other) occur in both first encounters. Here is Henry's first vision of Isabella:

> Indeed, the chamber was richly ornamented in the manner of Queen Elizabeth's time, with great stained windows at either end, and hangings of tapestry, which the sun shining through the coloured glass painted of a thousand hues; and here in state, by the fire, sate a lady, to whom the priest took up Harry, who was indeed amazed by her appearance.
>
> My Lady Viscountess's face was daubed with white and red up to the eyes, to which the paint gave an unearthly glare . . . She wore a dress of black velvet, and a petticoat of flame-coloured brocade. She had as many rings on her fingers as the old woman of Banbury Cross; and pretty small feet which she was fond of showing, with great gold clocks to her stockings, and white pantofles with red heels; and an odour of musk was shook out of her garments whenever she moved or quitted the room.
>
> (Bk. 1, chap. 3)

Each episode in Henry's memory, then, is always, strangely, a memory within a memory, never, in spite of its sensuous vividness and quality of immediate presence, only the recovery of an immediate presence. Even when it occurred the "first" time it was always already also a repetition. No originating first is recoverable, neither the first of fulfilled possession nor that of some traumatic loss which makes Henry, like his creator, like all men and women, it may be, creatures of unassuaged and unassuageable desire. That "first" moment of loss Henry can never give as such.

A final peculiarity of Henry's memory is the key element in the system, making the other features possible. This is the way Henry characteristically speaks of himself as if he were already dead. He views his past life from beyond the grave, from a point where the series is apparently complete, so that no more items may be added to change it. Until a man or woman is dead, something may happen to him or to her, he or she may do something which will change utterly the meaning of the long line of events which make up his or her life. The manner of a person's death, for example by suicide, has strikingly this power. Henry speaks repeatedly as if it were no longer possible for him to change the meaning of his life by adding a new episode to the series. The last element has been added, the line has been drawn, the portrait is complete, and Henry can look back at it from outside life entirely, seeing it as a perfected pattern. He claims to view it with complete objectivity, as if he were God or a resurrected soul joined to God: "To the very last hour of his life, Esmond remembered"; "her image was impressed upon him, and remained forever fixed upon his memory"; "And Harry remembered, all his life after." How can he know yet about the last hour of his life or about whether something is to last all his life, unless he is already dead?

The final image Henry gives of his memory in the series quoted above is the most important, the one that authenticates all its other qualities of accuracy, vividness, completeness, and totalizing meaning. His memory is the sort of total instantaneous recall, he says, we shall have after we have died and have been born again in heaven, when "the *reveillée* shall rouse us for ever, and the past in one flash of self-consciousness rush back, like the soul revivified." This is the function of the convention whereby Henry speaks of himself in the third person, as though he were the "omniscient narrator" of someone else's life. The old Henry, writing his memoirs or his "history" in Virginia, claims to be able to view his past self as though he saw it with godlike perfection of knowledge.

What that view is, the portrait that gradually emerges, as the line is drawn from one bright spot to the next, can be resketched here. Henry begins his life as a "nameless bastard" (bk. 2, chap. 8), in the state of need, desire, and abandonment he shares with his great prototype Oedipus. He seeks to find a name, a self, and a place in the world by discovering a legitimate authority in the world justified in giving him these securities. He seeks someone he can worship, someone like a king (or a queen), someone ruling by divine right, like a deity. He makes this search both in the political world and in the social one. He shifts from Rachel to Beatrix and puts his political faith first in James II, then in the Pretender, the second of each pair doubling the first in parody, just as Rachel already doubles Isabella and both double Henry's lost mother. Henry seeks everywhere some idol worthy of worship. He seeks someone who will have power to endow him with substance, with value, as a coin passes current when the king's countenance is stamped on it, or as the sun gives life to that on which it shines.

Henry's gradual discovery is that nothing and nobody outside himself are worth his worship. No one has the right to play the role of God to him in a world without God. Whatever golden luster this or that person has seemed to him to have—Rachel, or Beatrix, or that shabby prince—has been projected on them by Henry himself. The activity of Henry's narration, in relation to other people, is a process of unveiling, as he shows the tawdriness and vanity, the lack of intrinsic worth, in one person after another. The emblem of this process of demystification is that opening example of the undressing of the royal portrait of Louis XIV as Sun King. Henry reveals the little wrinkled old man underneath, pock-marked, with a great periwig and red heels to make him look tall.

Having undressed everyone else, having divested them all, one by one, of the auras they have seemed to have in his infatuated young eyes, Henry does not take the next step and undress also himself. He refuses to see that he, the emperor, also has no clothes. "De te fabula." He fails to see the relevance to himself of the epigraph from Horace for the imitation *Spectator* paper he writes attacking Beatrix. Having found nothing outside himself worthy of his worship, in the end he complacently allows others to kneel down and worship him. He takes his place as the head of the Esmond family, replaces all those who have been father-figures to him, marries the woman who has been in the place of a mother to him, and ends his life as the "king" of the new Castlewood in Virginia, revered by wife, children, servants, and slaves, the omnipotent sovereign of his own little kingdom. This he contrives to do without any apparent sense of guilt and without any awareness that he has been other than magnanimous and self-sacrificing, that he has ever been in the wrong.

He even manages to have it both ways in relation to the social sanction of his name and place. He discovers that his father had indeed married his mother and that far from being a "nameless bastard" he is the rightful heir to the Castlewood title. He is truly "the Right Honourable the Lord Viscount Castlewood," and Frank Castlewood only holds the title on his sufferance. He generously renounces his claim to the title in favor of Rachel's son Frank, burning the paper proving his identity at the same moment that he repudiates both Beatrix, his last amorous infatuation, and the Pretender, his last political mystification. Now he stands free of any belief in others, believing only in himself. At first he keeps secret his generosity in giving up the title, but gradually he lets it out, making sure that everyone knows who he really is. At the same time, since he has renounced the title, he can make good his project of being a self-made man and owing his value and selfhood to no one outside himself. This he expresses repeatedly by saying he intends to "make a name for himself." "If I cannot make a name for myself, I can die without one" (bk. 2, chap. 1), he says early in his career. Later he feels that he is no longer a "nameless bastard" but has "won myself a name" (bk. 2, chap. 8). Henry has the best of both ways. He is legitimately a nobleman, and so he has not arrogated to himself something society does not grant him the right to have. At the same time he has won himself a name. He is beholden to no one, not even to the family whose blood flows in his veins. He has cut off that genealogical line of succession. He has named himself, so to speak, and stands free of all, above all. He is a self-made man, a symbol of the rising bourgeois. Such is the grand portrait of himself Henry paints, tracing the line from point to point to its happy end in Virginia where Henry is, one might say, already out of this world.

The phantasmal, ironic presence of "Thackeray himself" behind every line Henry writes suffices to erase that line, to obliterate the kinglike portrait, and to draw another portrait in which Henry is indeed, like Louis, divested of poetry and shown to be but a little wrinkled old man, pockmarked, Henry is in fact quite short, as his daughter says in her preface, and his face was of course marked by the smallpox he brought home to the Castlewood household. Thackeray's pervasive irony has filled the text with details which have a double meaning, one ostensibly for Henry, one for the knowing reader. By tracing a new line from one to another of those second meanings, the reader can, if he accepts the author's invitation to do so, not only obliterate Henry's picture of himself, but also trace out the lines of an alternative portrait. The second image ironically doubles the first and undoes it.

Beatrix gives the most explicit sketch of this alternative face when she finally speaks her mind to Henry. She explains her sense of solitude, her jealousy of her mother Rachel, who has never liked her, and the reasons why she can never return Henry's love. Henry can succeed in discounting her unflattering portrait of him only by persuading himself and trying to persuade the reader that she is bad, wayward, untrustworthy, and destructive. In fact she speaks for the darkest insights into the human condition that this "melancholy" book provides. "You are a hypocrite, too, Henry," she says, "with your grave airs and your glum face. We are all hypocrites. O dear me! We are all alone, alone, alone" (bk. 3, chap. 3). Later, when she rejects his suit, she says:

> Of all the proud wretches in the world Mr. Esmond is the proudest, let me tell him that. You never fall into a passion, but you never forgive, I think. Had you been a great man, you might have been good-humoured; but being nobody, sir, you are too great a man for me; and I'm afraid of you cousin—there! and I won't worship you, and you'll never be happy except with a woman who will . . . Mamma would have been the wife for you, had you been a little older, though you look ten years older than she

does—you do, you glum-faced, blue-bearded little old man! You
might have sat, like Darby and Joan, and flattered each other;
and billed and cooed like a pair of old pigeons on a perch.

(Bk. 3, chap. 4)

Every word of this is true. Moreover, it seems to agree with Thackeray's
judgment of his hero as we have it on external evidence. Henry is indeed
a hypocrite. He has assumed the privilege of judging others, while refusing
to judge himself. He pretends self-righteously to be better than he secretly
knows he is. Like all the other characters he is alone and cannot, as he tries
to do, depend on others to build a complacent and solid image of himself
for himself. His self-righteousness does have something to do with the fact
that he begins life as nobody. Being nobody, he cannot afford any insou-
ciance. For him it is all or nothing. He therefore is a solemn man, a man
without irony. He is indeed a glum-faced, blue-bearded little old man, and
he is, as Beatrix says, finally happy only when Rachel worships him, when
they flatter each other, like Darby and Joan. Thackeray at various times called
Henry Esmond a "bore" and a "prig," "as stately as Sir Charles Grandison."
The novel as a whole he called "a book of cutthroat melancholy suitable to
my state."

The further outlines of the alternative portrait of Henry which emerge
from following ironic double meanings in his self-portrait may be quickly
traced. One form of this irony has already been identified. In analyzing the
lack of worth of all other people Henry unwittingly provides the reader with
the tools by means of which to identify Henry's own lack of worth. What
applies universally must apply to him too. This reversal of meaning can be
performed with any of the four systems of thematic recurrence which organize
the novel.

Henry, for example, discovers that no one outside himself has the ra-
diance of the true sun. He learns that the apparent location of golden solar
worth shifts according to his projections of desire. Rachel, once seemingly
the true sun, becomes in her turn the moon when Henry's infatuation shifts
to Beatrix: "And as, before the blazing sun of morning, the moon fades away
in the sky almost invisible, Esmond thought, with a blush perhaps, of another
sweet pale face [Rachel's], sad and faint, and fading out of sight, with its
sweet fond gaze of affection; such a last look it seemed to cast as Eurydice
might have given, yearning after her lover, when Fate and Pluto summoned
her, and she passed away into the shades" (bk. 2, chap. 9). Applied to Henry,
this suggests that any appearance of sovereign worth he has is only projected
into him by the admiration of others, for example by Rachel's "worship"
of him when they are married and live like Darby and Joan. All light is

reflected. There is nowhere any true sun, or genuine gold, or the ontological substance these stand for according to a system of figures going back, in the West, to Plato and the Bible and their precursors. Esmond's name does not contain "moon" (*Mond*) inscribed within it for nothing. He is, like everyone and everthing else in this novel, as fickle, as changeable, as secondary, as lacking in intrinsic light as the moon. He shines, like the moon, only with such reflected light as happens to come his way. In Thackeray's implicit deconstruction of the ancient system even the real sun, that light which illuminates the moon, is in its origin secondary. There is no sun in the sense of an independent sovereign head source of light, warmth, and value. There are only mock suns.

The same reversal may be performed with the other recurrent motifs. If there is no king who is not a "pretender," ruling without divine right only on the sufferance of those who have chosen him, then Henry has no right to claim to be the sovereign ruler of his little kingdom in Virginia. If Henry shows that in the social and family realms no man is intrinsically or by birth a nobleman, and no father lords it legitimately over his family, then he has no right to take the place of the father and head of his family, claiming that place both by inheritance of the bloodline and at the same time through his intrinsic merit.

The most elaborate redrawing of Henry's portrait of himself occurs when a different line is charted through all the literary allusions which punctuate the book. These include, as I have said, references to the Bible, to *Oedipus Rex*, to the *Aeneid*, and to *Hamlet*. All these stories are versions of that family romance of which the story of Oedipus is the "archetype," though the story of Rachel, Isaac, Jacob, and Esau is another version of it, as is of course *Hamlet*, and, in another way, the Aeneid. In its complete versions, this story involves father, mother, daughter, and son, or two jealous rival sons, like Henry's grandsons, children of that Rachel Esmond Warrington who writes the preface to *Henry Esmond* and so gives the reader the only perspective outside Henry's own as to what Henry was like. The story of those grandchildren is told in a later novel by Thackeray, *The Virginians* (1857–59). Like Eteocles and Polynices in the Oedipus cycle, they took opposite sides in a war, in this case the war for American independence. *The Virginians* demonstrates Thackeray's awareness that the Oedipal cycle was by no means closed by the "happy" ending of *Henry Esmond.*

The role of the Oedipus story as the key to a correct portrayal of Henry is indicated by the imitation *Spectator* paper Henry writes. This placement of the Oedipal story as archetype is already prepared for, near the beginning of the novel, along with an invitation to the reader to watch for puns and double meanings, in a curious interchange between Father Holt and Mrs.

Tusher. This interchange occurs at the time of Henry's first meeting with
Isabella:

> "Where I'm attached, I'm attached, Madame [says Mrs. Tusher
> to her mistress, Isabella]—and I'd die rather than not say so."
> "*Je meurs où je m'attache,*" Mr. Holt said with a polite grin.
> "The ivy says so in the picture, and it clings to the oak like a fond
> parasite as it is."
> "Parricide, Sir!" cries Mrs. Tusher.
>
> (Bk. 1, chap. 3)

Henry is in fact both parasite and parricide. He here unintentionally gives
the reader the labels which apply accurately to himself. Henry writes the *Spectator* paper as an attack on Beatrix, casting himself as author of the paper
in the role of "Oedipus" and naming Beatrix as a "Jocasta" who is so wayward
and inconstant that she has forgotten even the name of one of her suitors.
"Can you help us, Mr. Spectator, who know everything, to read this riddle
for her, and set at rest all our minds?" asks this "Oedipus" (bk. 3, chap. 3).
Though Henry puts the "de te fabula" of Horace as an epigraph to the paper,
and though he boasts of having an elephant's memory for accuracy and completeness, he has forgotten the way the fable he borrows can be made to apply
to himself, just as Lockwood, in *Wuthering Heights*, does not take seriously
the imputation of guilt in Branderham's "Thou art the man." Henry, like
Lockwood, gives the oracular saying but fails to read the riddle right. The
text of the *Spectator* paper gives the reader the elements necessary to make
that correct reading. It even indicates the principles on which the reading
should be based. As the interchange between Father Holt and Mrs. Tusher
depends on a pun whereby parasite and parricide are said implicitly to come
to the same thing, since they sound alike, so the *Spectator* paper also turns
on puns and double meanings. The paper has to do with a *lapsus*, a forgotten name which has been repressed, and of which Beatrix-Jocasta learns only
that it may be spelled either with an "i" or with a "y."

The false *Spectator* paper has two parts. The first section tells the story
of the forgotten name objectively and is signed "Oedipus." The second section tells the same story over again in the first person and is signed ostensibly by the man whose name Beatrix has forgotten, Cymon Wyldoats. The
double "author" of Henry's *Spectator* paper invites the reader to take it in
a double sense, to spell it out in one way according to Henry's intention and
in another way according to its application to Henry himself. The *Spectator*
paper is an emblem or parable of the way the whole of *Henry Esmond* should
be read. When the *Spectator* paper and the novel as a whole are read in this

second way, Henry is indeed an Oedipus, but an Oedipus manqué whose eyes remain blinded. He is an Oedipus who never reads the oracles right in their application to himself. He never understands his Oedipal guilt, though he gives the reader, in spite of himself, all the material for a correct reading. Henry means to be speaking of his faithful love for Beatrix when he says to her, "How long was it that Jacob served an apprenticeship for Rachel?" (bk. 3, chap. 3). Beatrix and the reader understand that Henry's true Rachel is Rachel Castlewood: " 'For Mamma,' says Beatrix. 'Is it Mamma your honour wants, and that I should have the happiness of calling you papa?' " (bk. 3, chap. 3). In the same way, Henry means Beatrix by Jocasta, but the reader understands that his true Jocasta is Rachel. Like the biblical Jacob, he has taken possession of a birthright which is not really his, even though it may be legally so, as Jacob has the inheritance legally after Esau has sold it. Like the biblical Jacob, Henry is self-righteously unscrupulous in his dealings with women, shifting from one to another and hungry for their complete submission, in spite of his willingness to define himself as their humble servant and worshiper.

If Henry ironically repeats Jacob in ways he does not recognize, this is even more true of his relation to Oedipus. Like the Oedipus of the legend, Henry has been responsible for the death of the man who stands in place of a father to him. He ultimately takes that father's place in the bed of the woman who has been a mother to him. The scandalized Victorian reviewers were right to see incestuous implications in the familial and emotional configurations of the novel. Henry is the parasite and upstart who has sprung from a collateral line of his family, even though his father, thinking himself dying, had legally married his mother, whom he had seduced and got with child. This child enters into the domestic enclosure of the family and like a true parasite upsets its economy, causing the death of the father and taking the sexual and material goods of that family to himself. Parasite and parricide, he is the intruder, the upstart usurper, the breaker of the family line.

The secret identity between Henry and Lord Mohun is affirmed not only by their similar functions as intruders alienating the proper affections of the women of the Esmond family, but also in the similarity of their names. Mohun (pronounced "moon") echoes *Esmond*. Both have "Harry" as given names. The significance of this is indicated when things Mohun has done or had done to him are thought to have happened to Harry Esmond: "Yes. Papa says: 'Here's poor Harry killed, my dear; on which Mamma gives a great scream; and oh, Harry! She drops down; and I thought she was dead too' " (bk. 1, chap. 13). Mohun is Henry's malign double. Acting as it were through Mohun, Henry is guilty in the two duels, the second repeating the first. First he kills his "father," Frank Castlewood, and then he kills Beatrix's fiancé,

Lord Hamilton, putting an end to her hopes for worldly advancement. What Mohun unsuccessfully attempts, the seduction of Rachel—Henry Esmond triumphantly accomplishes. Rachel's "guilt" has been her long secret love for Henry, a love which even from the beginning is far from maternal. Ultimately, like Oedipus, Henry does marry his "mother," and he fathers a new Rachel, the Antigone figure in the story, in this superimposition of biblical and Greek paradigms. Unlike Oedipus, however, Henry never comes to see his guilt and the havoc he has made in his family, though he has upset the generations and the line of succession, depriving each person of his or her rightful place.

This is the alternative portrait of Henry Esmond the reader is invited to draw by tracing another line through the data, the line indicated by all the ironic double meanings Thackeray has placed throughout the text. *Henry Esmond*, one might be tempted to say, is the indirect story or parable of this erasure of Henry's picture of himself and its replacement by another truer picture. The outlines of this other picture gradually emerge for the intelligent interpreter, as the narrative proceeds. The first picture loses its validity and disappears, like Eurydice fading back into the underworld, as Rachel does for Henry when she loses her divine glow. A good interpreter can read the signs right and make the right connections, threading his way correctly through all the clues. Though the method of *Henry Esmond* is irony, it would seem that irony in this case is used as the indirect expression of a wholly determinate and univocal meaning, a meaning which any good reader of the novel ought to identify. Is this so clearly the case, however? A further step into the novel will indicate that my triumphant replacement of a "mistaken" reading by the "correct" one can itself in turn be undermined or indeed undermines itself.

Parable is a way of saying one thing and meaning another. The usual German word for parable (in the sense, for example, of the parables of Jesus in the New Testament) is *Gleichnis*, "likeness."

Thackeray, in a letter to his mother I have already quoted, describes his portrait of Henry Esmond as "a handsome likeness of an ugly son of yours." A likeness too says one thing by means of another thing and draws its meaning from the correspondence, with more or less of difference, between the tow things. "Parable" and "likeness" seem appropriate terms to describe the procedure by means of which Thackeray says two things at once, creates one picture by means of another picture, says one thing and means another thing.

There is a difference, however, between saying two things at once and saying one thing and meaning another, and this makes all the difference. I have said that the instrument with which Thackeray creates for the reader the second truer picture of Henry is the trope of irony. Irony differs fundamentally from parable or from likeness. The latter leave the two pictures or the two narrative lines side by side, the one the support of the other. The moral or religious meanings of the parables of Jesus, however enigmatic those meanings are in themselves, or however enigmatic their relation to the story that supports them, do not question the referential validity of the realistic stories about fishermen, farmers, or ordinary folk which are the vehicle of their parabolic meanings. The one level of meaning is said to be genuinely "like" the other. The second meaning, the metaphorical or transported one, rests on the similarity as it is carried over. The meaning depends on keeping the validity of the vehicle untouched. In the case of irony, the second meaning undoes the first. As I have said, the second picture of Henry erases the first. It makes the reader see it as a hypocritical lie or self-deception.

In the definition of irony by Friedrich Schlegel, the master theorist of irony among the German romantics, the negativity inherent in irony is said to make it a permanent parabasis. According to Søren Kierkegaard's later definition, irony is "infinite absolute negativity." Parabasis is the rhetorical name for that suspension of dramatic illusion when one of the actors in a play steps forward on the stage and speaks "in his own voice" in commentary, as in the "Epilogue" to *The Tempest*. A parabasis momentarily suspends the line of the action. Irony is a permanent parabasis. This means it suspends the line all along the line. Irony is the one figure of speech which cannot be figured spatially or as any sort of geometrical line. Nor is it locally identifiable as a turn of language or "figure of speech." Irony may pervade a whole discourse, as it does in the case of *Henry Esmond*, exactly identifiable nowhere, but present everywhere as a persistent double meaning blurring the line of sense from one end to the other of the text.

In suspending the line, irony suspends also itself. In this lies its "infinite absolute negativity." According to two other traditional definitions, irony is a needle which with its eye sees two ways, or a knife that cuts in both directions. The ironist cuts up into little bits beyond hope of reassembling the coherence of the narrative or argument he ironizes. In doing so, he cuts also himself and the alternative narrative or line of argument he presents. Irony is a dangerous edge tool. He who lives by this sword dies by it too.

This does not mean that there may not be local ironies which are more or less limited or determinate. Such ironies may be contained within the larger framework of surface certainties about this or that fact—the fact, for example, that Beatrix tends to have a destructive effect on those around her. Most, though by no means all, good readers of *Henry Esmond* would agree that if the old Henry ironically undercuts the naiveté of his young self, that "he" of whom the "I" writes, the old Henry's judgments are in turn ironically undercut by an implicit circumambient judgment which can only speak indirectly, a judgment which may be called that of "Thackeray." To say that he who lives by irony dies of it too does mean, however, that irony, insofar as it has a tendency to spread out, proliferate, and pervade an entire discourse, as is the case in *Henry Esmond*, suspends the possibility of identifying certainly the underlying *logos* (cause, reason, meaning, or end) of the whole fabric which is woven of these smaller ironies. It takes away the reader's sense that he has somewhere solid ground to stand on from which to read the whole as a whole. Irony does this by putting in doubt those tools of interpretation—for example, seeing one thing as like another thing—with which the coherence of any interpretation is constructed, both the "first" and that "second" which is built on the ruins of the first, as well as the "third," and so on.

The way this happens in *Henry Esmond* is an admirable example of the self-destructive power of irony. This novel is one of the best texts in English fiction by means of which to explore the working of irony in narrative. Thackeray, I have said, sought authority over his own life by way of a detour representing that life in ironically displaced form in a fiction. He did this by means of the ventriloquism of an assumed voice and role. Thackeray wanted to understand and control his life by taking ironic authority over that assumed role and by showing the imagined person to have made a false interpretation of himself. Thackeray will present by irony the true interpretation and so indirectly a true interpretation of himself. He will come by way of the detour back to himself and so join himself to himself, taking possession of himself in a sovereign exercise of power. The reader is invited to follow in his turn this double line and to take full possession of the text of *Henry Esmond* in an authoritative interpretation based on his mastery of its ironical mode. He must replace one portrait by the other.

If irony is truly a permanent parabasis, this project cannot be carried out, either by the author or by the reader. Irony is the mode of language which cannot be mastered. It cannot be used as an instrument of mastery. It always masters the one who tries to master it or to take power with it. The means by which Henry paints his flattering portrait of himself is the taking of similarities as genuine identities. He not only claims to have a total memory of his own life, he also sees it as forming a coherent story, a "destiny" or "fate." He does this by identifying the various repetitions which make it hang together and link one part of it to another, as I have demonstrated by following out what Henry says of himself. An example is the way he sees himself as repeating Aeneas or sees each of his visions of Rachel as repeating the others. The alternative portrait traced out by the ironic double meanings uses exactly the same method of identifying similarities in order to draw a second line which replaces and erases the first. My drawing of the second portrait has depended at every point on the use of metaphorical similarities between one passage and another, one word and another, one narrative pattern and another. I have said, for example, that the second duel echoes the first, or that Esmond and Mohun are secretly identical in part because their names are similar. I have interpreted Esmond's life in terms of his unwitting reenactment of the story of Oedipus. In all this I have responded to invitations in the text. If Henry makes the mistake of seeing similarities as identities, I have done the same thing in my "second" reading. The reader is coaxed by the irony into replacing one metaphorical construction by another metaphorical construction. Henry paints a picture of himself as though he were already dead, embalming himself, so to speak. The reader brings him back alive once more beyond this death, but only to kill him once again in following out the ironic condemnation of him as an Oedipus manqué.

If the deconstruction of the first portrait depends on putting in question, by means of irony, the metaphorical connections Henry has made in order to draw a picture of himself, and if it unties all those connections, there is no reason why the same procedures should not be applied to the second metaphorical construction as have been applied to the first. What applies to the first must apply to the second. The undoing of the first by the second undoes also the second. The second destroys itself in the act whereby it fragments the first. If irony is "infinite absolute negativity," it can be in no way an instrument of tying up. It is only a power of dissolution, of analysis, or even of paralysis. If it is infinite negativity, it is also "absolutely" negative. It unties every line. Far from gaining mastery of himself by means of a detour through the ironic playing of a role, Thackeray remains permanently astray, distant from himself, unable to get back on the track and join his fictional self to his real self.

The same thing may be said, in a somewhat different form, of the way the fictional aspects of Thackeray's story seem to make themselves more solid and plausible, more real, by being woven with circumstantial accounts of battles, political events, and so on, events which the reader knows really took place in history. This relationship too works both ways. The effect is as much or more to make historical narrative seem phantasmal, fictional. It can never be more than a subjective interpretation telling the way things seem to have been to this or that person. History has the same kind of insubstantiality as Henry Esmond's false portrait of himself. A rejection of "official" history, for example of poetized history like Addison's "The Campaign," is one of the recurrent themes of *Henry Esmond.* Thackeray's argument against such history reflects back on his own procedure, which is to try to tell the truth about himself indirectly, through an imaginary story set in a real historical scene.

The same kind of disarming also dissolves the reader's power over the text. Far from mastering *Henry Esmond* by a recognition and interpretation of its irony, the reader remains lost in a work which is undecidable in meaning, except insofar as the negative workings of irony in it may be precisely defined. From Thackeray's own time to the present, criticism has vibrated between seeing his novels as "cynical" or faithless and seeing them as based on absolute standards by means of which English bourgeois society is judged as lacking, as a Vanity Fair. The disagreements among critics who have interpreted Thackeray are no accident. No reader can claim certain authority over *Henry Esmond*, or decide between the reading that sees Esmond as a hero and the reading that sees him as a prig. The line is interrupted, even the line the reader follows to reach the understanding of the undoing of the line. This might be formulated by saying that where there is irony there is no authority, not even the authority to know for sure that there is no authority. To put this another way, there is no way to be sure that Henry's flattering self-portrait is not meant to be taken "straight," as it has been taken by many readers and critics. It is impossible to be sure it is not Thackeray's true sense of himself, without irony, just as it is impossible to be sure that the Oedipal reading of the novel is the true one. The meaning vibrates among various possible configurations, since there is no solid base on which to construct a definitive interpretation.

*Henry Esmond* contains within itself, distributed here and there in the text, various emblems for this lack of ground and for the consequent fragmenting of any coherent line, even the line which puts in question the line. The story of Oedipus, for example, if it is taken as the archetype on which *Henry Esmond* is modeled, is, in Freud's interpretation of it, in that of Sophocles, or in the displaced version of the story in *Hamlet*, the narrative of the discovery that there is no authority, no father, no head source of meaning. It is the story of the discovery that one is oneself in the place of the father, but guiltily so, without any right to be there. The Oedipus story is the archetype of the discovery that there is no archetype.

It should be remembered that the "Oedipus complex" is itself an effect of language, whether in the person who suffers it or in an interpretation of the Oedipus story such as Thackeray's or Freud's. This is figured in the role of the various oracles, riddles, and prophecies in the story. These are, after all, linguistic formulations having performative power when they are read in one way or another. It is also figured in the mixing of generations and in the confusion or displacement of kinship names in the Oedipus story, where one man is husband and son of the same woman, and brother of his children. Such mixing occurs also in *Henry Esmond*. Who says the woman I love repeats my mother? Who says my life is governed by my rivalry for my father?

I do. Who said the experiences of Oedipus were the fulfillment of the oracles? Oedipus did. If he did not know it was his father he killed or his mother he married, how could he be guilty of incest and parricide? The crimes come afterward, when he puts two and two together, sets the oracles against the facts and condemns himself. His sufferings and his self-condemnation are a reading of his life in terms of those oracular texts. Oedipus sees his life as repeating the oracles, as Freud created the Oedipus complex by reading his own life in terms of his reading of Sophocles' play. The meaning of the Oedipus story lies neither in the first element, the oracle, nor in the second, its fulfillment, but in between. It lies in the gap between the two and in the filling of that gap which makes the first a prophetic sign fulfilled by the second. The Oedipus complex always goes by way of language. It is, like Henry's reading of himself or my second reading by irony, an error in interpretation. It falsely takes similars as equals. Such a reading leads to a recognition of a lack of authority, but even the line leading to that recognition is without authority. Henry in writing his imitation *Spectator* paper reads his life in terms of the story of Oedipus, as Freud also was to do. He creates in the paper a new oracle and then reads it. In the same way, the reader of the novel in his deeper insight into the implications of the *Spectator* paper reads it anew. The reader sets *Oedipus Rex*, *Hamlet*, *Henry Esmond*, and *The Interpretation of Dreams* side by side to make a story out of the lineup.

If the references to Oedipus and to his biblical and literary replicas in *Henry Esmond* function not to affirm a ground but to put the existence of any certain ground in question, three characters in the novel personify in different ways the interruption of the narrative line. They incarnate an energy of discontinuity which undoes the novel's coherence. One such character is Father Holt, the Jesuit master of disguise. Father Holt appears and reappears in many different costumes in his futile machinations for the Stuart cause. Holt, who had been Henry's mentor and a father figure to him in his boyhood, is proud of his omniscience. His knowledge, however, is a sham knowledge. He is always slightly wrong. He consistently makes a false story out of distorted facts. He is in this a parody of Henry's claims to a total memory and to an omniscient understanding, like God's, of his life. "A foible of Mr. Holt's," says Henry when he meets the priest again in Flanders, ". . . was omniscience; thus in every point he here professed to know, he was nearly right, but not quite . . . Esmond did not think fit to correct his old master in these trifling blunders, but they served to give him knowledge of the other's character, and he smiled to think that this was his oracle of early days; and now no longer infallible or divine" (bk. 2, chap. 13). "Nearly right, but not quite," and making a false claim to divine omniscience—these are good formulas for Henry's portrait of himself. In that portrait he makes a point of emphasizing his own shortcomings, but misses the most important ones, and falsely claims now to know it all.

The farewell to Father Holt, at the end of the book, emphasizes again Holt's indefatigable penchant for intrigue and disguise. It emphasizes also his failure to have obtained his goal by these strategies: "Sure he was the most unlucky of men: he never played a game but he lost it; or engaged in a conspiracy but 'twas certain to end in defeat. I saw him in Flanders after this, whence he went to Rome to the headquarters of his Order; and actually reappeared among us in America, very old, and busy, and hopeful. I am not sure that he did not assume the hatchet and moccasins there; and, attired in a blanket and war-paint skulk about a missionary amongst the Indians" (bk 3, chap. 13).

Another character who personifies the interruption of the narrative line is Henry's real father, Thomas Esmond. Thomas's gift for telling lies corresponds to another of Henry's habits, as well as to one of Thackeray's habits. Thomas Esmond could always talk himself out of a tight situation, for example the situation of having fathered Henry, by making up a circumstantial story. Father Holt tells Henry of this in the chapter where Holt recounts what he knows of Henry's origins:

> "I must tell you that Captain Thomas, or my Lord Viscount afterwards, was never at a loss for a story, and could cajole a woman or a dun with a volubility, and an air of simplicity at the same time, of which many a creditor of his has been the dupe. His tales used to gather verisimilitude as he went on with them. He strung together fact after fact with a wonderful rapidity and coherence. It required, saving your presence, a very long habit of acquaintance with your father to know when his lordship was l——,—telling the truth or no."
>
> (Bk. 2, chap. 13)

Here is an emblem of Henry's own narration. Like his father, Henry has the gift for stringing together fact after fact with solemn verisimilitude until it makes a coherent story. If Henry does this, so does Thackeray. He does it in a way even more like Thomas Esmond's storytelling than Henry's is, since Henry's narration is at least based on episodes that are presented as having really happened, whereas Thackeray's novel-writing, like novel-writing in general, is the making up out of whole cloth of plausible circumstantial stories. This is what Thomas Esmond does when he invents a previous life for himself, a father who is a Cornish squire, a shrewish wife there, and so on. Thackeray here momentarily brings to the surface, if the reader happens to think of the parallel, the lying or fictional nature of the text the reader

is at that moment reading, with all its "facts" about Henry's life. The notic-
ing of this parallel may remind the reader of the way Thackeray means to
use his detour into lie as a strategy for dealing with his own life, for retaining mastery over it and over other people, for duping his creditors. To reveal
the strategy in this way is to disable it. It makes the detour a permanent devia-
tion into fiction. The road is suspended by the indirect, ironic revelation of
its way of working.

The final and most important personification of this suspension is
Beatrix. Though her manifest function in the novel is as a displacement of
Henry's love for Rachel and as a means of dramatizing his tendency to love
someone because she is desired by others, she also functions, more covertly,
as his secret alter ego and as the embodiment of what is most negative in
Thackeray's view of life. Like Henry, she is a demystifier of the pretenses
of others, but she shows where such a procedure may lead if it is carried
all the way. Certainly she is not a model to admire and imitate. Rather she
is a demonstration of how destructive full clairvoyance about oneself and
about others is. It might be better to be fooled. The novel as a whole,
however, makes it difficult to go on fooling oneself, though readers who take
Henry as a positive characterization have succeeded in doing so. Beatrix, in
any case, is the embodiment in *Henry Esmond* of a dangerous feminine principle of skepticism. She represents a power of radical irony and faithlessness.
She disbelieves in any hierarchy or authority. She has a woman's cynicism,
a woman's knowledge that there is no king or legitimate male ruler, though
she is also an example of the need certain women have to possess the em-
bodiments of this pretended power, if only to destroy them.

She also knows there is no legitimate queen or goddess. "All the time
you are worshipping and singing hymns to me," she tells Henry, "I know
very well I am no goddess, and grow weary of the incense" (bk. 3, chap.
4). As Henry says, "She was imperious, she was light-minded, she was flighty,
she was false, she had no reverence in her character" (bk. 2, chap. 15). Beatrix
is Henry's unrecognized alter ego, his mirror image in a changed sex. If Henry
breaks the line of succession in his family, Beatrix is also destructive wherever
she enters. An example is the way she entices the Pretender away from London at the moment he might have seized the throne. In doing so she destroys
the possibility of a Stuart succession. The difference is that Henry does not
understand his destructive effects on those around him, while she does.
"Though we are here sitting in the same room," she tells Henry, "there is
a great wall between us" (bk. 3, chap. 4). The wall is also a mirror in which
he might see his secret face, the face he does everything to hide from himself
and from the reader.

Beatrix is in many ways the most complex and even attractive characterization in *Henry Esmond*, as Becky Sharp is in *Vanity Fair*, though it would be risky to have anything to do with such a person in real life. Beatrix and Becky are Thackeray's contributions to the long line of selfish and destructive women presented in English fiction. Such figures are among the most memorable invented by English novelists of both sexes, Rosamund Vincy in *Middlemarch*, for example, Lizzie Eustace in *The Eustace Diamonds*, or Estella in *Great Expectations*. Beatrix is as changeable and wayward as the moon, her emblem. She causes devastation wherever she goes. Neither Henry nor Beatrix's mother nor anyone else is able to master her. She is utterly selfish and faithless. She manipulates social codes for her own advancement without believing in them. She is therefore, beneath the surface of her beauty and her gaiety, deeply melancholy. She has the melancholy of her nihilism. She knows that we are all alone, alone, alone, and that no prize is worth winning. This is Thackeray's knowledge too. It lies behind that irony he wears like a cloak he cannot remove. Beatrix is the embodiment in the book of that principle of irony on which *Henry Esmond* is based. She puts before the reader the corrosive power of that irony, its ability to break every continuity and to reduce everything to naught. More than any other feature of *Henry Esmond* she exposes the pretenses of Henry's picture of himself. She reveals his priggishness.

Beatrix also casts an annihilating shadow on Thackeray's pretense of mastery, as well as on any pretensions of sovereignty in the understanding of the novel the reader may have. That chain of pretenses can only be sustained by repudiating Beatrix. She must be cast out of the novel like a scapegoat, with all the sins of society upon her. Henry in the end repudiates her as without value, as immoral, as not worth loving. Thackeray has her grow fat and marry Tom Tusher. He takes away all her lunar or solar glow. The reader in his turn must ignore the lesson she teaches if he tries with a clear conscience to present a coherent interpretation of *Henry Esmond*.

Henry's narrative is based on a claim of total memory, as Thackeray's must be, and as the reader's interpretation must be too. The New Criticism, for example, like the archetypal criticism of Northrop Frye, bases its claim for a complete reading on the possibility of a total simultaneous integrating recall of all the details of the text in question. Beatrix, on the other hand, is the personification of reading or narrating as forgetting. This is foregrounded not only in the story of how she forgets the name of one of her lovers, but also in the way she lives only in the present instant. She is ready at any moment to forget and to betray the last lover in order to be ready without memory and without past for the next. She gives herself without loyalty and, of course, without giving herself, either sexually, so it seems, or in any other way, to each lover in turn. She forgets in between. If Henry, Thackeray, and the reader are drawers of lines, weavers of webs, Beatrix is the unweaver. She is the undoer of all lines and of all figures made with lines. This is asserted in a passage which explicitly uses this figure. It may be taken as a final emblematic image of Beatrix's role as the embodiment of the disintegrative power of irony: "If [Henry] were like Ulysses in his folly, at least she was in so far like Penelope that she had a crowd of suitors, and undid day after day and night after night the handiwork of fascination and the web of coquetry with which she was wont to allure and entertain them" (bk. 3, chap. 3). *Henry Esmond* as a whole, insofar as Beatrix is the personification of the effects of irony in it, is, in its constant dismantling of itself, like that description of Proust's night work of forgetting given by Walter Benjamin. Benjamin, the reader will remember, uses this reversed image of Penelope's weaving and unweaving in a passage cited and discussed in the introductory chapter of this book.

Applied to *Henry Esmond*, Benjamin's distinction between the Penelope work of recollection and the Penelope work of forgetting leads to the following formulation: Henry's memory of his life is that false rationalizing daytime memory, stringing things together by way of what Benjamin elsewhere in his essay calls "identical" resemblance. The activity of irony in Thackeray's narrative, on the other hand, present everywhere in the book, but personified especially in Beatrix's disintegrating power, is that Penelope web of forgetting which works not by identities but by what Benjamin calls "opaque similarities" ("The Image of Proust"). Such similarities depend on difference and distance. They negate themselves in the same moment that they affirm themselves. Thackeray's irony continuously undermines the interpretation by way of repetitions the text nevertheless continuously invites the reader to make. *Henry Esmond*, in its totality, is therefore a large-scale expression of the negative relation between irony and repetition. If repetition creates meaning in fiction by making the forward movement of the narrative line turn back on itself and become significant thereby, irony loosens those connections. It makes the narrative line blur and finally break up into detached fragments. These may be put together this way or they may be put together that way, but never on the basis of that legitimate authority which, as I began by saying, *Henry Esmond* seeks.

BARBARA HARDY

# Thackeray: Inconstant Passions

Thackeray's analysis of feeling is comic and profoundly serious. "Pathos," he wrote, "I hold should be very occasional indeed in humourous works and indicated rather than expressed or expressed very rarely." He goes on to give a paradigm of pathos from *Vanity Fair*, "where Amelia is represented as trying to separate herself from the boy—She goes upstairs and leaves him with his aunt 'as that poor Lady Jane Grey tried the axe that was to separate her slender life' I say that is a fine image whoever wrote it (& I came on it quite by surprise in a review the other day) that is greatly pathetic I think: it leaves you to make your own sad pictures—We shouldn't do much more than that I think in comic books—In a story written in the pathetic key it would be different & then the comedy perhaps should be occasional. Some day—but a truce to egotistical twaddle" (*The Letters and Private Papers of William Makepeace Thackeray*).

*Vanity Fair* is a comic novel with many modulations to a pathetic key, but the earlier *Barry Lyndon*, written as an eighteenth-century pastiche, is the only work by one of the major Victorian novelists as totally comic as a novel by Fielding. Its medium is ironic, but it endows its comic hero with an emotional life, and is flexible enough to vary and complicate the record of Barry's feelings. The emotions of this autobiographical narrator are variously unreliable. Barry is a liar, a boaster, a self-flatterer and a sentimentalist, and his account makes an appeal which the reader recognizes as false, within a fiction of insincerity. Thackeray grants his hero and readers the lux-

From *Forms of Feeling in Victorian Fiction*. © 1985 by Barbara Hardy. Peter Owen Ltd., 1985.

ury of sporadic insight into underlying emotional truths. As one of E. M.
Forster's characters says in *Where Angels Fear to Tread*, "wicked people are
capable of love." Even George Eliot, who would scarcely credit this since
she saw wickedness as an incapacity for love, permits the villainous Demp-
ster in "Janet's Repentance," or Tito Melema in *Romola*, to participate in
a kind of loving. Thackeray was much clearer about love as what Joyce calls
"the word known to all men," partly because he thought of himself and others,
too, as bad—"take the world by a certain standard . . . and who dares talk
of having any virtue at all?" (*The Letters and Private Papers*). His moral pattern is therefore more cross-hatched than George Eliot's. There is no virtue
in Barry Lyndon, but he is endowed with some capacity for what we may
call "good" feeling. He is brilliantly shown as a master of almost all the forms
of false feeling, but is allowed genuineness when he feels nostalgia, filial
affection, paternal love, and hostility to war. These emotions are carefully
oriented. Thackeray is intent on drawing a portrait of a villain through the
subtle means of gauche confession. The autobiographer damns himself by
high praise. Barry is the opposite of an artist and his emotional narration
often imitates sentimental art, overreaching itself, for instance, with what
Thackeray called "mawkish" appeals to the reader. But most of the other
characters are sentimentally contaminated too, finding fine words for false
feeling. Barry's first love, Nora, and his rival, Quin, faintly echo the rhetorical
aspirations of Richardson's Lovelace as they address each other in poetic diction learnt from novels. "I vow before all the gods, my heart has never felt
the soft flame!" Quin announces, and "your passion is not equal to ours.
We are like—like some plant I've read of—we bear but one flower and then
we die!" stammers Nora (in chapter 1). Thackeray enjoys displacing the
rhetoric of predictable sentiment. Barry is allowed patches of candour, as
when he admits that amorous nostalgia and remorse are sentiments beyond
his experience.

Barry's first expression of intense feeling is fuelled by Thackeray's own
antimilitary anger and pity, which is half-assimilated to character. The account of the battle of Minden begins with blunt and matter-of-fact detail,
then makes a bid for pathos. Barry tells how he found in the pockets of the
ensign he had killed a purse of gold and a silver *bon-bon* box, moving trifles
twice repeated, and speaks of undignified recollections "best passed over briefly." Thackeray uses Barry's brusque callousness and sentimentality for
effectively understated pathos, and follows it with Barry's outburst against
war:

> Such knaves and ruffians do men in war become! It is well for
> gentlemen to talk of the age of chivalry; but remember the starv-

ing brutes whom they lead—men nursed in poverty, entirely ignorant, made to take a pride in deeds of blood. . . . It is with
these shocking instruments that your great warriors and kings have
been doing their murderous work in the world; and while, for
instance, we are at the present moment admiring the "Great
Frederick," as we call him, and his philosophy, and his liberali-
ty, and his military genius, I, who have served him, and been,
as it were, behind the scenes of which that great spectacle is composed, can only look at it with horror.

(Chap. 4)

Thackeray assimilates his own irony and compassion to the cynicism of Barry,
but to do so is to make Barry momentarily a better man than he is: "What
a number of items of human crime, misery, slavery, go to form that sum-
total of glory!" Thackeray ventriloquizes briefly, but at the end of this
declamatory passage he returns us to the characterized stream of feeling;
the experience described plausibly arouses distaste or remorse even in Barry
Lyndon:

I can recollect a certain day, about three weeks after the battle
of Minden, and a farmhouse in which some of us entered, and
how the old woman and her daughters served us, trembling, to
wine; and how we got drunk over the wine, and the house was
in a flame, presently: and woe betide the wretched fellow afterwards who came home to look for his house and his children!

(Chap. 4)

As Thackeray says about Amelia's rehearsal of grief, "it leaves you to make
your own . . . pictures." Like Sterne, whom Thackeray detested but in some
ways resembled, he knew the sentimental force of suggestiveness. Barry's hasty
summary of rape and murder is perfectly in character, and perfectly serves
the author's passionate sense of military waste and horror. This passion is
scarcely central to Barry's character, but successfully accommodated to it.
It perhaps does not quite fit Barry's report of his pleasure and profit in
plunder, but he is made to write about various stages of recollected emotion. His character is destabilized by role-playing and dishonesty, and his
contradictions and inconsistencies are used by Thackeray to express emotions discretely and discontinuously. But the assimilations are skilful. For
instance, two chapters after the description of the battle of Minden, Barry
speaks of having formed himself "to the condition of the proper fighting beast:
on a day of action I was savage and happy; out of the field I took all the
pleasure I could get, and was by no means delicate as to its quality or the

manner of procuring it." Barry's discrimination of "the proper fighting beast" is closer to Thackeray, in its irony, than to Barry, who is not usually "delicate" even off the battlefield. We may try to make the passage "realistic," by allowing for the protean attitudes of an unstable personality; or by seeing Barry's point of view as maturing in judgement. But there is an underlying difficulty in having Barry grow finer feelings with age, since in all other respects he appears to deteriorate in emotional scruple. Her certainly gives us no clue (as Jane Eyre does) to his emotional "development," and it seems that Thackeray, always peremptory in discounting order and convention, is cleverly creating a character of exceptional fragmentation, not to be judged by standards of realism.

Barry's erratic narrative is a vehicle Thackeray repeats from novel to novel, like the emotion of nostalgia. Some forms of nostalgia are in no way out of keeping with Barry's obtuse sensibility, and are entirely compatible with his facile and sentimental affections. Patriotism, filial love, and nostalgia are comically combined: "I had not seen the dear soul's writing for five years," he gushes over his mother's letter, which "created in my mind a yearning after home, a melancholy which I cannot describe" (chap. 7). He even gives up an engagement with Fraülein Lottchen, to pass "a long night weeping and thinking about dear Ireland." His tears are easily shed, and the combination of stimulants is irresistible: "All the old days, and the fresh happy sunshine of the old green fields in Ireland, and her love, and my uncle . . . and everything that I had done and thought, came back to me." Thackeray carefully places this sentimental outburst. The mother is replying to a diplomatic letter which Barry has designed to be read, to his own advantage, by his captain, and the night of weeping and thinking about "dear Ireland" is followed by the next day's recovery: "my spirits rose again, and I got a ten guinea bill cashed."

On another occasion, Barry's sentimentality is not criticized by Thackeray, but used for the double purpose of expressing congenial feeling, while effectively enlarging character. Barry shows the emotions of nostalgia and parental love, for instance, like Dobbin and Henry Esmond, in whom they are sympathetic and benign feelings, though not untouched by Thackeray's caustic irony. Here is a delicate moment of inner experience, showing the gross and vicious antihero overwhelmed by involuntary memory. He is not a monster, but remembers, and anticipates remembering again, with affection, chagrin, and fear:

> As for Castle Brady, the gates of the park were still there; but the old trees were cut down in the avenue, a black stump jutting out here and there, and casting long shadows as I passed in the

moonlight over the worn, grass-grown old road. A few cows were at pasture there. The garden-gate was gone, and the place a tangled wilderness. I sat down on the old bench, where I had sat on the day when Nora jilted me; and I do believe my feelings were as strong then as they had been when I was a boy, eleven years before; and I caught myself almost crying again, to think that Nora Brady had deserted me. I believe a man forgets nothing. I've seen a flower, or heard some trivial word or two, which have awakened recollections that somehow had lain dormant for scores of years; and when I entered the house in Clarges Street, where I was born (it was used as a gambling-house when I first visited London), all of a sudden the memory of my childhood came back to me— of my actual infancy: I recollected my father in green and gold, holding me up to look at a gilt coach which stood at the door, and my mother in a flowered sack, with patches on her face. Some day, I wonder, will everything we have seen and thought and done come and flash across our minds in this way? I had rather not. I felt so as I sat upon the bench at Castle Brady, and thought of the bygone times.

(Chap. 14)

Emotion is particularized in this charged descriptive set-piece, through the sacred objects and landscape of past youth. The moment is enlarged and dignified by generalization, in the observation about revived emotion, the suggestion that recurs in *Henry Esmond*, "I believe a man forgets nothing," and the comment on involuntary memory. The passage repeats one of Barry's pet adjectives, "old," later recalled by the attentive reader when Barry tells about his wanton and mercenary timber-felling. His sensitivity to place and nature is an easy encapsulation of nostalgia, making no demands. The significant details of the gambling-house, the finery, and the gilt coach, make their own terse contribution to an impression of Barry's nurture. The passage contains one of the deepest intimations of Barry's nurture. The passage contains one of the deepest intimations of Barry's lower depths in that grim reserve about a final total recall he would "rather not" experience. "I had rather not" is Thackerayan in its wry candour, but assimilated to Barry's remorse, which flickers briefly as it dies. When Barry recounts the death of his son, in chapter 19, the sorrow is not presented as excessive, feeble, or false. It is quietly but firmly marked by the characteristic pathetic adjectives "poor," "dear," and "little"—"My poor, dear little boy" and "There he lay in his little boots and spurs." "I could only burst out into tears" is followed by a characteristic motion of the egocentric narration. He tells the moving, self-congratulatory story of the little drummer-boy he was "fond of," to whom he ran to give water. As to remorse, he has boasted before of not feeling it. His son was killed because Barry bought him a dangerous horse and lay in a drunken sleep when the child went off to ride, hoping his "fond father" would remit the threatened horse-whipping. The death-bed scene is brilliantly controlled. Barry's feelings are never complicated by the pangs of guilt, only by those of self-pity, "Who cares for Barry Lyndon now?" and "what soul is there alive that cares for Barry Lyndon?" (chap. 14):

> During this time the dear angel's temper seemed quite to change: he asked his mother and me pardon for any act of disobedience he had been guilty of towards us; he said often he should like to see his brother Bullingdon. "Bully was better than you, Papa," he said; "he used not to swear so, and he told and taught me many good things while you were away." And, taking a hand of his mother and mine in each of his little clammy ones, he begged us not to quarrel so, but love each other, so that we might meet again in heaven, where Bully told him quarrelsome people never went. His mother was very much affected by these admonitions from the poor suffering angel's mouth; and I was so too. I wish she had enabled me to keep the counsel which the dying boy gave us.
>
> At last, after two days, he died. There he lay, the hope of my family, the pride of my manhood, the link which had kept me and my Lady Lyndon together. "Oh, Redmond," said she, kneeling by the sweet child's body, "do, do let us listen to the truth out of his blessed mouth; and do you amend your life, and treat your poor, loving fond wife as her dying child bade you." And I said I would: but there are promises which it is out of a man's power to keep; especially with such a woman as her. But we drew together after that sad event, and were for several months better friends.
>
> (Chap. 19)

The few traces of easy pity, "dear angel" and "poor suffering angel," pass almost without notice, as Barry's narration nearly rises to the occasion. (They are contaminated by many less discriminating uses.) The voice is solemn and restrained, but also egocentric and accusatory. Such episodes of feeling complete the picture of Barry's viciousness by adding to his falsities those of the sentimentalist, resilient, indulgent, more moved by past than present. Barry stands out amongst the emotional characters in Victorian fiction as a subtle study of weak and facile self-protection.

Thackeray is the Victorian novelist closest to Flaubert in being alive to the dangers of sentimentality. The cruelties and unrealities of the sentimentalist form a major theme in *Vanity Fair*. Amelia is introduced as the conventional heroine whose sweetness is dismissed as "twaddle" by the imaginary reader Jones, and affectionately defended, for the moment, by the narrator, but her character is developed as a blend of idolatry and nostalgia. Amelia's love for George Osborne is unreal and inactive, composed of the response to a social stereotype of masculine charm:

> This young person (perhaps it was very imprudent in her parents to encourage her, and abet her in such idolatry and silly romantic ideas) loved, with all her heart, the young officer. . . . She had never seen a man so beautiful or so clever: such a figure on horseback: such a dancer: such a hero in general.
>
> (Chap. 12)

This is cleverly called "Quite a Sentimental Chapter," the qualification clear in text as in title. The social typology at work in Amelia's feeling is composed of images of looks and motion, and underlined by comparisons with the Prince Regent and Beau Brummell. The only response which is not a physical one, "so clever," is wrong, though understandable, given her education and knowledge. The judgement ("silly" and "romantic") is endorsed by the banalities and raptures of the visions. Thackeray's preacher observes that such love "is in the nature and instinct of some women," but this regrettably unironic remark is not supported by the particular case. Thackeray can express strong feelings as he sees through them. For instance, he uses comic hyperboles which are teasing and sympathetic:

> The fate of Europe was Lieutenant George Osborne to her. His dangers being over, she sang Te Deum. He was her Europe: her emperor: her allied monarchs and august prince regent. He was her sun and moon.
>
> (Chap. 12)

The political scale of these comic grandiosities economically marks the limits of love and knowledge. Like Barry Lyndon, Amelia has no self-awareness. Like him, too, she finds it easier to feel for the past than the present.

After George's death, her feeling for him is replaced by an equally blind and selfish mother-love, sharply criticized for its self-indulgence. Amelia's strong feelings are contrasted with those of Becky Sharp, whose pretensions to wifely devotion and mother-love are also criticized. The narrator of *Vanity Fair* criticizes everyone, including himself, for vain feeling. But Becky is compared, as well as contrasted, with Amelia, to expose the superficialities and selfishness of Amelia's affections. Thackeray shows very clearly that a self-

congratulatory and sacrificial love can be cruel as it pampers the beloved
and neglects the unloved. Amelia's parental doting has much in common with
Barry Lyndon's. Her capacity for change is small but importantly present.
One of the people used and discarded by her is Dobbin, whose decision to
give up the patient suffering of romantic love comes as a relief and a release
for character and reader. Thackeray exposes Amelia's lack of generosity and
perceptiveness in a fine scene of love-reversal:

> "Have I not learned in that time to read all your feelings, and
> look into your thoughts? I know what your heart is capable of:
> it can cling faithfully to a recollection, and cherish a fancy; but
> it can't feel such an attachment as mine deserves to mate with,
> and such as I would have won from a woman more generous than
> you. No, you are not worthy of the love which I have devoted
> to you. I knew all along that the prize I had set my life on was
> not worth the winning; that I was a fool, with fond fancies, too,
> bartering away my all of truth and ardour against your little fee-
> ble remnant of love. I will bargain no more: I withdraw. I find
> no fault with you. You are very good-natured, and have done
> your best; but you couldn't—you couldn't reach up to the height
> of the attachment which I bore you, and which a loftier soul than
> yours might have been proud to share. Good-bye, Amelia! I have
> watched your struggle. Let it end. We are both weary of it."
>
> Amelia stood scared and silent as William thus suddenly broke
> the chain by which she held him, and declared his independence
> and superiority. He had placed himself at her feet so long that
> the poor little woman had been accustomed to trample upon him.
> She didn't wish to marry him, but she wished to keep him. She
> wished to give him nothing, but that he should give her all. It
> is a bargain not unfrequently levied in love.
>
> William's sally had quite broken and cast her down. *Her* assault
> was long since over and beaten back.
>
> "Am I to understand then,—that you are going—away,—
> William?" she said.
>
> He gave a sad laugh. "I went once before," he said, "and came
> back after twelve years. We were young, then, Amelia. Good-
> bye. I have spent enough of my life at this play."
>
> (Chap. 66)

Dobbin himself is criticized, in his turn, for his idolatries. He penetrates
the nature of Amelia's illusions and indulgences, but turns from woman-
worshipping to worshipping another idol, his child. All emotions are con-

taminated in *Vanity Fair*. The narrator's uncomfortable irony, not unrelieved by humour and sympathy, puts Amelia in her place.

> "It was time you sent for me, dear Amelia," he said.
> "You will never go again, William?"
> "No, never," he answered: and pressed the dear little soul once more to his heart.
> As they issued out of the Custom-house precincts, Georgy broke out on them, with his telescope up to his eye, and a loud laugh of welcome; he danced round the couple, and performed many facetious antics as he led them up to the house. Jos wasn't up yet; Becky not visible (though she looked at them through the blinds). Georgy ran off to see about breakfast. Emmy, whose shawl and bonnet were off in the passage in the hands of Miss Payne, now went to undo the clasp of William's cloak, and—we will, if you please, go with George and look after breakfast for the Colonel. The vessel is in port. He has got the prize he has been trying for all his life. The bird has come in at last. There it is with its head on his shoulder, billing and cooing close up to his heart, with soft outstretched fluttering wings. This is what he has asked for every day and hour for eighteen years. This is what he pined after. Here it is—the summit, the end—the last page of the third volume. Goodbye, Colonel. God bless you, honest William! Farewell, dear Amelia. Grow green again, tender little parasite, round the rugged old oak to which you cling!
>
> (Chap. 67)

The feelings of the reader are also put in their place; they are first amused by the narrator's wit and irony, then implicated in unreality, as the ending of the lovers' story is cleverly assimilated to the ending of the novel, declaring fictionality and mocking expectation. What is deluded but tolerated in the sentiments of Amelia and Dobbin is matched by our indulged sense of a happy ending. Thackeray says we have got to the last page before we actually do, cunningly displacing even further our newest expectations; when we really get to the last page of the third volume, Dobbin is implicated in new unreal emotions. In a neat stroke Thackeray praises him for not loving Amelia too much, and for perceiving the limits of her feeling, and implicates him in a parental idolatry of his "little Janey," of whom "he is fonder than of anything in the world." The refusal to make a tidy and moral ending compares the reality principle in the character with the reality principle in the novelist, and the reader. Thackeray distrusts closure and completion and likes to disconcert us when we expect solace. Here and in the teasingly reflexive ending of *The Newcomes* there is a final admission of fictionality. The characters in *Vanity Fair* are not only in love with vanities, but are mere puppets, as we expect in Vanity Fair. We have been criticizing idolatry, while caring about fictional images.

At the end of *The Newcomes*, Pendennis, Laura, Ethel and Clive "fade away into fable-land." The narrator observes of his characters: "They were alive, and I heard their voices; but five minutes since was touched by their grief. And have we parted with them here on a sudden, and without as much as a shake of the hand?" Arthur Pendennis is dismissed before he can tell if Ethel has married, without answering the reader's "sentimental question." Thackeray raises at the ending the question of that oddity, the author's and reader's feeling for fictions. Though the tone is teasing, it is also melancholy, as the illusion of reality shrinks into the admission of art. It shrinks too in *Vanity Fair*, where there is a double sadness, that of the character diminished to puppet, and that of the reader, invited to share the realization of vanity:

> Which of us is happy in this world? Which of us has his desire? or, having it, is satisfied?—Come children, let us shut up the box and the puppets, for our play is played out.
>
> (Chap. 67)

The awareness of the fiction plays its part within the emotional drama of the characters in *Pendennis*. Pen's amorous nights are marked by sound sleep, but the passions of Anxiety and Love are introduced, through the narrator's experience, in laconic and grave personifications:

> Even in later days and with a great deal of care and other thoughtful matter to keep him awake, a man from long practice or fatigue or resolution *begins* by going to sleep as usual, and gets a nap in advance of Anxiety. But she soon comes up with him and jogs his shoulder, and says, "Come, my man, no more of this laziness, you must wake up and have a talk with me." Then they fall to together in the midnight. Well, whatever might afterwards happen to him, poor little Pen was not come to this state yet; he tumbled into a sound sleep—did not wake until an early hour in the morning, when the rooks began to caw from the little wood beyond his bedroom windows; and—at that very instant and as his eyes started open, the beloved image was in his mind. "My dear boy," he heard her say, "you were in a sound sleep, and I would not disturb you: but I have been close by your pillow all this while: and I don't intend that you shall leave me. I am Love!

> I bring with me fever and passion: wild longing, maddening desire;
> restless craving and seeking. Many a long day ere this I heard you
> calling out for me; and behold now I am come."
>
> Was Pen frightened at the summons? Not he. He did not know
> what was coming: it was all wild pleasure and delight as yet.
>
> (Chap. 4)

Like the hyperbolic figure placing Amelia's passion, this is a fusion of traditional intensification with irony. Pen's image of the beloved fuses with the personification—"many a long day ere this I heard you calling"—to denote his love of Love as well as his delighted obsession. Irony is explicit, "There was no mistake about it now. He was as much in love as the best hero in the best romance he ever read," which insists on the flattery of our passions, and on their stereotypes, but the "wild pleasure and delight" are powerfully presented. Thackeray also uses scenes and images as Dickens does, creating a symbolism for feeling to which the characters are indifferent: "The blue waters came rolling into the bay, foaming and roaring hoarsely: Pen looked them in the face with blank eyes, hardly regarding them. What a tide there was pouring into the lad's own mind" (chap. 5). The comic medium is here also a sympathetic one, as the narrator approaches his character, then turns away a little to comment with the voice of worldly, but not cynical, wisdom. Thackeray does not ridicule or pity his characters, but holds ridicule and pity in a controlled suspension. Like the personification of Love, the image of the tide is intense and relaxed; Thackeray reverses Paul Dombey's appropriation of the metaphor of the waves, and shows the oddity of a character passionately ignoring the symbol created to express his passion. In the shift from the scene to the metaphor—"What a tide there was"—there is both affectionate intimacy and the assertion of fictional distance.

In *Pendennis* Thackeray pursues the inquiry into passionate sincerity which he began in *Barry Lyndon*. Pen and Blanche Amory (his second love) play at loving, as their narrator observes. Pen, like a flimsier Julien Sorel, acts himself into an approach to emotional reality, to be rejected by Blanche. When Pen makes her an offer of marriage without wealth, she gracefully simulates regret and self-pity. She puts on a similar performance for the benefit of another lover, Foker, in which her rounded periods, designed exclamations and falling cadences are contrasted with Foker's broken sincerities. After this, she and Pen have their last dialogue. She calmly takes him to task for having never cared for her, and explains her own incapacity for genuine feeling, "*Et moi, c'est différent*. I have been spoilt early. . . . If I cannot have emotions, I must have the world. You would offer me neither one nor the other"; when he comments on her *ennui*, she answers, "*Eh! Il me faut des émotions.*" (They both use French for elegant evasion and pose.) The narrator concludes:

> Pen had never seen her or known so much about her in all the years of their intimacy as he saw and knew now: though he saw more than existed in reality. For this young lady was not able to carry out any emotion to the full; but had a sham enthusiasm, a sham hatred, a sham love, a sham taste, a sham grief, each of which flared and shone very vehemently for an instant, but subsided and gave place to the next sham emotion.
>
> (Chap. 73)

Thackeray's problem is how to follow this, formally and psychologically, with Pen's final union with Laura. He begins with a preliminary understatement, just right as a contrast with false feeling and false speaking, in which the narrator shows Laura's pale face as Pen opens the door, asks, "May we follow him?" and rises to a balanced and solemn generalization:

> The great moments of life are but moments like the others. Your doom is spoken in a word or two. A single look from the eyes; a mere pressure of the hand, may decide it; or of the lips, though they cannot speak.
>
> (Chap. 74)

There is an abrupt cut to a later moment, when narrator and reader are allowed to "enter with her ladyship" to discover the lovers in a happy attitude; then the narrator swerves back to tell us what was omitted, to present, "In a word," Pen's brief proposal, and Laura's speechless reply. It is an arch device, making and breaking a promise of restraint, tiptoeing round the almost inarticulate lovers. Later in the scene Thackeray refuses to simplify, showing Pen's implicit apology for the "transaction" with Blanche, and reminding us of Laura's serious feeling for Warrington, her Bluebeard. Strong lines about Pen's awe "in the contemplation of her sweet goodness and purity," are qualified, relieved, and particularized by the narrator's speculative, "And she—very likely she was thinking, 'How strange it is that I should ever have cared for another; I am vexed almost to think that I care for him so little, am so little sorry that he is gone away.'" Laura's rapturous speech shows Thackeray's capacity for exaggerating sentiment without ironic comment:

> I care about nothing but Arthur; my waking and sleeping thoughts are about him; he is never absent from me. And to think that he is to be mine, mine! and that I am to marry him, and not to be his servant as I expected to be only this morning; for I would have

gone down on my knees to Blanche to beg her to let me live with him. And now—Oh, it is too much.

The language of feeling is placed, but not ridiculed.

Thackeray's greatest love story is *Henry Esmond*, a novel marked by the ruling passion of "cut-throat melancholy" in which as in *Pendennis*, Thackeray unbosomed himself of his love for Jane Brookfield, but more passionately. His letters to Jane, after what seems to have been an admission of affection, express the irony, stoicism, restraint and affection which colour *Esmond*:

> A change, a fine air, a wonderful sunshine and moonlight, and a great spectacle of happy people perpetually rolling by has done me all the good in the world and then one of the Miss Smiths told me a story which is the very thing for the beginning of Pendennis, which is actually begun and in progress—This is a comical beginning rather; the other, which I did not like, was sentimental; and will yet come in very well after the startling comical business has been played off.—See how beautifully I have put stops to the last sentence; and crossed the i's and dotted the t's! It was written 4 hours ago before dinner; before Jullien's concert, before a walk by the sea shore—I have been thinking what a number of ladies, and gentlemen too, live like you just now—in a smart papered room with rats gnawing behind the Wainscot. Be hanged to the rats! but they are a sort of company. You must have a poker ready, and if the rats come out, bang, beat them on the head. This is an allegory. Why, it would work up into a little moral poem, if you chose to write it. . . . I thought I would like to say good night to you.
>
> *(Letters and Private Papers)*

The first-person retrospect offered by the novel is a private memorial, a fantasy of unacted possibilities, and perhaps a melancholy message, like the letters. Nostalgia was one of Thackeray's favourite emotions, and the melancholy which is so strong in the remembrance of things past in *Henry Esmond* is not just a lament for Jane Brookfield. It marks a melancholy close to the sadness of those vanities in *Vanity Fair*, and here continues the theme of idolatry, dealing with it from the viewpoint of a latter-day Don Quixote, a man searching for name, title, legitimacy and identity. The use of the first-person pronoun is charged with emotional significance. The novel is melancholy but its passions are complex. It dramatizes and analyses a man's love for two women, with a remarkable imaginative coherence. The retrospective analysis of feeling in *Jane Eyre* and *David Copperfield* contrasts innocence with mature hindsight; in *Esmond* Thackeray deals with the complex experience of reviving past passion in memory. One of its dominant themes is the disturbed recollection of emotion, expressed in forms coloured by the narrator's experience, as dramatic utterance and knowledge.

Unlike *Vanity Fair*, *Esmond* no longer represents emotional constancy as sentimental, withdrawn, or unreal. Nostalgia is characterized through Esmond's retrospective narrations of love and grief. The introductory memoir by Esmond's daughter Rachel makes it clear that neither the physical deterioration of Beatrix Castlewood, referred to by her niece as "our other relative, Bishop Tusher's lady," and presented through the compounded jealousies of daughter and mother, nor Esmond's love for his wife, have dispelled past feelings: "papa said—'All women were alike; that there was never one so beautiful as that one; and that we could forgive her everything but her beauty.'"

The narrative is appropriately fragmented in several ways. Emotions are variably expressed as they are recollected in variable moods. For instance, Esmond narrates the discovery of Beatrix's intrigue with the Pretender jealously and angrily. He reports the porter's story of the Prince's kisses, in the severity of third-person form:

> Esmond darkly thought, how Hamilton, Ashburnham, had before been masters of those roses that the young Prince's lips were now feeding on. He sickened at that notion. Her cheek was desecrated, her beauty tarnished; shame and honour stood between it and him. The love was dead within him.
>
> (Chap. 13)

The narration continues to show anger and jealousy, so contradicting the flat statement "The love was dead." It recalls Esmond's sense of her treachery and his wasted time, "it was to win this that he had given a life's struggle and devotion," testifying to the animation of his feelings. These are not static, but fluctuate; his anger disappears as the Prince offers the reparation of crossing swords and puts honour before love, (rather belatedly) to touch Esmond "by this immense mark of condescension and repentance." A little later, when Beatrix glares at Esmond, looking "quite old," and hisses, "If I did not love you before, cousin . . . think how I love you now," in words which would have killed if they could, there is another assertion of the dead love:

> But her keen words gave no wound to Mr. Esmond; his heart was too hard. As he looked at her, he wondered that he could ever have loved her. His love of ten years was over; it fell down dead on the spot.

Esmond's repeated announcements of the death of love show love's resilience. There is a shift from the third to the first person, two sentences later, "I have never seen her from that day," and soon afterwards one more valediction, "the drama of my own life was ended." Esmond moves into the oblique and reticent narration of his second love and marriage:

> As I think of the immense happiness which was in store for me, and of the depth and intensity of that love which, for so many years, hath blessed me, I own to a transport of wonder and gratitude for such a boon.

The language is rapturous, pious, and exalted:

> In the name of my wife I write the completion of hope, and the summit of happiness. To have such a love is the one blessing, in comparison of which all earthly joy is of no value; and to think of her, is to praise God.

This praises a love which is more than profane love, and not for the first time. On earlier occasions he has clearly compared its sacred flame with his passion for Beatrix. He tells Rachel, for instance, that his fidelity to Beatrix "is folly, perhaps" and that she herself "is a thousand times better: the fondest, the fairest, the dearest of women." But he also tells her, "I cannot help myself. I love her." Under the running title, "Fidelity in Love," he mediates on the strangeness of fidelity, and the irrelevance of the beloved's faults. When the narrator reports emotion, he reports transience and momentariness. When he mediates on recollection he insists, like Barry Lyndon, on the way memory keeps faith, "We forget nothing. The memory sleeps, but wakens again" (bk. 3, chap. 7), and asserts:

> Years after this passion hath been dead and buried, along with a thousand other worldly cares and ambitions, he who felt it can recall it out of its grave, and admire, almost as fondly as he did in his youth, that lovely queenly creature. I invoke that beautiful spirit from the shades and love her still; or rather I should say such a past is always present to a man; such a passion once felt forms a part of his whole being, and cannot be separated from it.
>
> (Bk. 3, chap. 6)

His love is imprinted, like the scar from his Blenheim wound, and returns in celebrations and pains:

> It seemed to Esmond as if he lived years in that prison: and was changed and aged when he came out of it. At certain periods of life we live years of emotion in a few weeks—and look back on

those times, as on great gaps between the old life and the new. You do not know how much you suffer in those critical maladies of the heart, until the disease is over and you look back on it afterwards. During the time, the suffering is at least sufferable. The day passes in more or less of pain, and the night wears away somehow. 'Tis only in after days that we see what the danger has been—as a man out a-hunting or riding for his life looks at a leap, and wonders how he should have survived the taking of it. O dark months of grief and rage! of wrong and cruel endurance! He is old now who recalls you. Long ago he has forgiven and blest the soft hand that wounded him: but the mark is there, and the wound is cicatrized only—no time, tears, caresses, or repentance can obliterate the scar. We are indocile to put up with grief, however. *Reficimus rates quassas*: we tempt the ocean again and again, and try upon new ventures. Esmond thought of his early time as a noviciate, and of this past trial as an initiation before entering into life—as our young Indians undergo tortures silently before they pass to the rank of warriors in the tribe.

(Bk. 2, chap. 1)

Though the novel coherently joins the two kinds of loving, profane and sacred, the insistence on the inexorable recall of feeling, especially in a story offered neither as a fiction nor a private history but a family memoir, may seem strange. John Sutherland's analysis of deletions or slips in the manuscript of the novel (*Thackeray at Work*, 1974) has made it plain that Thackeray originally intended to make Esmond's "boyish adoration" for Rachel a "harmless childish flame" which passes away, and to replace it in proper sequence with the mature man's passion for Beatrix (originally a Dantean "Beatrice"). Revising and improvising as he wrote, Thackeray found the name Rachel for her mother (originally "Dolly"), to "keep alive the expectation of the ending by its faint biblical allusion to the long deferred marriage of Jacob and Rachel." Sutherland shows how, "by deliberate haziness, he manages to imply that Esmond is deeply in love with both at once," in what "is not a case of oscillation so much as emotional ambiguity." The novelist's creativity disinclination to make radical revision produced an ambiguity which, according to Sutherland, "enriched his novel with what he and most of his readers have felt to be his finest moments."

These "finest moments" create a tension between past and present passion, a refusal to simplify and separate acts of loving. Esmond has felt the goddess-like beauty of Rachel, his *dea certe*, from the beginning, and after her husband's death he proposes marriage, praising her as a boon and a blessing. His two loves continue for a while, their co-existence clarified and licensed by the distinction between sacred and profane. By refusing to be a story of emotional sequence, the novel breaks linear form to unfold the contradictions, tensions and fractures of emotion and emotional memory. Sutherland rightly singles out the scene in which Esmond sees Beatrix descending the great staircase:

> Esmond had left a child and found a woman, grown beyond the common height; and arrived at such a dazzling completeness of beauty, that his eyes might well show surprise and delight at beholding her. . . . As he thinks of her, he who writes feels young again, and remembers a paragon.
>
> (Bk. 2, chap. 7)

> And so it is—a pair of bright eyes with a dozen glances suffice to subdue a man; to enslave him, and inflame him; to make him even forget; they dazzle him so that the past becomes straightway dim to him; and he so prizes them that he would give all his life to possess 'em.
>
> (Ibid.)

The ungainly third-person form, "he who writes," comes into its own to make a precise and scrupulous admission of remembered and revived adoration. This time he remembers with delight, not pain. The recollection is clearly recognized as an act of loving praise. The narration of love's death was provisional, the product of a mood. There are no simple developments in *Esmond*, but a constant and complex return. This narrative evocation of past as present creates a new and sophisticated mode of representing memory; it breaks down the sense of a fixed actuality of action. The retrospect recalls the past differently in different moods, adopting for the purposes of narrative form what is a familiar experience outside fiction.

The representation of Esmond's feeling for Rachel is also productively equivocal in form:

> His mistress, from whom he had been a year separated, was his dearest mistress again. The family from which he had been parted, and which he loved with the fondest devotion, was his family once more. If Beatrix's beauty shone upon him, it was with a friendly lustre, and he could regard it with much such a delight as he brought away after seeing the beautiful pictures of the smiling Madonnas in the convent at Cadiz, when he was despatched thither with a flag; and as for his mistress, 'twas difficult to say with what a feeling he regarded her. 'Twas happiness to have seen

her; 'twas no great pang to part; a filial tenderness, a love that was
at once respect and protection, filled his mind as he thought of
her; and near her or far from her, and from that day until now,
and from now till death is past, and beyond it, he prays that sacred
flame may ever burn.

(Bk. 2, chap. 8)

The passionate adoration, desire, jealousy, anger, and regret which compose Esmond's love for Beatrix are narrated with passionate precision, but
the feeling for Rachel is presented more obliquely, with cunning evasiveness.
Here, for instance, is one of many ambiguous uses of "mistress," and the
topos of inexpressibility is convenient indeed, " 'twas difficult to say." The
emotion is strong but tranquil—" 'Twas happiness," " 'twas no great pang."
It is called filial, but the filial feeling is placed in the past, "as he thought
of her." The last sentence is true to the final feeling, with a suggestive but
non-committal echo of the marriage vow, "till death is past." The reader is
told a truth, to be fully discovered only on re-reading. The feelings in the
past are recalled fluidly, and those imputed to the present shown vaguely, not
to tell the whole truth, but still to tell a truth; past and present pivot on that
semi-colon in the last sentence. Thackeray's disordering of feeling is a brilliant,
intuitive discovery, disturbing simplicities and sequences of psychological and
artistic expectation.

CRAIG HOWES

# Pendennis *and the Controversy*
# *on the "Dignity of Literature"*

Much has been said about Thackeray's "weekday preacher" response to
the fame he gained through *Vanity Fair*. But another response was far more
controversial at the time: his position on the status of writers and the writing
profession, a position which embroiled him in what has been called the "Dignity of Literature" episode. The key text in this controversy is *The History
of Pendennis: His Fortunes and Misfortunes, His Friends and His Greatest
Enemy* (1848–50), Thackeray's first novel after *Vanity Fair*'s great success.
By parodying the Romantic artist's sentimental and bathetic sides in Pen's
early adventures, and by dramatizing the "true" market-determined conditions of literary production, Thackeray not only clarifies his own position
on his profession, but also provides us with the most detailed description
of the London literary world to be found in the writings of a major author.
Furthermore, when criticized publicly for this portrait while *Pendennis* was
still appearing, Thackeray reopens the issue right in the novel and attempts
to synthesize his most polemical insights—a move with important implications for his later writing. *Pendennis* is thus the turning point in Thackeray's
career. The novel's first half sketches out his professional understanding of
literature; its second half thoughtfully fills in this outline, as the sharp features
of his wily Manager of the Performance melt into those of his target turned
persona, Arthur Pendennis.

The question of the writer's place within society was particularly vexed
when Thackeray began writing in the 1830s. Dr. Johnson's famous tilt at

From *Nineteenth-Century Fiction* 41, no. 3 (December 1986). © 1986 by the Regents
of the University of California.

the Earl of Chesterfield is emblematic of a general eighteenth-century movement away from the patron and toward the marketplace as the surest source of support for writers. The open market seemed to promise a freedom of expression only those of independent means previously enjoyed. If you could sell it you could write it, and this latitude, coupled with the increasing public demand for literature, led Johnson to label his time "the Age of Authors."

But as England reacted to the French Revolution and Napoleon, to Wordsworth, Scott, and Byron, the market increasingly appeared to writers as another, more damaging form of slavery. One response to this situation was the Romantic mythos which portrayed writers as beings with greater sensitivity and powers of speech than other mortals—a position Wordsworth and Shelley proclaimed in their criticism, and Byron seemed to embody. When such prophets are poor or unrecognized, the fault is therefore not theirs. Authors' miseries are evidence of a philistine society. Claims of unrecognized merit, however, are nothing new among artists. At their most responsible, Romantic and post-Romantic writers described exactly how the prevailing economic system was perverting and debasing art. The marketplace values a different kind of profit, leaving literary legislators not only unacknowledged, but unpaid. The dark side of the artist's world is thus a realm where ignorant booksellers have replaced patrons, personal integrity has vanished in the press of the market, and prostitution has become the evil fact of literary life.

When authors like Bulwer, Forster and Dickens began to cry for literary reform, therefore, they set themselves the difficult task of determining the most equitable way for a profession of faith to function as a paying profession. For the sake of artistic integrity, income apparently must remain a secondary concern while writing, since payment comes from a world separate from and inferior to the creative universe. But secondary does not mean insignificant, and these same writers often bemoaned the fact that capitalism too often forces writers to meet standards other than their own, denies writers the time necessary to compose significant works, and cheats writers by siphoning the profits of their labor into the hands of booksellers. Without some kind of collective action, many writers believed, literature would become nothing but a commodity, and their labor merely one more exploited resource. For this reason, a number of writers' societies emerged. Their goals were highly pragmatic: a stricter copyright law was one; annuities, life insurance plans, and charitable foundations for writers were others. Hoping to brighten the writer's public image, these societies also lobbied for the same honors and preferments other professions already received. Those fighting collectively for the dignity of literature thus wished to ease the miseries of writers currently suffering for their art, to reveal how the present conditions of production impeded writers from making their essential contribution to society, and to explain how the creative and the commercial could come together in an honest profession.

Thackeray's literary apprenticeship lasted fifteen years, and he was personally familiar with the privations many writers faced, but his attitude toward the profession during this time is surprisingly ambivalent. His earliest works repeatedly attack the Romantic artist's most egregious pretensions. The crime is always the same: just as noblemen once claimed benefit of clergy to escape punishment, so many "literary" types claim their genius as an excuse for foolish or vicious behavior. Thackeray accuses George Sand of hiding hedonism behind a tawdry veil of sensitivity. He tars Byron with the same brush: in Thackeray's fiction anyone who tries to ape Byron's poetry or life is due for a fall. Finally, Thackeray's devastating attacks on Bulwer in a host of squibs and reviews, in *Catherine*, and in "Punch's Prize Novelists" are all responses to what Thackeray saw as conceited, precious writing masking ill-considered and dubious morality. The following travesty, delivered by the shop clerk, murderer and aesthete "George de Barnwell," gives us Bulwer's position as seen through Thackeray's distorting eyes: " 'Dog,' I said to the trembling slave, 'tell me where thy Gold is. *Thou* hast no use for it. I can spend it in relieving the Poverty on which thou tramplest; in aiding Science, which thou knowest not; in uplifting Art, to which thou art blind. Give Gold, and thou art free.' But he spake not, and I slew him."

Lampooning the artistic poses assumed by writers in their worst moments, however, is hardly a challenging task for a satirist as skillfull as Thackeray. A more reasoned critique, "A Brother of the Press on the History of a Literary Man, Laman Blanchard, and the Chances of the Literary Profession" (1846), reveals Thackeray's attitude toward the writing profession and his understanding of its relation to the marketplace just before the success of *Vanity Fair*. He says little about Blanchard's writing except that "His three volumes of essays, pleasant and often brilliant as they are, give no idea of the powers of the author, or even of his natural manner, which, as I think, was a thousand times more agreeable." Instead, Thackeray spends most of the review attacking Bulwer's appended Memoir, which presents Blanchard as a writer of great potential who fell victim to the literary marketplace.

K. J. Fielding has called Thackeray's review "eminently tactless," and perhaps he is right: it's always risky to take issue with an obituary. But Thackeray's indignation prevented him from leaving Bulwer's Memoir alone. The review first praises Blanchard, a "gay, gentle, and amiable" man who was beloved by both friends and family, and who also achieved some modest literary fame, though this is "the smallest matter of all." The review then accuses Bulwer of distorting a life "by no means deplorable" for polemical reasons. According to Thackeray, for most writers "the labour which is to answer the calls of the day is the one quite best suited to their genius." He continues this line of thought by equating the laboring writer with a bootblack—one would love to know Dickens's reaction to this—and by comparing their methods for meeting personal needs:

> I have chosen the unpolite shoeblack comparison, not out of disrespect to the trade of literature; but it is as good a craft as any other to select. In some way or other, for daily bread and hire, almost all men are labouring daily. Without necessity they would not work at all, or very little, probably. In some instances you reap Reputation along with Profit from your labour, but Bread, in the main, is the incentive. Do not let us try to blink this fact, or imagine that the men of the press are working for their honour and glory, or go onward impelled by an irresistible afflatus of genius. If only men of genius were to write, Lord help us! how many books would there be?

The review's message is thus a simple one: Bulwer's tale of suffering genius doesn't fit in the facts of Blanchard's life, whose "career, untimely concluded, is in the main a successful one." Though he would probably never have written a masterpiece, his priorities were in order: "he had a duty, much more imperative upon him than the preparation of questionable great works,—to get his family their dinner. A man must be a very Great man, indeed, before he can neglect this precaution." The great man in this case is of course Bulwer, and Thackeray accuses him of letting his literary hobby horse carry him down to the same "eminently tactless" level Fielding charges Thackeray with: " 'He neglected his talents; he frittered away in fugitive publications time and genius, which might have led to the production of a great work;' this is the gist of Sir Bulwer Lytton's kind and affecting biographical notice of our dear friend and comrade Laman Blanchard, who passed away so melancholily last year." Since the world seldom seeks the profound or the sublime, self-declared literary geniuses like Bulwer are therefore usually guilty of misunderstanding, sneering at, or ignoring both their audience and most of their fellow laborers.

At this point in his career, Thackeray was himself harnessed to the press, with little apparent hope for the kind of popular success *Vanity Fair* was to bring. Harsh personal discipline and the occasional thrashing of self-satisfied or posturing artists in print allowed him to maintain a philosophical attitude toward his own frustrated ambitions. Resentment appears in his letters, but Thackeray somehow resisted the temptation to turn on the reading public; more surprisingly, perhaps, he also refrained from joining other writers in their attacks on the system of literary production currently in place. Thackeray the periodical writer linked these apparently diverse positions into a loose survival strategy for himself, and for all hack writers: don't get full of yourself, don't turn on your audience, and don't bite the hand that feeds you, no matter how dirty it is. *Vanity Fair* altered many things in Thackeray's life, but his attitude toward literature as a profession was not one of them—at least at first. And in *Pendennis*, this newly famous prose laborer sets out to provide a detailed, even polemical account of the writer's task, an account now aimed at that large audience he had desired but never expected to find.

The first third of *Pendennis* could be subtitled "Portrait of the Man as a Young Artist," for Pen slavishly imitates the worst excesses of the popular poets. Pen has few role models, but a large library. His father raises him to be a gentleman, and his mother worships him as a demigod. Not surprisingly, then, Pen identifies strongly with those poets apparently sharing his narcissism and egotism. He may read Heber, Hemans, and Keble to his mother, but his favorites are less domestic; Moore's *Lalla Rookh* and Byron's romances make Pen "a sworn fire-worshipper and a Corsair." He models his own poetry on the popular verse of the day, publishing in the county paper such masterpieces as "To a Tear," "On the Anniversary of the Battle of Waterloo," "To Madame Caradori singing at the Assize Meetings" and "On Saint Bartholomew's Day." Pen's naïve self-assurance carries him easily through the trials of writing on religious, political and sentimental subjects he knows nothing about. Poetic genius apparently compensates for total ignorance; in fact, Pen believes some of his greatest contributions to world literature are already as good as written:

> He projected an epic poem in blank verse, "Cortez, or the Conqueror of Mexico, and the Inca's Daughter." He wrote part of "Seneca, or the Fatal Bath," and "Ariadne in Naxos"; classical pieces, with choruses and strophes and antistrophes, which sadly puzzled Mrs. Pendennis; and began a "History of the Jesuits," in which he lashed that Order with tremendous severity.

Poets shape Pen's behavior as well as his poetry. Adopting "a decidedly gloomy cast," he gallops over Dumpling Downs spouting his poems, "filled with quite a Byronic afflatus as he thought." His favorite writers also give Pen some welcome tips on how to act in society, for in their romances he learns how others with his genius are persecuted by an insensitive world. These models teach Pen that a poet's rudeness is candor, his pride a proper sense of self-worth, his egotism, genius. Thus Pen's unpopularity among his neighbors is actually proof of his social and artistic superiority. As a professional writer-in-the-making, Pen's task will be to grow out of these beliefs about poetic genius—those same beliefs that Thackeray had resisted, laughed at and attacked throughout his early career.

Love first challenges Pen's complacency. Having learned from his models that passion always overwhelms great poets, the schoolboy prepares for love as he would for an exam: "He read his favourite poems over and over again, he called upon Alma Venus the delight of gods and men, he translated Anacreon's odes, and picked out passages suitable to his complaint from Waller, Dryden, Prior, and the like." Pen clearly does not want a lover, but "a young lady to whom he could really make verses, and whom he could set up and adore, in place of those unsubstantial Ianthes and Zuleikas to whom he addressed the outpourings of his gushing muse." Pen finds his Dulcinea in the Fotheringay, whom he appropriately enough first sees on stage spouting Kotzebue, and feels all the ectasy his reading promised. "[A]s much in love as the best hero in the best romance he ever read," Pen cries out "Byron and Moore; passion and poetry" to the amiable, bovine Emily, and proclaims his passion in print: "Mrs. Haller," "Passion and Genius," and "other verses of the most gloomy, thrilling, and passionate cast" appear in Poet's Corner, all signed "EROS."

Most of the embarrassments resulting from this infatuation are predictably adolescent, and Pen's earnest devotion is touching as well as ridiculous. But even this early, the facts of life he learns through his poetical, self-dramatizing passion include the facts of the marketplace. Although he turns his eyes from the truth, his entire love affair is a transaction. He pays for his first glimpse of Emily when he enters the theater; her father Costigan sells him his introduction with a handful of benefit tickets; the fencing lessons he pays for are excuses to visit her; and Pen's prospects as his mother's heir buy his engagement. When Major Pendennis arrives to end the affair, his goals are simple: identify the principals in the transaction, and buy them out. The meeting resembles a bankruptcy proceeding, as Emily realizes: " 'Sure, if he's no money, there's no use marrying him, papa,' she said sententiously." Nor is Pen's early writing exempt from the deal. The Major pays Costigan's outstanding debts to regain Pen's legal tender, "them letters, and verses, and pomes," and Emily, now as always, treats his writings as commodities: "she wrapped up Pen's letters, poems, passions, and fancies, and tied them with a piece of string neatly, as she would a parcel of sugar." Without knowing it, then, Pen the poet has made his first sale—to himself.

This remarkably long opening episode introduces three quests Pen will undertake, and with difficulty complete. The first two—his search for a wife, and his education in the differences between true and sham gentility—have been amply discussed elsewhere, but the third, Pen's movement from one notion of the literary life to another, has not received as much attention.

Thackeray loses no time in starting this movement. He mocks Pen's early poems, lumping them "with his first socks, the first cutting of his hair, his bottle, and other interesting relics of his infancy." Through Pen's foolishness and subsequent discomfort in love, Thackeray also parodies melodramatic notions of writers and writing, thus preparing the way for Pen's encounter with the forces shaping literature most profoundly—the same market conditions that form both reputations and marriages in the Babylon world. Thackeray has therefore set himself a formidable task. To combat writers who take themselves or their profession too seriously, he will show the literary community in the starkest light he can—every wart in place, every injustice and meanness present. Only then can he go after Bulwer's persecution theory by showing through Pen how even merely competent writers can in fact survive and prosper within the artistic world and the larger society.

Demonstrating this takes up a good part of the novel's middle. After losing Emily, Pen believes his passionate life is over. Predictably, he loses his energy for writing as well. At Oxbridge he composes prize poems that lose, and at home his verses to Blanche Amory are lifeless things, written primarily to relieve boredom. Despite this emotional dryness, this period does have two things in common with Pen's earlier, impassioned time: he still has the freedom from want that Bulwer claims is essential for great writing, and he still produces writing as aimless and misdirected as his life—a truth Laura, his eventual wife, finds contemptible:

> "Look at him, dear mother!" said the girl. "We two women are no society for him: we don't interest him; we are not clever enough for such a genius as Pen. He wastes his life and energies away among us, tied to our apron-strings. He interests himself in nothing . . . He will never be happy while he is here. Why is he not facing the world, and without a profession?"

In fact, Pen does start recognizing certain literary truths which will prove essential for success in his eventual career. Though his affair's bitter aftermath makes him superficially cynical, the experience teaches him how to restrain his more excessive or fanciful literary posturing, thus providing him with some valuable distance from his writing. Pen also starts to realize that audience and occasion shape every act of writing. His earliest works felt spontaneous, but like most bad poetry they were actually grossly contrived. Pen aped the sorts of feelings that poets were supposed to have, then held out his derivative poems for public viewing; he now knows better. Though hardly a professional writer, and still ignorant of the literary world, Pen's experiences before London unmistakably prepare the way for his introduction to the literary life.

Pen stumbles into his proper professional niche within the London literary scene. Supposedly preparing for the bar, Pen does not begin considering the "Corporation of the Goosequill" until chapter 30, the first chapter to explore the author's trade. Writers emerge like ghosts out of the noise and smoke as Pen and Warrington sit drinking in the Back Kitchen. First come Hoolan and Doolan, bitter enemies in print, but best of friends otherwise; then Archer, a good-natured pathological liar. Pen finally learns to his surprise that Warrington writes as well. All three examples make the same point: authors don't necessarily resemble their works. Character assassination pertains only to another's written character; apart from his hyperbole, Archer is "both able and honest—a good man of business, an excellent friend, admirable to his family as husband, father, and son." As for Warrington, he treats his writing like a bad habit, hiding it from Pen, and becoming annoyed when Doolan praises him: " 'Why the devil will the fellow compliment so?' growled Warrington, with a sneer which he hardly took the pains to suppress." Real writers thus prove to be a rather common lot, hiding behind masks made of print, and considering this misrepresentation as essential to their craft.

This duplicity is also psychologically necessary, since economically writers are subordinates to the true powers of literary production. On the walk home Warrington introduces Pen to their professional mistress:

> They were passing through the Strand as they talked, and by a newspaper office, which was all lighted up and bright. Reporters were coming out of the place, or rushing up to it in cabs; there were lamps burning in the editors' rooms, and above where the compositors were at work: the windows of the building were in a blaze of gas.
>
> "Look at that, Pen," Warrington said. "There she is—the great engine—she never sleeps. She has her ambassadors in every quarter of the world—her couriers upon every road. Her officers march along with armies, and her envoys walk into statesmen's cabinets. They are ubiquitous. Yonder journal has an agent, at this minute, giving bribes at Madrid; and another inspecting the price of potatoes in Covent Garden. Look! here comes the Foreign Express galloping in. They will be able to give news to Downing Street to-morrow: funds will rise or fall, fortunes be made or lost; Lord B. will get up, and, holding the paper in his hand, and seeing the noble Marquis in his place, will make a great speech; and—and Mr. Doolan will be called away from his supper at the Back Kitchen; for he is foreign sub-editor, and sees the mail on the newspaper sheet before he goes to his own."

This impressive vision is inhuman—even satanic. Endless activity buzzes around a huge mindless force, the Press, which scatters human laborers in search of raw material for its maw. The goal is production, and writers are small cogs in the machine who become increasingly alienated from their labor as the machine's other servants—editors, compositors, and printers—transform words into commodities that provoke action in many spheres—most notably the economic, as the bribes, potatoes, and fortunes suggest. The resulting actions in turn stimulate further literary production. The blazing machine is therefore not only ubiquitous, but self-perpetuating—and no one controls it. Warrington does not admire the Press for its moral force or its humanizing influence. He marvels at its brute, thoughtless, yet sublime power.

Why then be its servant? Pen's empty purse is his main reason for becoming a professional writer, and Warrington declares that work is exactly what Pen needs: "A single man who has health and brains, and can't find a livelihood in the world, doesn't deserve to stay there." Clearly enjoying himself, Warrington suggests teaching, gambling, mail delivery, and chiropody before mentioning his own trade: " 'I write,' said Warrington, 'I don't tell the world that I do so,' he added with a blush. 'I do not choose that questions should be asked: or, perhaps, I am an ass, and don't wish it to be said that George Warrington writes for bread.' " Warrington's real reasons for anonymity emerge later; here he plays devil's advocate, treating authorship as one way among many to meet expenses: "When my purse is out, I go to work and fill it, and then lie idle like a serpent or an Indian, until I have digested the mass." Warrington then bluntly but expertly evaluates Pen's earlier writing, and his working potential:

> "Of all the miserable weak rubbish I ever tried, Ariadne in Naxos is the most mawkish and disgusting. The Prize Poem is so pompous and feeble, that I'm positively surprised, sir, it didn't get the medal. You don't suppose that you are a serious poet, do you, and are going to cut out Milton and Aeschylus? Are you setting up to be a Pindar, you absurd little tom-tit . . . ? No, my boy, I think you can write a magazine article, and turn out a pretty copy of verses; that's what I think of you."

Warrington places his friend's writing above his own—Pen's gift "is lighter, and soars higher, perhaps"—but the message is clear. Pen is not joining the ranks of the bards, but apprenticing himself to a trade; in the business of writing, a poet is simply someone who profits from a talent to amuse.

Pen's first sale, "The Church Porch," acquaints him personally with the nuts-and-bolts of his new trade. The subject, length, and deadline are all set beforehand—hardly the conditions for inspired writing—and the poem itself is greeting card verse: competent, but clichéd. Pen's own comment on the verses suggests their aesthetic value: "I screwed 'em out at last. I think they'll do." Thackeray spends as much time describing the marketing as he does the writing, indicating how much of a trade Pen's new profession is. Since Bacon the bookseller is functionally illiterate, quality has little to do with the transaction. Instead, Warrington sells the poem by emphasizing—or rather, exaggerating—Pen's social connections: "A man of property in the West, of one of the most ancient families in England, related to half the nobility in the empire—he's cousin to Lord Pontypool—he was one of the most distinguished men at Oxbridge; he dines at Gaunt House every week." The split between the market and private life is obvious: when dealing with Pen as his friend, Warrington attacks his pretensions; when dealing with the bookseller, Warrington inflates his "absurd little tom-tit" into a social lion to close the sale. All's fair in the marketplace.

While Warrington barters for the poem, Pen is outside, peering into the booksellers' windows. He soon recognizes that literature is not a homogeneous art, but a loose gathering of products meeting specific market demands. Periodicals, novels, books of poetry, Books of Beauty flood the market. The "Penny Horrific Register" and the "History of the most celebrated Murderers of all Countries" pander to the sensation-loving; "The Raff's Magazine" and "The Larky Swell" cater to those who enjoy low-life frolics. Dissenters, Catholics, or Church of England devotees find works suited to their tastes as well. Booksellers are clearly more important players in the literary scene than writers, since they deal with its entire range of products. Though the writer produces what is needed, the bookseller recognizes or creates the need.

The bookseller is in short a capitalist, as Pen's visit to Fleet Prison points out. The writer-prisoner Captain Shandon scribbles furiously, the pages falling wet to the ground, while porcine Bungay the bookseller looks on, highly pleased with the arrangement: " 'when the Captain's locked up,' he said, 'we are sure to find him at home; whereas, when he's free, you can never catch hold of him.' " The instant Shandon finishes his piecework, Bungay pays him without even looking at the product. This prison scene is a painfully literal but precise allegory of the writing profession, and it also exposes some of the trade's least admirable qualities. First of all, writers need not be honest. Shandon's prospectus describes the *Pall Mall Gazette*'s contributors as "gentlemen of England" important in both Houses and in Europe's major diplomatic circles. Nor is this gammon condemned—Pen, Warrington and Shandon all find it funny. Second, only the current market determines a writer's value. If titled writers are in vogue, a successful magazine will have its stable of nobility, though they will ideally contribute nothing but their names: "Lady Hipshaw will write: but she's not much, you know, and we've two lords; but the less they do the better." Third, the greatest of the Muses is financial need, as Warrington, Pen, and now Shandon all bear witness to.

Thackeray sharpens these points in the next two chapters. He abandons the implicit commentary he makes by juxtaposing young Pen, galloping and versifying across Dumpling Downs, with Captain Shandon, desperately writing in prison while his employer looks on. Instead, Thackeray moves toward polemic, arguing through Warrington that writers are and should be governed by the same economic realities as the rest of the world. Writers have no claim to privilege; as common mortals they tread on the ground, Bulwer notwithstanding. To make this argument, Thackeray places Bulwer's expressed opinions about literary genius and the marketplace into Pen's naïve mouth:

> "No man shall tell me that a man of genius, as Shandon is, ought to be driven by such a vulgar slave-driver as yonder Mr. Bungay, whom we have just left, who fattens on the profits of the other's brains, and enriches himself out of his journeyman's labour. It makes me indignant to see a gentleman the serf of such a creature as that, of a man who can't speak the language that he lives by, who is not fit to black Shandon's boots."

The snobbish attitude toward bootblacks recalls the Blanchard review, and Pen speaks as a pseudo-Bulwer on other issues as well—for instance, when he excuses Shandon's drunkenness on aesthetic grounds: "the very ardour and enthusiasm of temperament which makes the author delightful often leads the man astray." Pen's diatribe ends with a ringing condemnation of the literary marketplace, couched in the terms of a good student of radical political economy: "I protest against that wretch of a middle-man whom I see between Genius and his great landlord, the Public, and who stops more than half of the labourer's earnings and fame."

Warrington then opens fire on the innocent, and his response echoes Thackeray's in the Blanchard review. Warrington denies "that there are so many geniuses as people who whimper about the fate of men of letters assert there are," and insists that most writing is mechanical and commonplace: "There are thousands of clever fellows in the world who could, if they would, turn verses, write articles, read books, and deliver a judgment upon them; the talk of professional critics and writers is not a whit more brilliant, or profound, or amusing, than that of any other society of educated people." He then pounces on the argument that writers should be saved from the uncertainties of the marketplace:

"What is it you want? Do you want a body of capitalists that shall be forced to purchase the works of all authors who may present themselves manuscript in hand? Everybody who writes his epic, every driveller who can or can't spell, and produces his novel or his tragedy,—are they all to come and find a bag of sovereigns in exchange for their worthless reams of paper? Who is to settle what is good or bad, saleable or otherwise? Will you give the buyer leave, in fine, to purchase or not?"

This passage digs at Pen, whose own epics and tragedies have already been laughed at, but it also raises an important question: who sets the standards for literary excellence? Bacon and Bungay certainly prove that booksellers are poor judges in themselves; nevertheless, Warrington follows Dr. Johnson by giving the laurel to the general reading public, whose taste the bookseller makes it his business to know, if not to understand: "I may have my own ideas of the value of my Pegasus, and think him the most wonderful of animals; but the dealer has a right to his opinion, too, and may want a lady's horse, or a cob for a heavy timid rider, or a sound hack for the road, and my beast won't suit him." One maxim can sum up Warrington's—and Thackeray's—position: pity the writer's individual failures, but never claim more for writers as a group than they gain in the world through their own efforts.

This maxim becomes drama in "A Dinner in the Row" (chap. 34)—the chapter which set off a different kind of row among Thackeray's contemporaries. This scene proves that Warrington is correct: writers don't respect each other, or care much about writing at all—like anyone else, their concerns tend to be money and social reputation. Mrs. Bungay provides the first standard for evaluating writers in this scene when she ranks her guests by family background or size of coach. She prizes the nobleman novelist Percy Popjay, but she barely tolerates those working full time as literary men: Doolan, whom she can't abide; Mr. Bole, "the real editor of the magazine of which Mr. Wagg was the nominal chief"; and the recently released Captain Shandon. Just below Popjay in her hierarchy come Wenham and Wagg— and in that order, for Wenham knows duchesses, but Wagg only knows baronets. Pen and Warrington are mysteries to her, but when Popjay greets them their stock soars, and when Wagg and Wenham recognize Pen, he rises even further: Mrs. Bungay communicates "her ideas to Bungay, afterwards, regarding the importance of Mr. Pendennis—ideas by which Pen profited much more than he was aware."

The scene itself makes fun of Mrs. Bungay, but shares her lack of concern for the guests' writing ability. Dull and foppish Popjay, for example, emerges as a congenial figure: "Heaven had not endowed young Mr. Popjay with much intellect of his own, but had given him a generous faculty for admiring, if not for appreciating, the intellect of others." Miss Bunion is another positive portrait. A "large and bony woman in a crumpled satin dress, who came creaking into the room with a step as heavy as a grenadier's," she may differ from her "Passion-Flowers" literary persona, but her sensible, unpretentious nature is finally more attractive. As Miss Bunion rises, however, the mighty fall. Wagg's most damning quality is his tireless attempt to sound like his writing. Though there are hints of a human side, of "personal calamities or distresses (of which that humorist had his share in common with the unjocular part of mankind)," the way he exercises his wit condemns him to the lowest place on Thackeray's scale. The problem lies in the way Wagg chooses his targets: he toadies to the aristocrats who scorn him, and attacks his social inferiors even when they do him a kindness. Wagg's talk has a flashiness to it that Thackeray must have enjoyed writing, but for all his literary fame, Wagg is essentially mean.

The moral that Warrington rather sententiously draws from the scene is as obvious as it is expected. Mrs. Bungay's social rankings are suspect, but judging writers by their reputation or ability is equally questionable, since the most successful author, Wagg, is the least admirable, and the most brilliant, Shandon, is also the weakest person. If writers must be judged, then, let it be simply as people struggling in the world all share, subject to the same passions, responsibilities, and temptations all others must live with. The chapter closes with a denial of literary privilege so absolute that it almost certainly represents the last word Thackeray intended to say on the subject in *Pendennis*:

> "And now," Warrington said, "that you have seen the men of letters, tell me, was I far wrong in saying that there are thousands of people in this town who don't write books, who are, to the full, as clever and intellectual as people who do?"
>
> Pen was forced to confess that the literary personages with whom he had become acquainted had not said much, in the course of the night's conversation, that was worthy to be remembered or quoted. In fact, not one word about literature had been said during the whole course of the night:—and it may be whispered to those uninitiated people who are anxious to know the habits and make the acquaintance of men of letters, that there are no race of people who talk about books, or perhaps, who read books, so little as literary men.

With this, Thackeray's portrait of literary life is more or less complete. After a short chapter about Pen's duties for the *Pall Mall Gazette*, the novel returns to its primary concern: Pen's personal fortunes.

To this point in the novel, Thackeray has said nothing about his profession that he has not said before; *Pendennis* is simply a more extended and emphatic statement. He had always ridiculed artists' egotism and imaginative excesses. In the London scenes he dramatizes the profession itself, with all its characters and in all its drudgery. What is so striking about this part of the novel is Thackeray's deep conviction in the equity of his profession. He exposes the puffery, the exploitation, and the injustice, yet he sees these as obstacles Pen must negotiate through rather than hope to change, obstacles in this sense quite similar to the social snobbery and mania for wealth which block his advancement in other aspects of his life. A writer can make a decent living as a writer, and be decent while making it: this is as much as Thackeray will claim for literature as a profession.

But for many of Thackeray's peers, the monthly numbers of *Pendennis* seemed like large and ungrateful bites of the hand which now fed him so richly. Their response was immediate, provoking first Thackeray's anger, but then his industry. In a move with important implications for his career, Thackeray midway through the novel rethinks in far greater detail his attitudes toward his profession.

The "Dignity of Literature" story has been told many times. In early January of 1850, when *Pendennis* was halfway through its run, a *Morning Chronicle* article argued that pensions and public honors would not help the literary profession's poor reputation. John Forster responded immediately in the *Examiner*, defending pensions but agreeing that the profession's reputation was not good, and that in *Pendennis* Thackeray was guilty of "a disposition to pay court to the non-literary class by disparaging his fellow-labourers." Thackeray was furious. "If I stoop to flatter anybody's prejudice for some interested motives of my own, I am no more nor less than a rogue and a cheat; which deductions from the *Examiner's* premises I will not stoop to contradict, because the premises themselves are simply absurd"—so he wrote in "The Dignity of Literature," published January 12 in the *Chronicle*. In this letter he also repeats his Blanchard review argument that the popularity many writers enjoy makes weeping about public prejudice not only "absurd" but "ungrateful." Finally, Thackeray echoes Warrington: "The only moral that I, as a writer, wished to hint in the descriptions against which you protest, was, that it was the duty of a literary man, as well as any other, to practise regularity and sobriety, to love his family, and to pay his tradesmen."

The most intriguing statement in this response, however, appears in a paragraph Thackeray slips into the middle, where he warns against making any final statements about his attitudes while *Pendennis* is still appearing: "Who knows what is coming in the future numbers of the work which has incurred your displeasure and the *Examiner's*, and whether you, in accusing me of prejudice, and the *Examiner* (alas!) of swindling and flattering the public, have not been premature?" This is a remarkable thing for a writer to do: Thackeray promises to answer his critics right in the novel. He clearly had finished with the subject of the literary profession, since the controversial September number containing "A Dinner in the Row" ends by moving toward the Blanche-Pen-Foker triangle which the recently-published January issue discusses exclusively. But sure enough, the February issue contains a chapter reopening and debating precisely those issues both Forster and the *Chronicle* had raised.

"Contains a Novel Incident" (chap. 41) has long been a locus classicus for Thackeray's opinions about literature; it becomes even more significant when we remember that he is answering specific charges made not only against the first half of *Pendennis*, but his entire career. To this point *Pendennis*'s course has been direct and sure, as Pen passes through a series of initiations—from the Fotheringay to Oxbridge, from Blanche and Laura to London. Equally sure has been Thackeray's treatment of artistry and the profession of art, as he draws on his own experience and previous writing to create a vivid picture of Pen's initial sense of literary art, and his later introduction to the actual commercial world of literature. But the attacks on Thackeray, which basically amount to the charge of philistinism, clearly jolt him into realizing that his debunking wit has caused him to draw a literary world which appears to rule out the possibility of genius, or even feeling. "The words in Pendennis are untenable be hanged to them," Thackeray writes in a letter when the debate is at its hottest, "but they were meant to apply to a particular class of literary men, *my* class who are the most ignorant men under the Sun, myself included I mean. But I wrote so carelessly that it appears as if I would speak of all, & even if it were true I ought never to have written what I did." In the earlier sections of the novel, Thackeray through Warrington insists that personal decency and dignity are possible within the literary scene. Unfortunately, by insisting that writing is a job like any other, a claim made to undercut Pen's egotism when imitating the most ridiculous excesses of his artistic models, Thackeray overstates his case, and thus undervalues those qualities of genius, feeling, and expression which he does believe are integral components of his profession. "Contains a Novel Incident" attempts to rectify this mistake by showing just how art's creative dimension adapts itself to survive with integrity in the world of commerce.

This chapter, an extremely tight, self-contained narrative, abruptly announces that Pen has dusted off the manuscript of a novel written before his move to London. *Walter Lorraine* is predictably a "very fierce, gloomy, and passionate" account of Pen's youthful loving and writing. Time, disillusionment, and London, however, have granted him some distance from his manuscript. Just as Thackeray's narrator looks ironically but kindly on Pen's early escapades, so Pen himself glances back on his youth while rereading, aware of the faith and ardor now lost, yet touched by his own earnestness on the page. He may have outgrown his love for Byron, but Pen still finds his own Byronic novel moving because of its personal significance: "he remembered what had been the overflowing feelings which had caused him to blot it, and the pain which had inspired the line." Thackeray makes a crucial move here. To this point he has emphasized the disjunction between personal history and what an author writes. Introducing *Walter Lorraine* allows him to discuss past experience as a suitable source of material for the professional writer. Warrington's and Pen's conversation about this novel will stand as Thackeray's answer to his critics.

Pen first confesses to his friend that the novel makes him ashamed of his memory, and Warrington agrees, mocking Pen by reading some of *Walter Lorraine*'s dreadful melodramatic dialogue aloud. But for the first time, Pen fights back effectively, claiming he has the right to profit from his past emotions—first, because they are his, and second, because time has softened any pain his portraits of Emily and Blanche might cause. Having reread his boyish manuscript, he has no qualms whatever in making it public: "do you know, outrageous as it is, it has some good stuff in it; and if Bungay won't publish it, I think Bacon will."

The expected squelch, blunt and mocking, follows:

> "That's the way of poets," said Warrington. "They fall in love, jilt, or are jilted: they suffer and they cry out that they suffer more than any other mortals: and when they have experienced feelings enough they note them down in a book, and take the book to market. All poets are humbugs, all literary men are humbugs; directly a man begins to sell his feelings for money he's a humbug."

The first half of this passage sums up Pen's life so far—love, lose, write, sell—and the second half repeats the kind of statement that provoked "The Dignity of Literature" controversy in the first place. By responding forcefully to this attack, Pen not only gains an authority of his own, but also becomes a spokesman of sorts for Thackeray's opponents, making this speech one of the most important in the novel:

> "I suppose a poet has greater sensibility than another man," said Pen, with some spirit. "That is what makes him a poet. I suppose that he sees and feels more keenly: it is that which makes him speak of what he feels and sees. You speak eagerly enough in your leading articles when you espy a false argument in an op-

ponent, or detect a quack in the House. Paley, who does not care for anything else in the world, will talk for an hour about a question of law. Give another the privilege which you take yourself, and the free use of his faculty, and let him be what nature has made him."

The Wordsworthian echoes are striking; the first three sentences virtually paraphrase the "Preface" to *Lyrical Ballads*. Though Pen compares his talent with the lawyer's or political writer's, his gift makes him more human— superior in sensibility, in capacity for feeling, in eagerness and ability to speak. A poet *is* a natural, set apart by essence. Though clearly fond of his hero, Thackeray in the first part of the novel lampoons Pen's pretensions to genius or fine feeling. He has accused Bulwer of the same pretensions for years. But in this chapter, he allows Pen's statement to stand.

Thackeray then goes further, as he lets a newly assured Pen justify selling his emotion recollected in tranquility to the highest bidder:

> "Why should not a man sell his sentimental thoughts as well as you your political ideas, or Paley his legal knowledge? Each alike is a matter of experience and practice. It is not money which causes you to perceive a fallacy, or Paley to argue a point; but a natural or acquired aptitude for that kind of truth: and a poet sets down his thoughts and experiences upon paper as a painter does a landscape or a face upon canvas, to the best of his ability, and according to his particular gift."

Pen here is forging links between his earlier passionate writing and Warrington's hard-headed market approach—the two dimensions of writing Thackeray has to this point largely set at odds. Pen's argument is thus an apologia for both himself and Thackeray. The inspired pre-market writer is a more sensitive, more talented individual. The economic facts of literary production, however, create the post-market figure, a laborer responsible for turning commodities to order. In the first half of *Pendennis* Thackeray never blends these types. The poet grows out of one and into the other as Pen himself passes from childhood to maturity. But in chapter 41, Thackeray ties these stages together through the great Romantic bonding force of memory. Thackeray here claims that the poet is a pre-market writer when first composing, but that once this first flow of creation ends, the writer must revise and refine with the market in mind. An older, more cynical Pen will shape the young man's manuscript, and this time gap proves very convenient and profitable for Pen and Thackeray both, since it allows for a relentless parody of literary genius found in the portrait of Pen's youth, but also for a nostalgic glow when, many chapters later, the worldly professional author looks for publishable material in his trunk.

As the chapter continues Warrington himself reveals that he too believes in a union between the emotional and the market. He sees and values the genuine feeling to be found in *Walter Lorraine*: "'I can't read any more of that balderdash now,' he said; 'but it seems to me there is some good stuff in it, Pen, my boy. There's a certain greenness and freshness in it which I like somehow. The bloom disappears off the face of poetry after you begin to shave.'" Warrington then gives himself over to helping Pen transform the novel into a product. To underscore the mechanical nature of the revision—and perhaps to slip away from his own admiration of Pen's sentimental writing—he couches his tips in a facetious market rhetoric and worse. The biblical allusion to Joseph and the literally cosmetic nature of the revisions he suggests link selling a novel to betraying a relative, auctioning a slave, or pimping a prostitute:

> "We will carry him to the Egyptians, and sell him. We will ex-change him away for money, yea, for silver and gold, and for beef and for liquors, and for tobacco and for raiment. This youth will fetch some price in the market; for he is a comely lad, though not over strong; but we will fatten him up, and give him the bath, and curl his hair, and we will sell him for a hundred piastres to Bacon or to Bungay. The rubbish is saleable enough, sir; and my advice to you is this: the next time you go home for a holiday, take 'Walter Lorraine' in your carpet-bag—give him a more modern air, prune away, though sparingly, some of the green passages, and add a little comedy, and cheerfulness, and satire, and that sort of thing, and then we'll take him to market, and sell him. The book is not a wonder of wonders, but it will do very well."

Pen will therefore remain a writer of the emotions, but with a twist. He eagerly makes the revisions Warrington suggests, and the result is truly odd: a naive and self-indulgent, but "fresh" and sincere pre-market novel becomes through revision a garish child whore, left to the public's tender mercies after the canny mercenaries exchange him for what they can. One passage can thus provide the moral for this chapter: "it is one thing to write a novel, and another to get money for it."

Having answered his critics by reinserting passion and individuality back into his portrait of the literary profession, but without conceding his point about the inflated artistic ego or the grindingly commonplace operations of the literary marketplace, a relieved Thackeray brings this subject quickly to a close. Pen's fashionable connections and the Bacon-Bungay feud are again the real reasons for the price his manuscript draws, and the chapter ends by insisting that Pen's success is uncommon, that publishing a novel is next to impossible, and that the chances of publishing a second one are even less likely. In short, though it shows Thackeray as definitely believing that writers are often gifted, distinctive beings, "Contains a Novel Incident" returns to the Blanchard review's position that professional success is ultimately "the smallest matter of all":

> There are some natures, and perhaps, as we have said, Pennen-nis's was one, which are improved and softened by prosperity and kindness, as there are men of other dispositions, who become arrogant and graceless under good fortune. Happy he who can endure one or the other with modesty and good-humour! Lucky he who has been educated to bear his fate, whatsoever it may be, by an early example of uprightness, and a childish training in honour!

This chapter is crucial not only to *Pendennis*, but to Thackeray's later fiction as well. Throughout his career he has openly and unapologetically discussed the mercenary nature of his work, and scorned those who scorned it. But in January 1850 the public attacks on his integrity and his own second thoughts lead him to reconsider his own status as a writer. He realizes that after many years in "The Corporation of the Goosequill," he has earned through his success the artistic freedom Bulwer and others claim is essential for enduring work. Chapter 41 begins the process of releasing Pen as well, as his role shifts from satiric butt to spokesman. At least on literary matters, Pen now has a kind of authority—we hear for the first time the voice that will explicitly "narrate" *The Newcomes* and *Philip*, and implicitly *Henry Esmond* and *The Virginian*. That this altered position is identical to Thackeray's own becomes apparent in the novel's "Preface," where he comments almost defensively about his popularity:

> I can no more ignore good fortune than any other chance which has befallen me. I have found many thousands more readers than I ever looked for. I have no right to say to these, You shall not find fault with my art, or fall asleep over my pages; but I ask you to believe that this person writing strives to tell the truth. If there is not that, there is nothing.

In describing how he will achieve this truth, he calls *Pendennis* "a confidential talk between writer and reader," commenting that "In the course of his volubility, the perpetual speaker must of necessity lay bare his own weaknesses, vanities, peculiarities." Leaving aside the astonishing fact that this voice emerges from the same man who spoke as *Vanity Fair*'s elusive Manager of the Performance, the description here, though accurate for *Pendennis*'s second half, badly misrepresents the first thirty-five chapters. *Vanity Fair*'s energy results in part from the narrator's confidence as he moves his puppets. Though he may constantly undercut his own authority, he retains a firm grip on his narrative, and the same kind of vivacity drives the first half of *Pendennis* forward. Though the characters are complex, their edges are sharp—even Laura has a sarcastic, penetrating quality of mind that withers away later in the novel. This narrator exposes *Pen*'s "weaknesses, vanities, peculiarities" to a clear, kind, but unambiguous light. Think of Pen's obnoxious behavior at the Clavering ball, or his insufferable self-satisfaction when he first proposes to Laura. But by granting Pen some authority in chapter 41. Thackeray starts the process which reshapes his own narrative voice. His formerly confident storyteller becomes like his hero: uncertain about his own genius, confused about his aesthetic values, and ambivalent about his profession, but committed to the idea of integrating all three.

By novel's end, Pen has all but taken up his creator's task. In chapter 61, the much-debated "philosophical" chapter in Thackeray's most "philosophical" novel, a manifesto for the novelist's hard-won and honest confusion emerges from Pen's, not the narrator's, mouth:

> "The truth, friend!" Arthur said imperturbably; "where is the truth? Show it me. That is the question between us. I see it on both sides. I see it on the Conservative side of the House, and amongst the Radicals, and even on the Ministerial benches. . . . If the truth is with all these, why should I take side with any one of them? Some are called upon to preach; let them preach. Of these preachers there are somewhat too many, methinks, who fancy they have the gift. But we cannot all be parsons in church, that is clear."

The narrator claims these opinions are "delivered dramatically, the writer being no more answerable for them than for the sentiments uttered by any other character of the story," but the assurance that led Thackeray in 1847 to comment that "Satirical-Moralists" follow a profession "as serious as the Parson's own," the artistic sureness he displayed in *Vanity Fair*, and the vigor he shows in *Pendennis*'s own first half all undeniably fade away as his narrator increasingly identifies himself with Pen. Perhaps the most ironic moment in this transition comes in a letter of July 1853, where Thackeray confesses to feeling "immensely relieved" after deciding to make Pen the narrator for *The Newcomes:* "by the help of this little mask (w.h I borrowed from

Pisistratus Bulwer I suppose) I shall be able to talk more at ease than in my own person." Thus his most ambivalent creation becomes his mask, and the idea comes from Bulwer. Thackeray subsumes himself in the thoroughly ordinary artist Pen.

Many have commented that *Pendennis*'s second half lags, and generally attribute this to Thackeray's serious illness. But Thackeray is quite deliberately not the same writer when he finishes this novel. He writes his next one, *The History of Henry Esmond*, in a single sustained effort, free from the direct market pressure serial publication imposes; in short, he writes it the way Bulwer said novels should be written. The tentative, digressive quality of Thackeray's prose increases markedly in the novels supposedly written by Pen, though this tendency culminates in the impotent Prufrockian narrator of *Lovel the Widower*. More seriously, the commitment to personal truth Thackeray champions in the "Preface" to *Pendennis* and ultimately in its main character eventually leads to intriguing messes like *Philip*, where Pen the narrator openly discusses his mercenary motives for writing, his mental fatigue, his lack of interest in the plot. *Pendennis* is thus one of the most personally defining and transforming works a major novelist has written. Thackeray begins his task with the same cutting tools and feelings which had led to his success; he finishes it wearing the blurred, indecisive, troubled, but genial, sympathetic and "true" mask of the successful professional artist he had become:

> Turning over the leaves of "Pendennis" as it lay on the table beside him, [Thackeray] said, smiling, from time to time:
> "Yes, it is very like—it is certainly very like."
> "Like whom, Mr. Thackeray?" said my mother.
> "Oh, like me, to be sure; Pendennis is very like me."
> "Surely not," objected my mother, "for Pendennis was so weak!"
> "Ah, well, Mrs. Baxter," he said, with a shrug of his great shoulders and a comical look, "your humble servant is not very strong."

# Chronology

| | |
|---|---|
| 1811 | William Makepeace Thackeray born on July 18 to Richmond Thackeray, a British Civil Servant, and Anne Becher Thackeray, in the British colony of Calcutta. |
| 1815 | Richmond Thackeray dies of a fever. |
| 1817 | William is sent to school in England. |
| 1822–28 | Attends the Charterhouse School in London, where he circulates drawings and writes a poem called "Cabbages," a parody of a popular sentimental poem of the time. |
| 1829 | Enters Trinity College, Cambridge, where he contributes to the magazines *The Snob* and *The Gownsman*, his first publication being a poem, "Timbuctoo," in mockery of the year's Prize poem competition. In the summer, Thackeray makes his first trip to Paris. |
| 1830 | In June, after losing £1500 by gambling, Thackeray leaves Cambridge without earning his degree. In July he travels to Germany, where he spends a year. Meets Goethe in Weimar. |
| 1831–32 | Returns to London, where he enters the Middle Temple to study law. Passes the summer of 1832 in Paris. |
| 1833 | From May to August Thackeray writes and studies art in Paris. Loses the bulk of his inheritance because of a bank failure in India. |
| 1835 | Meets Isabella Shaw. |
| 1836 | Thackeray's first book, *Flore et Zephyr*, a set of comic lithographs of ballet dancers, is published. In August, marries |

Isabella Shaw in Paris. Writes as Paris correspondent for *The Constitutional* and contributes to several other magazines.

1837–38    The Thackerays settle in London. *The Yellowplush Correspondence* appears in *Fraser's Magazine*.

1839–40    *Catherine; a Story* appears in *Fraser's*.

1840    Thackeray's first book published in England, *The Paris Sketch Book*. Continues to contribute comic pieces and art criticism to several journals. Harriet Marian (Minny) Thackeray is born; Isabella Thackeray suffers a nervous breakdown which leads eventually to permanent insanity.

1841    *Comic Tales and Sketches*, edited and illustrated by Mr. Michael Angelo Titmarsh, appears in two volumes.

1842    Thackeray contributes "The Legend of Jawbrahim-Heraudee" to *Punch*, his first known work for the magazine.

1843    *The Irish Sketch Book*, by M. A. Titmarsh; this is Thackeray's first book to contain his own name, in the dedication.

1844    *Barry Lyndon* appears in *Fraser's Magazine* from January to December, with an interruption in October; because of its limited popularity, Thackeray cannot find a publisher for it. Thackeray works variously as a reviewer, political correspondent, and translator.

1845    Several publishers reject the first chapters of *Vanity Fair*.

1846    *The Book of Snobs*, in *Punch*. Produces his first Christmas book, *Mrs. Perkin's Ball*, by M. A. Titmarsh.

1847–48    Bradbury and Evans, the publishers of *Punch*, release *Vanity Fair. Pen and Pencil Sketches of English Society* in twenty parts, from January 1847 through July 1848 (final double number). The novel appears in book form as *Vanity Fair. A Novel without a Hero*. Thackeray begins *Pendennis*.

1850    *Pendennis* concluded.

1851    Thackeray lectures on the eighteenth-century English humorists. Begins *Henry Esmond*. Resigns from *Punch* in December.

1852    *Henry Esmond* is published in three volumes by Smith, Elder. Thackeray visits America for the first time.

1853    Thackeray returns to England. Begins *The Newcomes*. The first of twenty-four parts appears in October, published by Bradbury and Evans.

1854    Thackeray produces *The Rose and the Ring*, the last of his Christmas books, and writes a comedy entitled *The Wolves and the Lamb* (later novelized as *Lovel the Widower*).

1855    *Miscellanies: Prose and Verse* is published by Bradbury and Evans. Thackeray concludes *The Newcomes*. Makes second trip to America. Lectures on the four Georges.

1857    Runs for Parliament from Oxford, unsuccessfully. The first number of *The Virginians* appears.

1859    *The Virginians* concluded.

1860    The first issue of *The Cornhill Magazine*, edited by Thackeray, appears. Thackeray's contributions include *Lovel the Widower* (in six numbers) and *The Four Georges*.

1861    *The Adventures of Philip* appears in *Cornhill*.

1862    Resigns editorship of *Cornhill*, concludes *The Adventures of Philip*. Begins writing *Denis Duval*.

1863    *Denis Duval* (uncompleted) appears in *Cornhill*. On the morning of December 24, Thackeray dies at the age of fifty-two.

# Contributors

HAROLD BLOOM, Sterling Professor of the Humanities at Yale University, is the author of *The Anxiety of Influence*, *Poetry and Repression*, and many other volumes of literary criticism. His forthcoming study, *Freud: Transference and Authority*, attempts a full-scale reading of all of Freud's major writings. A MacArthur Prize Fellow, he is general editor of five series of literary criticism published by Chelsea House. During 1987–88, he was appointed Charles Eliot Norton Professor of Poetry at Harvard University.

ROBERT KIELY is Professor of English and American Literature and Language at Harvard University. He is the author of *Modernism Reconsidered*, *Beyond Egotism: The Fiction of James Joyce, Virginia Woolf and D. H. Lawrence*, and *The Romantic Novel in England*.

R. D. McMASTER is Professor of English at the University of Alberta.

WOLFGANG ISER teaches English and Comparative Literature at the University of Konstanz, in Germany, and at the University of California, Irvine. A pioneer of "reception aesthetics" criticism and a founder of the "Poetics and Hermeneutics" research group, he has written books on Fielding, Pater, Spenser, and Beckett as well as *The Act of Reading*, *The Implied Reader*, and *Der Appelstruktur der Texte*.

INA FERRIS is Associate Professor of English at the University of Ottawa. She is the author of several articles and a book on Thackeray.

JOAN GARRETT-GOODYEAR teaches English at Smith College.

PETER K. GARRETT is Professor of English at the University of Illinois. He has written on James Joyce and is the author of *The Victorian Multiplot Novel: Studies in Dialogical Form*.

MARIA DiBATTISTA is Associate Professor of English at Princeton University. She is the author of *Virginia Woolf's Major Novels: The Fable of Anon*.

JULIET McMASTER is Associate Professor of English at the University of Alberta. She is the author of *Thackeray: The Major Novels, Trollope's Pallisader Novels: Theme and Pattern,* and *Jane Austen on Love.*

GEORGE LEVINE is Professor of English at Rutgers University. Author of *The Boundaries of Fiction,* he has published widely on Victorian prose writers and fiction.

RICHARD W. ORAM is Associate Professor of English at Smith College.

J. HILLIS MILLER is Professor of English and Comparative Literature at the University of California, Berkeley, and President of the Modern Language Association. His studies of Victorian and modern literature include *The Disappearance of God, Poets of Reality,* and important books on Charles Dickens and Thomas Hardy. He has also written extensively on William Carlos Williams and Wallace Stevens.

BARBARA HARDY is Professor of English Literature at Birbeck College, University of London. She is the author of *The Exposure of Luxury: Radical Themes in Thackeray* and of critical studies on George Eliot and Jane Austen.

CRAIG HOWES is Assistant Professor of English at the University of Hawaii at Manoa. He has published essays on Poe and Wordsworth and is currently at work on a book on English radical satire, 1789–1860.

# Bibliography

Baker, Joseph E. "Thackeray's Recantation." *PMLA* 77 (1962): 586–94.

Baun, Stephen. "L'Anti-histoire de Henri Esmond." *Poétique* 9 (1972): 61–79.

Bledsoe, Robert. "*Pendennis* and the Power of Sentimentality: A Study of Motherly Love." *PMLA* 91 (1976): 871–83.

Burch, Mark H. " 'The World Is a Looking Glass': *Vanity Fair* as Satire." *Genre* 15 (1982): 265–79.

Cabot, Frederick C. "The Two Voices in Thackeray's *Catherine*." *Nineteenth-Century Fiction* 28 (1974): 404–16.

Carey, John. *Thackeray: Prodigal Genius.* London: Faber & Faber, 1977.

Chapman, Raymond. *The Victorian Debate: English Literature and Society 1832–1901.* New York: Basic Books, 1968.

Colby, Robert A. "Thackeray Studies 1979–1982." *Dickens Studies Annual* 12 (1983): 341–56.

———. *Thackeray's Canvass of Humanity: An Author and His Public.* Columbus: Ohio State University Press, 1979.

*Costerus* n.s. 2 (1974). Special Thackeray issue.

Dodds, John W. *Thackeray: A Critical Portrait.* New York: Oxford University Press, 1941.

Dooley, D. J. "Thackeray's Use of Vanity Fair." *Studies in English Literature 1500–1900* 11 (1971): 701–13.

Douglas, Dennis. "Thackeray and the Uses of History." *The Yearbook of English Studies* 5 (1975): 164–77.

Ennis, Lambert, *Thackeray: The Sentimental Cynic.* Evanston, Ill.: Northwestern University Press, 1950.

Ferris, Ina. "Narrative Strategy in Thackeray's *The Adventures of Philip*." *English Studies in Canada* 5 (1974): 448–56.

———. "Realism and the Discord of Ending: The Example of Thackeray." *Nineteenth-Century Fiction* 38 (1983): 289–303.

———. *William Makepeace Thackeray.* Boston: Twayne, 1983.

Fielding, K. J. "Thackeray and the 'Dignity of Literature.' " *Times Literary Supplement* 19 and 26 September 1958.

Frazer, John P. "George IV and Jos Sedley in *Vanity Fair*." *English Language Notes* 19, no. 2 (1981): 122–28.

Garson, Marjorie. " 'Knowledge and Good and Evil': Henry and Rachel in *The History of Henry Esmond.*" *English Studies in Canada* 9 (1983): 418–34.

Greig, J. Y. T. *Thackeray: A Reconsideration.* London: Oxford University Press, 1950.

Hagan, John. "*Vanity Fair*: Becky Brought to Book Again." *Studies in the Novel* 7 (1975): 479–505.

Harden, Edgar F. "The Discipline and Significance of Form in *Vanity Fair.*" *PMLA* 82 (1967): 530–41.

———. *The Emergence of Thackeray's Serial Fiction.* Athens: University of Georgia Press, 1979.

———. "Esmond and the Search for Self." *Yearbook of English Studies* 3 (1973): 181–95.

———. *Thackeray's English Humorists and Four Georges.* Newark: University of Delaware Press, 1985.

———. "Theatricality in *Pendennis.*" *Ariel: A Review of International English Literature* 4, no. 4 (1973): 74–94.

Hardy, Barbara. *The Exposure of Luxury: Radical Themes in Thackeray.* London: Peter Owen, 1972.

Harvey, John. *Victorian Novelists and Their Illustrators.* London: Sidgwick & Jackson, 1970.

Jeffers, Thomas. "Thackeray's Pendennis: Son and Gentleman." *Nineteenth-Century Fiction* 33 (1978): 175–93.

Klein, J. T. "The Dual Center: A Study of Narrative Structure in *Vanity Fair.*" *College Literature* 4 (1977): 122–28.

Lerner, Lawrence. "Thackeray and Marriage." *Essays in Criticism* 25 (1975): 279–303.

Lester, John A., Jr. "Thackeray's Narrative Technique." *PMLA* 69 (1954): 392–409.

Loofbourow, John. *Thackeray and the Form of Fiction.* Princeton: Princeton University Press, 1964.

Lund, Michael. "Reading Serially Published Novels: Old Stories in Thackeray's *The Newcomes.*" *Philological Quarterly* 60 (1981): 205–25.

Manning, Sylvia. "Incest and the Structure of *Henry Esmond.*" *Nineteenth-Century Fiction* 34 (1979): 194–213.

Martin, Bruce K. "*Vanity Fair*: Narrative Ambivalence and Comic Form." *Tennessee Studies in Literature* 20 (1975): 37–49.

Mauskopf, Charles. "Thackeray's Concept of the Novel." *Philological Quarterly* 50 (1971): 239–52.

McMaster, Juliet. "*The Rose and the Ring*: Quintessential Thackeray." *Mosaic* 9, no. 4 (1976): 157–65.

———. *Thackeray: The Major Novels.* Toronto: University of Toronto Press, 1971.

———. "Thackeray's Things: Time's Local Habitation." In *The Victorian Experience: The Novelists,* edited by Richard A. Levine. Athens: Ohio University Press, 1976.

———. "Theme and Form in *The Newcomes.*" *Nineteenth-Century Fiction* 23 (1968): 177–88.

Miller, J. Hillis. *The Form of Victorian Fiction: Thackeray, Dickens, Trollope, George Eliot, Meredith and Hardy.* Notre Dame, Ind.: University of Notre Dame Press, 1968.

Milner, Ian. "Theme and Moral Vision in Thackeray's *Vanity Fair*." *Philologica Pragensia* 13, no. 4 (1970): 177–85.

Monod, Sylvère. "Brother Wearers of Motley." *Essays and Studies* 26 (1973): 66–82.

Monsarrat, Ann. *An Uneasy Vision: Thackeray the Man, 1811–1863*. New York: Dodd, Mead, 1980.

Musselwhite, David. "Notes on a Journey to Vanity Fair." *Literature and History: A Journal for the Humanities* 7, no. 1 (1981): 62–90.

Paris, Bernard J. *A Psychological Approach to Fiction: Studies in Thackeray, Stendhal, George Eliot, Dostoevsky, and Conrad*. Bloomington: Indiana University Press, 1974.

Parker, David. "Thackeray's Barry Lyndon." *Ariel: A Review of International English Literature* 6, no. 4 (1975): 68–80.

Phillips, Kenneth C. *The Language of Thackeray*. London: André Deutsch, 1978.

Rawlins, Jack P. *Thackeray's Novels: A Fiction That Is True*. Berkeley: University of California Press, 1974.

Ray, Gordon N. *The Buried Life: A Study of the Relation between Thackeray's Fiction and His Personal History*. Cambridge: Harvard University Press, 1952.

———. *Thackeray: The Uses of Adversity, 1811–1846*. London: Oxford University Press, 1955.

———. *Thackeray: The Age of Wisdom, 1847–1863*. London: Oxford University Press, 1958.

———, ed. *The Letters and Private Papers of William Makepeace Thackeray*. Cambridge: Harvard University Press, 1945.

Redwine, Bruce. "The Uses of Memento Mori in *Vanity Fair*." *Studies in English Literature* 17 (1977): 657–72.

Rogers, Katherine M. "The Pressure of Convention on Thackeray's Women." *Modern Language Review* 67 (1972): 257–63.

Rogers, Mary. "Perspective on Henry Esmond." *Victorian Newsletter* 56 (1979) 26–31.

Rogers, Winslow. "Thackeray's Self-Consciousness." In *The Worlds of Victorian Fiction*, edited by Jerome Buckley. Harvard English Studies 6. Cambridge: Harvard University Press, 1975.

Scarry, Elaine. "*Henry Esmond*: The Rookery at Castlewood." In *Literary Monographs 7*, edited by Eric Rothstein and Joseph Anthony Wittreich, Jr., 1–43. Madison: University of Wisconsin Press, 1975.

Segel, Elizabeth T. "Truth and Authenticity in Thackeray." *Journal of Narrative Technique* 2, no. 1 (1972): 46–59.

Shillingsburg, Peter L. "*Pendennis* Revisited." *Etudes Anglaises* 34 (1981): 432–42.

Stevenson, Richard C. "The Problem of Judging Becky Sharp: Scene and Narrative Commentary in *Vanity Fair*." *Victorian Institute Journal* 6 (1977): 1–8.

*Studies in the Novel* 13, nos. 1–2 (1981). Special Thackeray issue.

Sudrann, Jean. " 'The Philosopher's Property': Thackeray and the Use of Time." *Victorian Studies* 10 (1967): 359–88.

Sundell, M. G., ed. *Twentieth Century Interpretations of* Vanity Fair. Englewood Cliffs, N.J.: Prentice-Hall, 1969.

Sutherland, John A. "The Expanding Narrative of *Vanity Fair*." *Journal of Narrative Technique* 3, no. 3 (1973): 149–69.

———. "*Henry Esmond* and the Virtues of Carelessness." *Modern Philology* 68 (1971): 345–54.

———. *Thackeray at Work*. London: Athlone, 1974.

Talon, Henri-A. "Time and Memory in Thackeray's *Henry Esmond*." *Review of English Studies* n.s. 13 (1962): 147–56.

Taube, Myron. "Contrast as a Principle of Structure in *Vanity Fair*." *Nineteenth-Century Fiction* 18 (1963): 119–35.

Tillotson, Geoffrey. *Thackeray the Novelist*. Cambridge: Cambridge University Press, 1954.

———. *A View of Victorian Literature*. Oxford: Clarendon, 1974.

Tillotson, Geoffrey, and Donald Hawes, eds. *Thackeray: The Critical Heritage*. London: Routledge & Kegan Paul, 1968.

Tillotson, Kathleen. *Novels of the Eighteen-Forties*. Oxford: Oxford University Press, 1956.

Van Ghent, Dorothy. *The English Novel: Form and Function*. New York: Holt, 1953.

Vega-Ritter, Max. "Women under Judgement in *Vanity Fair*." *Cahiers d'Etudes et de Recherches Victoriennes et Edouardiennes* 3 (1976): 7–24.

Welsh, Alexander, ed. *Thackeray: A Collection of Critical Essays*. Englewood Cliffs, N.J.: Prentice-Hall, 1968.

Wheatley, James F. *Patterns in Thackeray's Fiction*. Cambridge, Mass.: M.I.T. Press, 1969.

Williams, Ioan. *The Realist Novel in England: A Study in Development*. London: Macmillan, 1974.

Wolff, Cynthia, Griffin. "Who Is the Narrator of *Vanity Fair* and Where Is He Standing?" *College Literature* 1 (1974): 190–203.

Worth, George J. "The Unity of Henry Esmond" *Nineteenth-Century Fiction* 15 (1961): 345–53.

# Acknowledgments

"Victorian Harlequin: The Function of Humor in Thackeray's Critical and Miscellaneous Prose" by Robert Kiely from *Veins of Humor* (Harvard English Studies 3), edited by Harry Levin, © 1972 by the President and Fellows of Harvard College. Reprinted by permission of Harvard University Press.

"The Pygmalion Motif in *The Newcomes*" by R. D. McMaster from *Nineteenth-Century Fiction* 29, no. 1 (June 1974), © 1974 by the Regents of the University of California. Reprinted by permission of the University of California Press.

"The Reader as a Component Part of the Realistic Novel: Esthetic Effects in Thackeray's *Vanity Fair*" by Wolfgang Iser from *The Implied Reader: Patterns of Communication in Prose Fiction from Bunyan to Beckett* by Wolfgang Iser, © 1974 by the Johns Hopkins University Press, Baltimore/London. Reprinted by permission of the Johns Hopkins University Press.

"The Breakdown of Thackeray's Narrator: *Lovel the Widower*" by Ina Ferris from *Nineteenth-Century Fiction* 32, no. 1 (June 1977), © 1977 by the Regents of the University of California. Reprinted by permission of the University of California Press.

"Stylized Emotions, Unrealized Selves: Expressive Characterization in Thackeray" by Joan Garrett-Goodyear from *Victorian Studies* 22, no. 2 (Winter 1979), © 1979 by the Trustees of Indiana University. Reprinted by permission of the author and the Trustees of Indiana University.

"Thackeray: Seeing Double" by Peter K. Garrett from *The Victorian Multiplot Novel: Studies in Dialogical Form* by Peter K. Garrett, © 1980 by Yale University. Reprinted by permission of Yale University Press.

"The Triumph of Clytemnestra: The Charades in *Vanity Fair*" by Maria DiBattista from *PMLA* 95, no. 5 (October 1980), © 1980 by the Modern Language Association of America. Reprinted by permission of the Modern Language Association of America.

"Funeral Baked Meats: Thackeray's Last Novel" by Juliet McMaster from *Studies in the Novel* 13, nos. 1/2 (Spring/Summer 1981), © 1981 by North Texas State University. Reprinted by permission.

"*Pendennis*: The Virtue of the Dilettante's Unbelief" by George Levine from *The Realistic Imagination: English Fiction from* Frankenstein *to* Lady Chatterley by George Levine, © 1981 by the University of Chicago. Reprinted by permission of the University of Chicago Press.

" 'Just a Little Turn of the Circle': Time, Memory, and Repetition in Thackeray's *Roundabout Papers*" by Richard W. Oram from *Studies in the Novel* 13, nos. 1/2 (Spring/Summer 1981), © 1981 by North Texas State University. Reprinted by permission.

"*Henry Esmond*: Repetition and Irony" by J. Hillis Miller from *Fiction and Repetition: Seven English Novels* by J. Hillis Miller, © 1982 by J. Hillis Miller. Reprinted by permission of the author and Harvard University Press.

"Thackeray: Inconstant Passions" by Barbara Hardy from *Forms of Feeling in Victorian Fiction* by Barbara Hardy, © 1985 by Barbara Hardy. Reprinted by permission of the author and Peter Owen Ltd., London.

"*Pendennis* and the Controversy on the 'Dignity of Literature' " by Craig Howes from *Nineteenth-Century Fiction* 41, no. 3 (December 1986), © 1986 by the Regents of the University of California. Reprinted by permission of the University of California Press.

# Index

Abrams, M. H., 175
Addison, Joseph, 12, 180
*Adventures of Philip, The*: autobiographical elements in, 148–52; cannibal theme in, 142–45; characteristics of, 61; critical comments on, 149–50; death images in, 137–38, 145–47; Dr. Firmin's role in, 139, 140–41, 145–46; narrative style of, 253; narrator's role in, 59, 147–48, 185; and Pendennis as projection of Thackeray, 149–52; and Pendennis's view of Philip, 150–52; and Philip Firmin as projection of Thackeray, 148–52; pretension versus reality in, 138–42; skepticism in, 68; violence and pain as images in, 141–42
*Aeneid, The* (Virgil), 195, 201
Aesop, 11
*Agamemnon, The* (Aeschylus), 132, 136
Arnold, Matthew, 160
Austen, Jane, 17, 123

Baker, Joseph, 149–50
Bann, Stephen, 179
*Barchester Towers* (Trollope), 157
*Barry Lyndon*, 215–20
Barthelme, Donald, 13
Beerbohm, Max, 184
Benjamin, Walter, 213
Bennett, Arnold, 39

Blake, William, 13
Boethius, 27
*Book of Snobs, The*, 184, 186–87
Booth, Wayne, 38–39, 48–49
Boswell, James, 5
Boyes, J. F., 169–70
Brecht, Bertolt, 3
Brontë, Charlotte, 1, 42, 124, 136
Brontë, Emily, 180
Brookfield, Jane, 73, 165, 179, 227
"Brother of the Press on the History of a Literary Man, A," 235–36
Browning, Robert, 177
Buckley, Jerome, 169
Bulwer-Lytton, Edward: as influence on *The Newcomes*, 253; memoir of Blanchard by, 235–36, 243; on need for literary reform, 234; parody of, 184; Thackeray's view of, 15–17, 20, 235, 249; view of literary profession of, 235–36, 239, 243
Burne-Jones, Edward, 24
Butor, Michel, 42
Byron, George Gordon, Lord, 234, 235

Camus, Albert, 35
Carey, John, 150
Carlyle, Thomas, 160–61
*Catherine*, 235
Cervantes, Miguel de, 25
Chesterton, G. K., 1, 92, 169
*Cid, Le* (Corneille), 34
Coleridge, Samuel Taylor, 11

267